Helen Hazlett

Glennair; or, Life in Scotland

Helen Hazlett

Glennair; or, Life in Scotland

ISBN/EAN: 9783743341722

Manufactured in Europe, USA, Canada, Australia, Japa

Cover: Foto ©ninafisch / pixelio.de

Manufactured and distributed by brebook publishing software (www.brebook.com)

Helen Hazlett

Glennair; or, Life in Scotland

GLENNAIR;

OR,

LIFE IN SCOTLAND.

BY

HELEN HAZLETT,

AUTHOR OF "HEIGHTS OF EIDELBERG," ETC.

"Let us walk together as friends, in the shaded paths of meditation,
Nor judgment set his seal until he hath poised his balance;
That the chastenings of mild reproof may meet unwitting error,
And charity not be a stranger at the board that is spread for brothers."

PHILADELPHIA:
CLAXTON, REMSEN & HAFFELFINGER,
819 & 821 MARKET STREET.
1869.

INTRODUCTION.

THE complaint has been made of late, perhaps not without reason, that distant lands are portrayed and antique subjects chosen, when the pen of the author would glide more smoothly and be more acceptable to the community, if confined to familiar home scenes. The apology offered in thus braving the literary world is, that the authoress has been led to wake up in memory those who lived among Scotia's hills, the home of her own ancestry, and from whose lips much of 'Scottish life' has been gathered.

GLENNAIR.

CHAPTER I.

"Now — courage again!
And, with peril to cope,
Gird thee with vigor,
And helm thee with hope."

I SHALL assuredly enroll you among the insane, if you insist on braving this tempest, Duncan; and must exert my influence with your sister, to prevent her accompanying you."

"My father's note admits no option, uncle," returned the young man addressed. "His charge is, to bring my sister *home*, regardless of the storm, or Mr. and Mrs. Rushbrook's importunities. The bearer was a stranger; it was handed to me as I was leaving the bank, toward evening. Father has entire reliance on my obedience; would you have me lessen his future confidence, Uncle Ralph?"

A faint smile played for a moment over the features of the youth, as his dark-gray eyes rested inquiringly upon Mr. Rushbrook.

"It would be difficult to arouse distrust in *you*, Duncan, in the family or community; but does it not appear to you singular your father gives no reason for his peremptory summons?"

2   13

"I do not doubt, uncle, my father's explanations will be quite satisfactory; he is never unreasonable. But here is Amy, equipped, — and, has she convinced Aunt Louisa, though against her will, that we are right — if perversely so?"

"Aunt Louisa pronounces father intensely absurd, and is equally complimentary to his son and daughter for following his mandates," replied a bright, happy-looking girl of apparently eighteen years. "I have no idea of the why, but the motive must be cogent to induce father ever to allow us to battle with this storm. We are ready, Duncan; good night, Uncle Ralph. Aunt Louisa looks determinately opposed; you will at least exchange a parting kiss, auntie?"

"I would I had power to oppose this rash step, Amy," said Mrs. Rushbrook; "remonstrance has failed."

"And I have expended all *my* arguments, and shall not urge another word," pursued Mr. Rushbrook. "Will has been trying various ways of getting the carriage out for you, children, but the drifts are so heavy he cannot succeed; and, indeed, it would be quite impossible and useless to attempt to drive any vehicle to-night. So, Duncan, if you are resolved, there is no choice — you must *walk*."

"Father writes that Lochiel will meet us with the' sleigh the other side of the brook," replied the young man, calmly.

"Your brother will manifest less wit than has usually been ascribed to him, if he ventures such a risk; yet, you are all young and strong, and the elements are under the direction of a merciful God. May He be your covert this night, children."

After a few inquiries respecting the security of his sister's apparel against the anticipated contest with the northern blast, and an interchange of kind adieus, Duncan Graeme and his sister Amy set forth.

"How dark and dreary it is, Duncan," she murmured, when with difficulty they had gained about a quarter of a mile. "My courage would fail were it not balanced by our experience of father's unerring judgment."

"How I wish I could carry you, Amy," said the brother, gently, "but these drifts half bury me. Cling close to my arm, and I can then lift you as often as I extricate myself. Cheer up, Amy, it is only one mile to the Grotto; Loch. is not one to disappoint us."

"The Grotto! Not Elfin Grotto!" she exclaimed, half releasing the arm she held. "Why appoint *that* place, Duncan? a night among these drifts would be preferable to such a refuge." A strong blast at that moment separating and whirling them at a distance from each other, all else was forgotten in the strenuous efforts to recover a footing.

"I am almost exhausted, Duncan," Amy exclaimed, when her brother had once again joined her, and the fierce wind had in a measure subsided, "and I do not hear the bells of Lochiel's sleigh."

"And will not, this night, Amy. It would be utterly impracticable to reach us — the roads are impassable."

"Oh! brother, what will become of us?"

"Had we our father's hope, faith, and assurance of a heavenly home, or mother's unwavering trust and confidence in the Scripture promises, we might follow your suggestion, to sit down passively, and yield the victory to King Boreas."

"Is there no alternative except—"

"The Grotto is our sole security, Amy. We have, to the letter, obeyed our directions; further we cannot proceed. The foot-bridge is carried away, Amy."

Amy had the arm of her brother in a close clasp, but she answered not. "There is no prospect of an abatement of the storm," he continued. "Choose, Amy,—death, or the haunted cavern. I shall not leave you, whatever may be your decision." The wild sighing of the winds through the forest, the crashing of the limbs and bending of the surrounding trees, were fearful. "Here, Amy, we are exposed to the fury of the hurricane; we can but die, should we realize all you fear, in the cave."

"Lead where you will, Duncan; in a very little while I shall be unable to follow you."

He waited for no more. Quickly passing his arm round her, and lifting her over the low brushwood, he glided with his precious burden down a narrow by-path, to the much-dreaded and ever-avoided "Grotto of the Elfin."

"I had not supposed the wild legends and dark doings of the Glenlock fairies could have taken possession of the strong mind of Amy Graeme," her brother observed pleasantly, as he placed her before the door they were now to enter.

"I would disabuse your mind of any such belief,

Duncan," she replied. "I have no fear of other than *incarnate* spirits ; I *do* believe some of the worst of the human race infest this spot, and have never thought otherwise. The land of spirits — or fairy-land — has in it nothing terrible for me."

"Perhaps hospitality may be the redeeming trait of this band of savages," said her brother, laughing. "We will hope so, and make our entrance."

The door opened as though by a sesame, at the first touch. After passing down a short flight of steps, the brother and sister found themselves in a large room, partially lighted by a swinging lamp, and warmed by a large coal-stove. The apartment was furnished, too, rudely, but comfortably. Miss Graeme could not repress an exclamation of amazement on entering.

"A very unique style of banditti, we must confess, Amy," observed her brother ; "not a weapon of offence. Let us take advantage of their comforts," he added, taking from his sister her cloak and hood, and hanging them near the fire. "I would advise a rest upon that divan, until claimed by a fairy or a felon ; and I will usurp this chair, and play monarch for the time there, — really, *you* might pass for an Elfin Queen, so delightfully enveloped in those cushions. But what have we here on these shelves ? Books, — some scientific, some poetic, and — a Bible !"

"How strange ! Duncan. Who can the inmates be, and why not here on this inclement night ?"

"This is obviously not the only apartment, and our host has too much propriety to intrude upon his guests. With your consent, Amy, I will touch this. It mayhap be a wand to gather the family in groups."

"It is a bell, Duncan. Not for the earth," she whispered, eagerly.

"Who knows but his Majesty might furnish some mode of our getting home? Had I not better seek, if I may not summon him?"

"What is the hour, Duncan?"

"Half after nine,—cne hour and a half since we left Uncle Ralph's,—a twenty minutes' walk, ordinarily."

"Hark!" exclaimed Amy, in a hushed voice,—"what was, what *is* that, Duncan?"

"Only the wail of the winds, my nervously excited sister." Yet he drew nearer the corner from whence the sound proceeded. "We might imagine all the goblins from all lands; or that the inmates of Pandemonium itself held a convention at this spot to-night. You are pale and exhausted, Amy; I wonder if to sleep were quite impossible."

The only reply was a nervous shake of the head. Amy sat intently listening. "I cannot be mistaken," she said at length; "there *are* human voices mingling with the noises of the elements."

"When similarly situated, Amy," he returned, "I have been almost inclined to answer to my own imaginings. Depend upon it, Amy, those voices will subside with the gale."

"Duncan Graeme! there are human footsteps approaching!" she almost shrieked, burying her face in her hands in terror.

"Amy, dear Amy!" whispered her brother, sitting

down closely beside her; "whatever your eyes or ears may witness here, you and I are perfectly secure. Have I ever deceived you, my sister? Further revelation would be perjury."

The hands fell from her face. Amy lifted her eyes to her brother in astonished inquiry, while the compressed lip 'and ghastly cheek evidenced the anguish his words had occasioned.

"Amy," he said, placing his arm caressingly around her and speaking cheerfully, "my associations with this place do not render me unworthy of your affection and confidence; my reputation would remain unsullied were it proclaimed throughout our country; yet, so peculiarly am I circumstanced, that even you may not yet listen to the detail of events that link me, for the present, to the tenant of the 'Cavern.' Shall I ask my sister's silence, and also that she will remain satisfied with mine until the period arrive when I may, without injury to others, reveal all?"

Amy raised her head from the shoulder upon which it was resting, and faintly asked, — "Is Edith Lincoln in possession of your secret, Duncan?"

There was a sudden start, yet as suddenly checked. Leaning down and fondly kissing her forehead, he replied, — "She *is* aware of my frequenting this Grotto, and holds me guiltless. Can not you, Amy?"

A burst of bitter weeping was the answer. "Forgive me, Duncan," she murmured, after a long interval, dashing back the tears as she spoke; "it would be difficult to convince me there could be anything censurable in your motives, but I was so startled, so stunned. Yet, Duncan, it is passing strange that Edith never herself ventures near this Grotto, nor suffers others to do so. She has frequently obstinately persisted in riding several miles out of the way, rather than cross Elfin Bridge. If conscious of security, why is this, Duncan? Edith is incapable of duplicity —"

"I do not consider my accountability embraces all the fantasies of others, Amy. Edith Lincoln is beyond even the suspicion of insincerity; whatever be her reasons for concealment, they must not suggest an evil thought of her."

"I *love Edith*, Duncan; we *all* love her, and deeply mourn the unhappy occurrences which have separated her from us so irretrievably. We only do not often *speak* of her, Duncan, because we know how intensely you suffer."

"Do not use the word irretrievably, Amy dear; the reputation of Hugh Lincoln is not a total wreck. There are many as sanguine as myself that his character will be re-established, and he reinstated in his position in society and in the Bank. The time may not be near; I do not think it very far distant. Edith, and her Aunt Cameron, bask in the hope; they are perfectly assured of his innocence, and —"

"But, Duncan, the proofs of his guilt are so obvious; and his mysterious disappearance reflects only culpability — anything, surely, than conscious innocence. Father thinks him a bad, designing man; and father has considerable discernment, Duncan."

"No question of it, Amy; yet *my* intimacy in the family has given me special opportunity of watching his traits of character. Religion sits so naturally, so easily upon him ; his amiability is so winning, — such a father could not be a bad citizen. I suppose it was known his disappearance was owing to the perilous threats of the populace. Should his life *now* be sacrificed, he will lie forever in a dishonored grave, and the name of Lincoln be branded infamous ; but credit me, Amy, there are those who *can*, who *must*, and who *will* shed light on this dark affair. These proceedings against poor Lincoln will yet be stayed ; he will stand as honored and respected throughout his country as now defamed."

" Poor, dear Edith ! Father has not prohibited your visiting there, although he has Lochiel and me."

" I should have a terrible conflict with the Fifth Commandment, in such a case, Amy. I fear there would be only nine left on the decalogue for *me*."

" Why is the house so entirely deserted, if others hold your good opinion of Mr. Lincoln, Duncan ?"

" Public sentiment keeps his friends politically silent. The favorable day is yet to dawn, but it *will* dawn, believe, my Amy."

" There is that singular noise again, dear Duncan ; it cannot be the wind ; it is enclosed with us," interrupted the sister, tremblingly.

Removing a stone, young Duncan revealed a small black cord. Drawing the end, hastily, he again closed the aperture and resumed his seat. " Our host supposes strangers have been driven in by the storm, and is trying the effect of his music. It will cease now ; they will not molest us."

Miss Graeme saw and heard her brother in amazement. "Why, Amy," he resumed, "I should be dismissed from the Bank did I give public expression to my opinion, — to *father*, I *have* — he thinks me excessively sanguine, and believes it is entirely on account of my position in the family — but it is not. I would defend him as an innocent man had he no daughter."

"Some little influenced by that, nevertheless," returned his sister. "Edith's loveliness is very attractive. Even father, when he forbade my intercourse with her, said with tears, 'It is a sad necessity, my child; I think I am as much attached to Edith Lincoln as Duncan himself.'"

A smile of momentary brightness played over the features of the youth, but the voice was sad, and in broken accents he said, —

"Only *I* could not have deprived her of the solace and companionship of an almost sister. *She* admits the propriety; *I* have never been reconciled to the withdrawal of our family; only a thistle-hedge has divided our homes since infancy; that should have been thrown down in this ordeal, rather than a greater barrier placed there; but father acts from principle; he does not intend to induce sorrow. Father cannot do wrong wittingly, nor would Mr. Lincoln. Edith is supported by a large proportion of pride, in the neglect of her former associates. She receives very few visits, and makes none. But, dear Amy, how weary and pale you are; let me arrange your cushions once more, and oblige me by trying to sleep. I shall resort to the soldier's custom when I see you more composed."

In a little while he had the satisfaction of seeing her yield to " tired nature's sweet restorer." Throwing his own cloak upon the floor, he was himself, in a short time, profoundly sleeping. Whatever might have been the strife of the elements, the silence of death reigned in the cave. For hours there was no sound save the breathing of the sleepers.

The flicker of the expiring lamp awakened Duncan. None but the initiated could have procured a substitute. Removing a stone from the side of the wall, from a shelf behind he produced candles and matches. Lighting and introducing one into the neck of an old bottle, he extinguished the lamp before the smell of the smoking oil should arouse his sister. The fire required fuel, but that could not be replenished as noiselessly, and was allowed to tarry. His watch told the morning dawn. Through no crevice in the mystic cave could the day break ; no sunlight ever shed a gleam of brightness there. While his sister still slept, young Graeme passed a slip of paper through another secret opening. In reply, a stone was removed from the opposite side, and crackers, cheese, dried mutton, ham, nicely chipped, and milk, were handed through into the apartment, — then all silently closed. Having spread the articles over the table, near the light, Duncan Graeme sat down by the side of the couch of his sister. It was not long before she raised her head, and glancing around in slight alarm, said, —

" Where ? — yes, — yes, — I have been sleeping, Duncan — dreaming. Where is mother, Duncan ?

She was here, surely, or was it the cry of the Benshee? No, no; that is fabulous; I was only dreaming." With a strong effort to smile, she asked, —
"What have we here, Duncan? The Elves have
not been sleeping."

The thoughts of the brother had kept pace with
the words of Amy. He, too, had dreamed of their
mother. He felt that *she* was somehow certainly
connected with their night wanderings; yet he replied with well-feigned cheerfulness, —

"The Benshee did better than cry; she has pitied
our condition and brought us food." He filled a
glass as he spoke, and Amy drank the milk only
because he held it to her lips. A bright fire once
again lighted the room; and except for the time-
riveted associations of the "haunted Grotto," and
the peculiarity of their sojourn there, it might have
been deemed cheerful. Breakfast was very soon
over, and now the possibility of reaching home was
discussed. Refusing to listen to reason while her
brother took an observation from the door, Amy
accompanied him up the steps, and through the
passage they had entered the preceding night. A
scene of desolation presented itself. The storm was
still raging; the winds howled over and around
them; broken branches lay heaped up on all sides,
obstructing the pathway.

"Effectually blockaded!" exclaimed young Graeme,
"and a question whether the larder of the Elves will
stand a siege! Shall we return to our quarters,
Amy? There seems no other resource."

Amy stood with folded hands, gazing wistfully

upon the prospect. "We can only go back and bide our fate," she replied, after a lengthy pause. "Our anxiety cannot exceed their at home. Oh, Duncan, what could have happened to have rendered this disastrous journey necessary?"

"I dread to learn, Amy; yet, as this result could not have been foreseen by father, we may greatly exaggerate the occasion. Let us endeavor to hope so, Amy dear. The team will be sent in quest of us so soon as there is a possibility. Shall we go in? The wind is too keen for you here."

Miss Graeme turned mechanically. "Is there no other way of egress?" she inquired, after they had been some time sitting silently by the fire.

"Not by land, Amy; and there would be more risk than I would like you to encounter, as the passage to the sea is very dark and dangerous to other than Elves," he added, pleasantly.

"I would hazard all the dangers. The anticipation of reaching home banishes every fear, Duncan. I could brave the tempest of last evening again, to look upon mother's face once more, and to know I have a mother still."

"Still wandering over the regions of superstition, Amy. You *cannot* give credence to the laments, the wails and the waifs, the legends repeated around Scottish hearth-stones?"

"Perhaps not actual belief, Duncan; but my nerves are weakened by the singular adventures of the night, and my *mind*, too, probably," she said, mournfully.

"I do not blame you, Amy," he replied, soothingly.

3

" No wonder your imagination has been wrought upon by the seemingly strange proceedings of the night. I much regret the necessity that led to your witnessing them. Yet, Amy, there is nothing mystical here; nothing superhuman acted in this place. As it has been *our* refuge for *one* night, so the refuge of the unfortunate it has been and will be, I trust, ever. It certainly never was my intention to introduce my sister into the cave, or to its inmates, but it seems I am driven to both. For a few moments he stood irresolute, then suddenly, with an evident effort to appear calm, he stepped forward, and striking a spring-bell, placed it again on the ground, and sat down on the couch near his sister, who was intently watching his operations. The vibrations of the bell had not ceased when the same large stone through which had issued the provisions an hour before, was slowly removed, then one below it, then another and another, until an aperture was made sufficiently large to admit the person of a robust, athletic man. His countenance bespoke the extreme of sadness as he stood mutely awaiting orders.

" The boat and a torch, Roger ! My sister cannot be wanted at home any longer. Speed you, my good fellow."

" Nae morrow for the ain that wull fly the oar the morn ; for *me* 'tis nae muckle ill, yet the *bairns* might bide life for the love of it."

" The distance is short, Roger, and the barque stout. We shall skim round the Lynne and over Loch Muir speedily, and safely, too. Is Norval here ? "

" I need not Norval, if I gang; the *wind* drives. No oars will be needed, I trow."

" My sister cannot walk, and no wheels could find passage. Roger, we have no choice; by driving out we will be safe."

" I trow not, Maister Duncan; but I bide your bidding."

" The torch, then, good Roger. We will walk to the outlet and view the dangers first." The sturdy Roger disappeared only a minute, returning with a lighted torch which he handed to the youth. He remarked, — " *I* maun guide the leddy through the pass. Amy instinctively followed. She noticed in the next apartment three cot-beds, and that two figures stood in the shadowy niches. There was no word spoken until they reached the bottom of a flight of steps formed of stones of various shapes and sizes, when her escort said, — " I maun carry you, lassie, it is sae slippy here." Unresistingly, Amy was borne through the dismal avenues, her brother cautiously bending the light into the difficult windings, obviously himself perfectly familiar with the way. After an irksome travel of half an hour, the light suddenly broke upon them, and they stood before the broad ocean; but the rocks sheltered them securely from the strong blast. A heavy boat rocked at the mouth of the cave.

" Oh, Duncan ! " whispered his sister, shuddering; " is it well to venture? yet how can we return ? "

" Even *this* contrasts favorably, Amy dear. We will choose the least evil in your view," he answered affectionately. " The boat, Roger; we can put in at Maelaine inlet if we are conquered."

"It is nae far frae the manse of Maister Graeme, the hame of your father, Maister Duncan; yet I trow there is anither hame we'll nae miss if we meddle with the billows this morning. Will I loose her? The surges will be doubtful anchorage."

"Launch her, Roger; I feel we shall arrive safely. We *must* get home; by land is impracticable for my sister. The sea is not so much troubled, and the wind has lulled considerably since dawn."

"*Ye* ken, Maister Duncan, I dinna," returned the man, swinging the boat from its moorings with the same nonchalance. Young Graeme lifted his sister over, stepped in, and the three commenced the hazardous enterprise. Amy sat in the centre of the boat, her head resting on her hand, watching the movement of the oars with mingled hope, fear, and occasional despair, as the strong man struggled with the angry waves.

"We maun drift into smoother water; the underflow is powerfu', the air strong an' the Lynn yawnin'. Mair than ane of my name ha' gane there, nor shroud, nither coffin. An awfu' coast on a foul morn, Maister Duncan, but —"

"There is a gun, — hark! Neilson, — another and another; throw up the oar for a flag-staff; Amy's scarf will serve for an ensign."

"The Lynn afore the maircy of Glennair's Laird," he bitterly ejaculated as he obeyed, "he wull hae nae muckle for Roger Neilson; yet sae let it be, twa for the ane."

In an instant the scarf was torn from the pole. "Forgive me, Roger," said young Graeme, "I

thought only of home, and judged the firing proceeded from thence. Are we nearing the Laird's
inlet?"

"Nae, nae, Maister Duncan, there's a heavy balance of blessin's fa' ye, agin a' I ha' to forgie, but
ye canna ken, nor I canna speak the hate of the
mon fa' the name of Roger Neilson. Lincoln is nae
mair to his mind. I would nae like to luke him in
the een."

"And *shall not*, good Roger," replied the youth
warmly. "Yet, Roger, the Laird errs ignorantly;
the development of the truth will send him to seek
your pardon for his part in the transaction — turn,
quickly! Roger!" he exclaimed, suddenly rising,
"there is a heavy swell on us — northward, or we
will be bilged." Seeing their danger at a glance,
the skilful pilot threw his boat over the wave, and
the next moment she glided into the inlet of Glennair.

"We are here, an' maun make the best of it; —
we had nearly toppled. It is cauld for the bonnie
lassie; spring up, Maister Duncan, an' I will hand
Miss Amy tae ye."

"And yourself, Roger?"

"Tak' agin to the waters. Loch Muir is nae far;
unco' kind wull be the greetin' o' Allen Dhu an' his
auld wife, an' our ain cave will nae want me the
eve, if my oar ha' its strength."

"My kindest wishes will accompany you, Mr.
Neilson," said Amy, offering her hand, which was
warmly clasped. "I have reason to be thankful to
the cave, to the boat, and to its owner. May you

3 *

be as safely delivered from all your trials as we
from ours, of last night and this morning."

"Many thanks, leddy. Ye wad nae ha' had the
racket we gie to the foe an' the stranger, if Maister
Duncan had nae forgot the signal; it was nae
meant for ye."

"It was only a momentary shock."

"I could not have struck the gong, without occa-
sioning greater terror, Roger. It was not remiss-
ness; it was the choice of evils--your goblinism
seemed preferable; but pass up my sister, and take
to your craft, before the brighter light of morning
tells the tale we would fain keep from the ear of
Glennair's proprietor."

As Neilson lifted Amy, he whispered, "Mind
Roger Neilson in your prayers, leddy: at the askin'
of some, the light may gleam through even sic' as
covers Hugh Lincoln an' mysel'. Bonnie lassie,
farewell," he added, as her brother received her on
the beach. "Gude bye, Maister Duncan; when ye
stumble on us agin,' gie us the signal."

"Good bye, Roger," returned the youth; "a
summer day will be dawning." Neilson, raising
his cap, looked an almost smiling adieu upon his
young friends, and turned his boat silently from the
spot, as the two stood as silently gazing after him.

"Amy"—the brother spoke huskily. She looked
up inquiringly. "No mention of places or persons
you have unwittingly encountered since yester's
sunrise."

"Concealment with mother I have never practised, Duncan; mother will disclose nothing that I
would not."

"To none else, Amy?"

"I promise you, Duncan. Why should I desire to reveal that I would so gladly be ignorant of myself?"

"Undeniably, Amy, appearances against Lincoln are as dark as the cave, and nothing has occurred to strengthen your confidence in his guiltlessness. Mayhap your mind is disquieted concerning your brother, also, Amy? No marvel it were."

"Duncan, dear Duncan," she replied with energy, yet falteringly; "might I ask why *you*, of all others, are so connected with these fugitives from justice? and why you, and no other, regard them innocent of such widely credited accusations? and why rigidly honorable persons, as Mungo Robertson and Robert Dunbar, have not a sparkle of lenity toward him or his family?"

"Universally, Amy, those who suffer in their coffers from the supposed delinquency of a fellow-man, are the last to inquire into his relative virtues. Men of as firmly established reputation as either Dunbar or Robertson, may as readily become the victims of designing villains, in an unguarded hour, as Hugh Lincoln or poor Roger."

"How is Neilson implicated? What situation had he in your banking-house?"

"A very inferior officer; yet, although subordinate, his undoubted reliability gave him free access to every part of the building, and he is suspected of affording Lincoln opportunities of executing his infamous purposes, in the absence of the other officers. Certainly Mr. Lincoln could have accom-

plished nothing without an agent; and on account
of his gigantic physical strength, suspicion has fallen
upon Neilson as his abettor. As if to confirm this
opinion, bolts and bars have been proved no bar-
riers, and a large chest was conveyed away without
any extraneous aid. Yet, Amy, all this is pre-
sumptive evidence, and on only such the voice of
the community utters its maledictions against men
who were never known to deviate from the very
straightest path of rectitude. I dare not openly,
but secretly I will defend and succor them while I
have breath. I feel sanguine the hour is not far
distant, when the hills and rocks of our beautiful
Caledonia will echo and re-echo their triumphant
acquittal from all participation in this mysterious
affair; the heartless perpetrator will be brought to
justice, and his deeply laid villany proclaimed from
our lofty towers. But here we are, Amy, and the
gates are barred."

"I saw Miss Gertrude appear at a window for a
moment. I am convinced she recognized us, and
will doubtless have us admitted immediately."

"Miss Amy Graeme!" exclaimed the young lady
who had accompanied the servant she had summoned to give them entrance; "why so early, so
far from the manse, and why — but let all your
reasons rest for the moment — you are cold and
weary; — Kenneth, add logs to the fire." (There
was always a noble bank of ashes from the preceding evening.) "Now, Amy, sit you down on this
couch,—throw off your camlet. Master Duncan,
take father's arm-chair; — Kenneth, hasten breakfast, and tell father."

"No, no! Lady Gertrude," interrupted Mr. Graeme, "do not, I beseech. Former experience induced us to expect a hospitable reception; but we shall regret this step, if you swerve from your customary regulations. The snow-drifts have prevented our reaching home. After we have rested, and-partaken of some refreshment —"

"Very questionable hospitality that would defer either rest or refreshment to this chilled mortal, Mr. Duncan. You miscalculated your strength, Miss Amy, when you ventured a contention with the drifts this morning; but place your feet upon this cushion, and give me your mufflers, and all discomforts shall be forgotten."

"Your kindness, Miss Gertrude, would thaw an iceberg," returned Miss Graeme, as she gave her hood and cloak into the young lady's hands.

"With the auxiliary of one of Kenneth's fires," she said, laughing and pointing her little dimpled fingers in that direction. "Nine logs, *only;* it is a pity the size of the chimney-place should restrict him; papa is sure he would pile in a whole fir-tree, but for lack of space. Percy suggests an enlargement."

"Kenneth's fire is refreshingly comfortable to half-frozen wanderers," Miss Graeme observed,— "and so totally unexpected as we were, it seems the production of magic."

"No, Kenneth always has a tower of coals, in case of sickness in, or surprise outside the house. We have so long laughed at his preparations, that he is in a state of excited exultation at having occasion to open the hall, and his ashes, for the perishing stranger!"

"Good morning, Amy; good morning, Mr. Duncan. Was it you firing us up at early dawn?" These inquiries and salutations were made by a bright, sweet-looking girl, a brunette of about fifteen, who entered the apartment with a gleesome laugh, first kissing Miss Graeme, then cordially shaking the hand of her brother.

"Not quite so discourteous as *that*, Lady Ellen, although we have laid siege at no timely hour, and have made no apology —"

"And will leave it unmade, Mr. Duncan," interrupted Miss Ellen; "what is inevitable needs none, neither what is agreeable,—and your visit combines both. Perhaps *my* undue curiosity may demand an apology—indeed, I cannot restrain my inquisitiveness to learn why you selected such a morning and such an hour to visit Glennair?"

"Ellen!" whispered her sister, rebukingly.

"Necessity, Miss Ellen," replied young Graeme. "I cannot tell you how, or why. Amy and myself have yet to be instructed in the reason, or the reasonableness, of being summoned from Everbright on this inclement night. You shall be among the earliest initiated — nay, Miss Gertrude, I consider the question perfectly natural, — reproof is needless."

"Ellen is so thoughtless; she is invulnerable to reproof: yet, Ellen, I did not fear you would be regardless of others' feelings."

"Nor has she, Lady Gertrude," interposed the

youth, rising, and drawing her arm in his, in answer to the sound of the breakfast-bell.

"The Laird is ready for breakfast," said a voice at the door; "shall you be ready to have it served, my ladies?"

"Now for questions, and *no* apologies," said the lively little lady, — "but you understand papa, Mr. Graeme?"

Duncan inclined his head, but the sad expression that fell upon her from those deep gray eyes surprised Ellen; she meant what she said, playfully. Silently they followed the others to the breakfast-room.

"I hope we have not interfered with any of your arrangements, my Lord Glennair," Duncan observed, advancing to receive his graceful welcome.

"You could not, Master Duncan Graeme; the son of your worthy father could not be intrusive, no matter what the hour. And Miss Amy," he continued, taking her hand in both of his, "is a pleasant substitute for the sunbeam we lack this morning. I hope to learn our pastor, and your excellent mother, are enjoying a large measure of health; and Lewellyen — no, Lochiel, you call him — I venture to say *he* is enjoying all he can of life, if at the expense of all others; his best friends, I believe, are no surety — eh, Miss Amy?" he asked, as he drew the chair nearer himself, which was placed for her.

"Lochiel has no *better* reputation than he merits," laughed Miss Graeme; "and my Lord Glennair has a worse opinion of him than he really deserves."

"I am not in the minority, Miss Amy; yet he is

a favorite, too. He is brave, even to daring; noble-
hearted, generous, but reckless. Were he here,
instead of conversing as Duncan is, and eating his
breakfast, some misdemeanor would have enraged
me, and sent him from the table; this, Miss Amy,
has occurred several times."

"His parentage has not so effectually rendered
him innoxious to the Laird of Glennair," she observed, archly; "but, indeed, Lochiel's frailties
spring from an overflowing mirthfulness, and his
better feelings are quite accessible. These annoying
propensities, I am confident, will die out with his
years. I have entire reliance in the strength of
character of both my brothers." The color mounted
as she met the glance of Duncan, who had heard,
and been arrested by the last sentences. His face
reflected her own; the confusion was momentary
and unnoticed — the Laird immediately replying:

"Do not quarrel with mutton hash, Miss Amy,"
he said, helping her plentifully, and then himself;
"it is very wholesome, and so are Mrs. Carter's bis-
cuit. As to the lad Lochiel, there is little need to
battle for him; I am sure as yourself he will out-
grow his quirks; but I had as leave bide his absence
till he do. Gertrude, dear, replenish Miss Amy's
cup before you send mine; and, Kenneth, learn what
prevents Master Percy's more timely compliments
to our guests."

"He was disturbed by the firing, papa, or rather
by the inquirers about it. His apartment," she said,
turning again to Mr. Graeme, "is the only one over-
looking the sea, and we were anxious to ascertain

whether some fellow-being required assistance. Did
you notice it, Mr. Duncan?"

"I heard the gun, but supposed it proceeded from
the shore."

"Some fool firing at gulls, I warrant," rejoined
the Laird.

"So Percy suggested in no meek spirit or voice,"
remarked the younger lady, "and would give none
of us admittance."

"It is said evil spirits always appear when their
qualities are being discussed,—which of mine are
worthy of the remarks of Ellen Dunbar?" inquired
the young man in question, entering the room.
With perfectly easy address, he bowed generally to
the group, and then cordially welcomed the visitors.

"You were perversely determined there should be
distress upon our coasts this morning, Ellen," he remarked playfully, as he took his accustomed seat by
her side; "I would not have delayed giving the
alarm, had *your* aid been required, my dear little
sister."

"You might have opened your door, and not have
resisted all my importunities," she said, half petu-
lantly, pushing his hand from her head and bending
low to prevent his intended kiss.

"Was there nothing to be seen, Percy Dunbar?"
asked his father; "*your* eyes were our only medium."

"Dreaming ears, eyes, and lips, I do trust, are irre-
sponsible agents, father, or I have much incivility to
answer for. Ellie here is totally unforgiving, and
no doubt thinks I deserve the tower for not spying
a wreck, and not illuminating the observatory to

4

help the sun-rising ; and sister, her sentence is no breakfast for her heartless brother."

" *You* may be the best judge of your delinquencies and deserts, brother," returned Gertrude, laughing, " but I have sent for coffee and hot cakes for you."

He playfully bowed his thanks, and addressing Miss Graeme, said courteously, " he flattered himself she was to be their guest several days ; the weather certainly is propitious to that happiness, Miss Amy."

" Such an arrangement would be very agreeable to me," she answered ; " but it is necessary we should be at home even now, Mr. Dunbar."

" How ! what ! " exclaimed the Laird ; " you must not think of travelling where a vehicle cannot. Who talks of venturing on foot, to-day ? "

" We must do other than talk, my Laird," interposed Duncan. " We are needed at home, and speedily. The drifts prevented our reaching there last night."

" And will prevent your *sister* to-day, also. If so determined, tramp it alone — or with Percy. Amy Graeme is my guest until she can leave here with comfort and in safety."

" My father — "

" Say to him I am surety for every inconvenience I may occasion ; and I tell you, Duncan Graeme, your sister is the captive of Robert Dunbar so long as the roads between here and the manse are inaccessible to a horse and carriage. Are you going home, or to the Bank ? "

" I will be there in the course of the day. Our

operations are suspended until the officers examine the papers."

" I believe it is fully ascertained half a million is irretrievably lost."

" *Robertson's* estimate is £300,000. *He* advises less harshness with regard to Lincoln ; he proposes to delay the confiscation of his property until it is known how far available, — his library especially."

" Humph ! Though the blood of the Camerons flow in my veins, nevertheless I say to the death ! — and to the last farthing ! — and both speedily ! Extension, forsooth ! has Robertson a watchword to stay the clamors of creditors, too ? Will he have *me* part with Glennair to save Thistle-hedge Hall ? And will he have the miscreant, — the felon Lincoln, go free ? Hugh Lincoln was not ignorant of the penalty ; the sin of a man has ever been and must ever be the inheritance of his children. Edith Cameron Lincoln must wear the brand her father has imprinted upon her ; she will sink into obscurity somewhere far from her native place ; mayhap will change her name and be, with her father, forgotten. He has escaped to the Continent, I presume."

" Father !" observed young Dunbar, after a long interval of silence, " the exalted virtues, the beauty, the gentleness, the purity, the Christian forbearance of Miss Lincoln, will never, *can* never fade from the remembrance of Glennair and its vicinity."

Every eye, save that of Duncan Graeme, was turned toward the Laird. The gathering wrath left his son a few moments unanswered. At length, in tones deep with contending emotions, he returned,—

"Percy Dunbar! as you value my affection and dread my resentment, never, in my presence, mention any one of that doomed family with respect, or even with lenity. I lament, I pity the poor bairn; yet had I the authority, the death-warrant of the father, for forgery and defrauding, would have my seal fixed to-day. I am glad to know, children, that our pastor has laid his interdict also upon all communication with the family of this infamous man."

"I would disabuse your mind on that point, my Lord," returned Duncan, raising and dropping his spoon repeatedly into his cup while speaking. "Miss Edith Lincoln declines almost any intercourse with the human family; my father has recommended a cessation of my sister's visits for a' time; Lochiel has imbibed the universal impression; I cannot, myself, understand how it can be salutary to the guilty, to ourselves individually, or to the nation, to thus confound the innocent with the criminal."

"Human nature has not been very extensively studied by my opponent," answered the Laird, haughtily. "Man would be encouraged to transgress under your lenient policy. Depend upon it, young man, the more stringent the law, and the more rigid its enforcement, the stronger the barrier to these outbreaks. Strange such a man as Lincoln, such a *father*, could have plotted so much criminality, knowing his *family* would be involved in his disgrace; strange *that* had not deterred him."

"How terribly Edith must feel, as being the innocent occasion of fastening suspicion upon her father," observed Miss Gertrude. "The notes found by

Edith were confirmatory of his guilt; a correspondence between him and Neilson about the removal of the trunk, and all those checks, failing to counterfeit correctly the signatures of father and Mr. Robertson. Poor Edith, little supposing papers directed to the bank porter could involve her father in any trouble, innocently gave them into the hands of the Bailie."

" Yes, it was to support her own firm conviction of his ignorance of the whole affair which led to the production of the papers confirming his guilt. Has it yet been discovered what became of those documents, papa ? "

" Very well· known, Gertie, but never proved. They disappeared with Lincoln. Of course, they are in his possession, or his daughter may — "

" No, my Lord, no ! " burst from the lips of young Graeme. " That name and reputation has hitherto been unsullied, and I trust ever will escape the voice of calumny."

" Mayhap the *father* may find an advocate in the assistant cashier of our wicked bank ; can a syllable be written in extenuation or palliation of *his* guilt, Duncan Graeme ? "

" *Possibly, many,* my Lord, were permission given to investigate the whole business, and placed with judicious, unprejudiced persons." A touch under the table from the boot of Percy, checked Duncan. Smiling, he gravely added, — " From childhood, our families have been almost as one ; it is difficult to awaken or harbor a thought derogatory to so early a friend. Time will make its own developments."

4 *

"*Time* will, no doubt, and will exhibit unequivocally the real villain ; and it will be prudent to spare the espousal of his cause till those he has wronged discover they have erred most singularly in their judgment. Personal interest has misled you, young man. Be cautious where you utter such sentiments ; you may become entangled in the net this *early friend* has woven ; but no more of it."

He pushed his chair back hurriedly and arose.

The cheek of Duncan paled with indignation, but an entreating look from his sister, and the hint from the monitor beneath the table, held back his response.

" Kenneth," inquired young Dunbar of the person removing the chairs from the table, " could the horses be possibly attached to the heavy wagon this morning ?"

"Naithing mair possible, Mister Dunbar ; but how muckle mair I dinna ken ; hae ye a mind to try ?"

" Yes, yes ! let us all try, papa ; do permit us," exclaimed Miss Ellen.

" *I* must go too, then, Ellen — "

" *You?* oh ! no, dear papa, some evil might befall you ; I could not hazard that," she said, throwing her arms caressingly around him.

" What greater, dear, than happening to one of you ? Suppose I were bereft of my second Ellen, what would life be to Robert Dunbar ? Let Duncan Graeme and your brother take each other for company ; the steeds may have more wit than to trifle with their *own* necks."

"I cannot bear to vex you, my Lord," said Amy, meekly, laying her fingers on his arm, "and am really loth to leave you all; yet I feel so apprehensive of some calamity at home, that every moment I linger seems an age. I would not incur your anger willingly, but how can I remain?"

"Take the risk, then, Miss Amy," he replied, gently, patting her hand; "but say to your mother you were carried away by your own waywardness, disdaining my dissent. Go find your trappings; mind they be warm; and take my forgiveness," he added, kissing her forehead.

"I declare, they are nearly ready," cried Gertrude from the window. "The young gentlemen are directing Kenneth, and he is evidently protesting against it, though harnessing with all his might. Nymph stands gently enough, but Pitt is restive."

"Restive!" exclaimed the Laird, advancing hastily and throwing open the casement. "Out with Pitt," he commanded, "and bring Leon. Miss Graeme's neck is worth the saving, if her wits have followed the sun this morn."

The exchange was made; Laird Glennair was summoned to a private interview with a man in the library; so, without further interruption, Amy was equipped for the journey of seven miles, and bade farewell, for a season, to the daughters of the haughty yet kind, inexorable yet just, stern yet tender-hearted, Laird of Glennair.

CHAPTER II.

"Angels are 'round the good man, to catch the incense of his prayers,
And they fly to minister kindness to those for whom he pleadeth;
For the altar of his heart is lighted, and burneth before God continually,
And he breatheth, conscious of his joy, the native atmosphere of heaven."

A BROAD glare of light gleamed from the manse upon the road through which the travellers were to pass. Lamps had been placed in every window as beacons to guide the missing ones. A young man, apparently about sixteen, with hurried and excited step, paced the hall, repeatedly opening the front door, anxiously endeavoring to scan into the distance; but the violence of the hurricane hurling myriads of snow-flakes against him, obliged him to seek a retreat within. The wind, whistling around, shook the house to its centre, and an old tree that had graced the ground for centuries, moaned and shivered, and bent its huge frame as though it felt and acknowledged its danger.

"Duncan — Amy!" he murmured, clasping his hands in agony. "Where are you? where, oh! where? And my precious mother!" Throwing himself into the corner of an old settee, his head bent low upon his knee. There was a footstep upon the stairway; it was unheeded. A hand was laid upon his shoulder.

"Your mother mentions the name of Lochiel

44

inquiringly. She evidently desires your presence, my boy."

The youth started to his feet. "What of my mother, Dr. McMillan? Will she live? Will she be spared us? Tell me, oh! tell me, must I be bereft of hope?"

"While life continues, the Great Shepherd suffers us to hope, Lochiel."

"But what is your candid opinion?" he inquired, fixing an intent gaze upon him.

The head of the physician was shaken despondingly. His eye sought the floor, as, for a few moments, he stood in silence.

"Tell me the worst, doctor; suspense is intolerable."

"It is your mother's wish, and, I believe, her Saviour's will, that she should soon enter her eternal rest."

A burst of grief followed — uncontrolled, violent; the frame of the youth trembled with emotion.

Again the kindly hand rested upon his. "Lochiel, my boy, your mother anxiously awaits you. Delay not for Duncan and Amy; this tempest renders their return impracticable. They doubtless are still under the shelter of your uncle's roof. The storm must have been pending when the message was received."

"They have set out," replied the boy vehemently, at the same time dashing his cap heavily upon the floor, "or my name is not Lochiel Graeme. The message was peremptory; and when did Duncan disregard the slightest wish of his father? Would that I could bear the same testimony to his brother's obedience," he added, mournfully. "I will follow you, doctor."

"And promise composure? Agitation might produce serious results."

The head was bowed in acquiescence, although the lip quivered while the promise was given. Both entered the chamber.

The stillness of death was there. Mr. Graeme, bowed with grief, was seated at the side of the bed, the hand of his wife resting within his own. A faint smile played over the countenance of Mrs. Graeme as Lochiel approached. Throwing himself impetuously upon his knees beside her, he silently bathed her hand with tears.

"My beloved, precious boy," she murmured.

"Can you forgive me, my darling mother; forgive my waywardness, my disobedience; forgive the many cruel pangs I've cost you?"

"All, all," she answered feebly, "and love you with all the strength of a dying mother's love. But Duncan,—Amy?"

"The storm has prevented their return, my darling," Mr. Graeme replied.

A shade of disappointment crossed her pallid face. "May the blessing of the Triune God be with my precious ones," she ejaculated.

The head of Lochiel was buried in his hands; a low sob only broke upon the stillness of the apartment. The hand of the invalid was slightly raised. Mr. Graeme, reading her wish, gently placed it upon the head of Lochiel.

"May the star of Bethlehem guide my latest-born," she almost whispered; "and may he take refuge under the shadow of the cross. May his parents' God be his God, and may he experience, in a dying hour, the same perfect peace he has vouch-safed me at this moment."

"I will, mother; I will," gasped the youth. "I will be all you wish, wish —" The power of utter-ance failed; a gush of feeling followed.

Gently, very gently, the hand of the kind physi-cian was laid upon his shoulder. "Lochiel," he whispered, "have you forgotten your promise?"

There was no reply; but rising immediately, he busied himself arranging the pillow for his mother.

"Have you no blessing for *me*, Agnes?" inquired Mr. Graeme, again taking the hand he had relin-quished.

The countenance was almost beaming as she faintly replied, "Those who turn many to right-eousness, will shine as the stars in the firmament. Many jewels you have been permitted to place in the diadem of your Redeemer. Do you need a fur-ther blessing, my Malcolm?"

"Yes," he murmured, in broken accents; "grace and strength to bow to this sore bereavement."

There was a radiant smile as she pointed upward, saying, "Home,—home,—Je—" The smile remained, but the word died upon the lips; the spirit, without a struggle, had winged its way to the home, where Jesus was awaiting, with hosts of angels, to wel-come it.

Mr. Graeme arose, and laying his hand upon the

polished forehead, beautiful even in death, meekly said, " The Lord gave, the Lord has taken —" His voice faltered. " Blessed be his name," added Dr. McMillan, as he gently closed the eyes of his beloved patient, and drew the arm of his pastor within his own, to lead him from the room.

With a loud wail, Lochiel threw himself upon the body. " My mother,— oh! my mother!" he exclaimed. " Speak but one word to your boy, your son, your Lochiel."

A deep groan told the feelings of the father, as he bent his head upon the shoulder of Dr. McMillan.

" The Lord loveth whom he chasteneth," whispered the physician in the ear of the boy. " Can you not put your trust in so good, so merciful a being, dear Lochiel ? "

" What is mercy ? " he inquired, sullenly. " The exertion of power to bring blight and ruin in our midst ? "

" Do not arraign the Almighty, my darling son," said Mr. Graeme, as tears, unbidden, coursed down his face. " What I do, thou knowest not now ; but thou shalt know hereafter."

At the sound of his father's voice, the youth raised his head reverently, and meeting the heavenly expression upon the face of his mother, his attention was riveted ; he gazed —gazed intently.

" May God forgive my rebellious spirit," he said, mournfully, as he rested his cheek upon that of his mother, and wet her face with his tears. " Your God shall be my God, mother ; your slightest wish shall be laid up in my remembrance, and I here solemnly vow to honor your religion for your sake. So help me, my mother's Redeemer."

Dr. McMillan was about replying, but checked himself, merely remarking,—"It would be her wish, Lochiel, that you would now endeavor to be the stay and solace of your bereaved father."

The lad immediately arose and silently laid his arm around the neck of Mr. Graeme.

The doctor led the way into the adjoining apartment.

With countenances in which the deepest sadness was depicted, two faithful domestics performed the last rites for all that remained of their beloved mistress.

"There will be monny a sair heart to mourn her loss, Kathleen," the elder woman remarked.

"But nan sae sair as our ain Mr. Lochiel, Maggie," was the reply; "it near breaks his heart, this partin';" then lowering her voice, she added, "and a mighty thorn he was in his mother's side, bein' sae awfu' wilful."

"He's a bonny bairn, Kathleen," her friend returned, warmly, "though as wild as the rocks around him; but frae the time his mouth first lisped the name of Margie, to this melancholy day, he has never crossed the path of his old nurse, Margaret MacDee."

"And has Margaret MacDee e'er said nae to her bonnie bairn?" Kathleen inquired, pleasantly.

"It wud nae be the kind thing o' ye, Kathleen," she returned with an offended air, "tae think he

5 D

put a nail in his mother's coffin. After all the sights and sounds afore her death, nothin' could hae saved or harmed her. Did Rob Roy howl for naethin'? I trow nae. And did the auld clock's weight fa' like a death damp, an' nae bidden either, Kathleen?"

"I dinna ken, Margie; I trow our blessed Lord dinna need dumb creturs to speak his will. When he sends swift messengers, is it auld clocks and howlin' dogs that does his biddin'?"

"Twenty winters passed o'er my head afore ye were rocked upon yere mither's lap, Kathleen MacLeod; and is n't the Benshee's cry that came to my ears sae often, and the monny deaths that's came after them, of nae account wi' ye? And dinna them of your own clan that 's came afore ye, tell ye the same truths that I tell ye at this moment? Yere ain gude Book says,—'Be not faithless, but believing.'"

"Truly it does, Margie; the words of our ain Redeemer. Believe in the Lord Jesus Christ, and all faith in sights 'ill flee awa'. We are not to add or take from that gude Book."

"Ye are a puir MacLeod, Kathleen; the first heathen e'er raised among them."

A sad smile passed over the face of Kathleen. "Would that ye would study yere Bible, Margie," she returned; "that Bible tells—" The door opened, and Dr. McMillan entered.

"The light is just dawning, my good women," he remarked; "you must take some rest for a few hours; nothing is needed for the present. I will remain, and my man is here to answer any necessary calls."

With a lingering look toward their mistress, they quietly, but with evident reluctance, withdrew from the chamber, and the Doctor threw himself upon the couch in the same apartment. Lochiel had left his father's chamber, and his hurried step might now be distinguished pacing the hall below. A fervent petition was offered by Dr. McMillan, that this heavy bereavement which now pressed with such weight upon the spirit of the youth, might tend to attune that heart to gladness, and enable him to praise and magnify the name of his Redeemer, and find a radiance shed over his now darkened path.

The gray dawn had scarcely appeared; the white and heavy clouds moving rapidly over the mountains, tokening another fall of snow. The wind had partially lulled, but a dreary waste lay before the vision.

The Doctor arose, and stood viewing the gloomy prospect, when the hall-door, closing heavily, arrested his attention. On hearing his name mentioned at the chamber-door, he immediately opened it. A tall, brawny Irishman stood before him.

" What is it, Bernard ? " he inquired.

" It's a dreary marnin' for Misther Lochiel, I'm afther thinkin', yere honor, an' he'll be head over hales out of his depth afore he can make a calkilation. Now I could n't make free to spake, but maybe a word frum yere honor would do the thing, and kape him frum reskin' sich a wa bet of a neck in sich elements. He's got the strength of a giant packed up in a wa bit of a frame that would n't do much wark in this hurricane, I'm thinkin'."

Before the door was reached, Lochiel had proceeded some steps, and was carefully picking his way toward a drift at the side of a mountain. His head was almost buried in a high coat-collar with a felt hat drawn about his ears; a gun was carelessly laid across his shoulder. At the voice of Dr. Mc-Millan, he turned. "You will accomplish nothing by this risk, Lochiel," he called; "and your father will be rendered yet more unhappy from the suspense he will endure for your sake."

His eye rolled wildly as he replied, "I will bring Duncan and Amy to him. *They* can comfort where I cannot."

"But your own precious life, my boy?"

"That is valueless; if I cannot save, I can only perish with them."

"And are you ready to yield that spirit to your mother's God, young man?" asked the Doctor solemnly, as he came forward and laid his hand upon his arm.

A blast of wind moaned past them, almost overturning the slight frame of the youth, who was forced to cling to a jutting rock for support, and with bended form await until it had spent its force. When he again arose, he threw his head impetuously upon the shoulder of his friend, and gave way to a torrent of grief.

"Can any future woe surpass my present suffering?" he inquired.

The head was drawn very closely, as the kind physician returned gently: "'Come unto me all ye that are weary, and I will give you rest.' Return with me, dear Lochiel; you are not fitted this day to brave the hardships before you. And your efforts would not avail."

"No, Doctor, no. Do not detain me; I must atone for the trouble I have caused my now only parent. I will restore to him his children; I will render his declining years comparatively happy. I have trodden every foot of ground and rock for miles around, and can with —" A sudden thought seemed to pass through his mind; a low whistle brought an immense dog to his side, bounding joyfully upon the shoulders of his young master.

"Hist! Rob," he whispered. "Lost, lost." The dog looked intelligently, then darted forward, returned, wagged his tail, growled, again darted forward, and was soon lost to view. At a signal from the Doctor, Bernard disappeared, and returned equipped with a large coat, flapped hat, and gun. There was a glance of gratified surprise as the man joined him, but no word passed, and they hastily pursued the way down the road, while the Doctor, with a sad heart, retreated into the house, and joined Mr. Graeme in the sitting-room.

Lochiel and Bernard had proceeded but a short distance, when a tall, slight female figure, wrapped in a large plaid shawl, turned the corner of the rock. She started, and the deep color mounted to her cheek as they approached; but the cap, slightly raised, was the only recognition, and the head of Lochiel again sank upon his bosom. With a deferential bow, Bernard advanced to meet her.

5 *

"Is it afther the Doctor ye are, Miss Edith?" he inquired.

"Yes, Bernard, little Helen is quite ill this morning, and Aunt Cameron wished to see him immediately. Is he still with Mrs. Graeme?"

"An' it's a long time I'm a-trustin', Miss Edith, afore he reaches that same home where her spirit's now a-restin'. He'll give many a d'rap o' comfort to all around him afore that day arrives, I'm thinkin'."

"Bernard!" exclaimed the young lady, clasping her hands together, "Mrs. Graeme is not dead; surely you are mistaken."

The man shook his head. "It's too true, Miss Edith; I had it from the Doctor's own lips, and Margie and Kathleen."

With her face buried in her hands, she stood silent a few moments, then hesitatingly inquired, "Has Miss Amy yet returned?"

"No; nor Mr. Duncan nither, Miss Edith; the Docther's afther a-thinkin' it will be an awful blow, if they ever rache the manse, which sames rather doubtful. And for the raisin we are now in sarche of them, I can't be afther tellin' the Docther you nade him."

"They were yesterday at Mr. Rushbrook's," she replied, with forced calmness, though her voice trembled with agitation. "Why do you suppose them in danger?"

"I don't know the grounds of the case, Miss Edith; but Mr. Lochiel is on a wild-goose chase, an' I'm a-follerin' afther him, with my ordthers, to

peck the wee thing out when he's head over haels
in snow; but we'll soon be brought up by the sac,
I'm thinkin'."

"But would it not be possible to force a way to
Mr. Rushbrook's?" she inquired, with a face of
ashy paleness. "The team?"

"*He's* a manin' for all his doin's," he replied,
pointing his finger toward the now almost invisible
figure of Lochiel. "He has his own plans laid, I'm
thinkin'; and I'll follow him through arth and
wather, always provided he steers clare of the Elfin.
I've pretty strong nairves, Miss Edith; but a stout
heart might be afther quakin' at the unarthly sights
in that quarter, fet to make the hair of one's head
stand upright, and fasthen in the other end. But
we'll musther strong, if there's a nade be, and drive
out all the men, an' sperits, too, afore Mr. Duncan
and Miss Amy shall be the worse."

An involuntary start was not noticed by Bernard.

"But it's quite and intirely time I was kapin' in
the wake, Miss Edith, for Misther Lochiel might
be buried up, for all the care I'm takin' of him."

So saying, with another low bow, he left her, and
hastened to rejoin the young man, who was entirely
out of sight.

"Will yees be afther cuttin' across to Misther
Rushbrook's, Misther Lochiel?" he inquired.

"The snow would prevent the possibility. We
will take MacLoughlin's boat, and endeavor to find
some safe landing-place."

"A man bred to the sac would kape clear of the
shore, instead of venturing on it, Mr. Lochiel."

"We may possibly throw up the boat upon the sand beach to the right of the Elfin. The forests in the neighborhood may afford them shelter, though no sustenance."

"The Elfin!" exclaimed Bernard. "A sorry place to enter for safety; we nade a sarch-warrant from the divil for that expedition, I'm thinkin'."

"If you and John have any fear, you can remain in the boat, while I enter the forest in search of them. There are many caves beside the Elfin; I scarcely think, myself, that Duncan would venture there."

"Sich a cowardly step's not in my natur, Misther Lochiel. No, no, my strong foot may do some sarvice, if his riverence does n't interfere on the side of his friends; at any rate, it sha'n't be said that Bernard O'Dougherty desarted a bet of a streplin' in his utmost nade."

There was a flash in the eye of the youth; it was momentary; for despair, which had set its seal upon that brow, resumed its place.

"I will never return without them," he murmured; "never, never."

The tone, rather than the words, fell upon the ear of Bernard; feeling that they were not addressed to him, he forbore reply.

After much difficulty, they at length reached the hut of the fisherman, which stood upon a bluff, about a quarter of a mile from the ocean. A loud halloa brought him to the door of his cabin.

"Misther Graeme is wantin' your services, John MacLoughlin," called Bernard; "jist step this way, man, and don't be sleepin' to 'tarnity."

The person addressed, a sour, crusty-looking man, came forward, having evidently just risen at the call of his friend.

"Yere makin' an unco' noise aboot naethin', Bernard O'Dougherty," he growled. "I 'll rise wi' the sun, or when it's gaun awa', an' nae settlement wi' ye, nither."

"Well, come, be afther makin' a sittlement with Misther Lochiel, who 's down on the wather's edge a-waitin' to strike a bargain wi' yees. You always was good in that line, Misther MacLoughlin," he added, slapping the ill-natured man upon the shoulder.

".Ye 'd mickle better make a settlement wi' yere own tongue, Bernard O'Dougherty; there 's nae mon but mysel' wad hae carried Norval Neilson far frae danger, an' the tender mercies o' my Laird Glennair."

"And were ye afther doin' the thing handsome, John, an' did n't ye grip the last bawbee from the poor divil's pocket? I'd hae been the last man would cast it up in yere tathe, but it was a mane pace of business, ye can't deny it, can ye? The stuff would burn in my pocket, I tell ye."

"Make yere ain bargains, and mind yere ain affairs," he remarked, breaking from him angrily, and advancing to the spot where Lochiel was standing.

"Wull ye aught wi' me, Maister Graeme," he inquired.

"Let your boat be launched at once, John, and provide me a strong oarsman."

"In sic a blaw, Maister Lochiel?—and the puir auld craft is sae ailin'; she canna hauld water, salt or fresh; she's mickle the waur for the last wurk she tried upon the waters."

A shade of bitter disappointment crossed the face of the young man. "And can no boat be obtained?" he inquired. "Where is Aleck Edgar?"

As he spoke, his eye carefully scanned the waters. A small speck at some distance met his view. It was pointed out to Bernard.

"It's nae mair than a sea-bird, dippin' for its ain dinner," MacLoughlin remarked.

The practised eye of Lochiel saw differently, as much of his leisure time had been passed in watching boats and shipping as they gradually neared the shore. Taking a small glass from his pocket, he brought it to bear upon the object.

"There is a boat," he observed, after a few moments' intent gazing, "evidently endeavoring to effect a landing. Their danger is imminent; here the waves are comparatively smooth; fire quickly, Bernard; let them know they are observed."

The order was immediately obeyed, and the echo reverberated from rock to rock.

Suddenly the glass was grasped tightly, while an exclamation of horror escaped him.

"It is — it is!" he gasped.

The glass was grasped by Bernard, as his strong arm was placed around Lochiel to support the trembling boy. A signal was plainly seen — a curiously wrought crimson scarf, which Bernard well remembered having seen upon the neck of Miss Graeme.

"Another look, in mercy! Bernard."

The glass was again placed to the eye of Lochiel.

For a moment the scarf fluttered upon the breeze, then suddenly disappeared, as though intentionally it were carefully removed from view.

The strained eye of Lochiel intently watched the boat, as he clung to the arm of Bernard for support; an immense surge rose higher and higher, becoming more terrific every moment, then bursting upon the little boat, engulfed it within its bosom.

Lochiel saw no more, but with a wild shriek, fell senseless upon the ground. His faithful dog — who had been scenting every nook throughout their journey, and as often returning to the side of his master, eagerly watching every movement — threw himself, with a piteous whine, upon him.

"John MacLoughlin, if ye have any pity in yere heart," shouted Bernard, as he gently raised the unconscious boy, "let your boat — lake or no lake — be launched, and save the precious lives of Misther Duncan and Miss Amy. This moment, or ye will be too late," he added, with feverish impatience, as he saw the man still linger.

"And wha wi' ha' a care for the risking of the life o' John MacLoughlin?" he inquired, sneeringly, "and wha wi' hae a look tae his bairns, if the morn see him in the bottom of the Lynn? Tell me that, Maister Bernard O'Dougherty."

"Launch at once, MacLoughlin," he shouted, as (taking his cloak from his shoulders, and gently laying the youth upon it, under shelter of a rock) he advanced and seized the side of the boat, while great drops stood upon his forehead, from the excitement of the moment. "Lend a hand, man, and throw her into the dape, and I 'll take all the risk, if you 'll lend an eye to the lad yonder."

"And wha wuld be the profit of that, wi' a dead boy to scare the auld woman and bairns."

"Then handle the oar," he cried, impatiently, as he almost threw the man into the boat, now floating upon the angry billows, "and I 'll promise you a full pocket for all your trouble."

. The man surlily obeyed, and in a few moments was springing the breakers and breasting the waves in a manner that showed him no novice in his vocation.

"And yere childer might be more scared with yere ugly visage, you craven," Bernard murmured, as he resumed his burden and proceeded to the hut of MacLoughlin.

The tap at the door being unanswered, the latch was lifted and he entered. A dirty bundle of straw in the corner of the room appeared to have been just vacated, and a tall, lank, bony woman was crouching over some smouldering embers, which she was endeavoring to light by the aid of some chips which lay beside her. An infant a few months old, wrapped in a tattered spread, was lying upon the floor, feebly making known its wants, while several children — the eldest not over six — were clamorously surrounding their mother for something to eat. A dirty table, devoid of cloth, was standing beside the wall, with a few fragments — the remnants of last night's meal. Crumbs and grease had fallen, and were scattered in various directions around.

"Out upon ye, every mither's son o' ye," she

shouted, seizing an old shoe, and testing its strength over the back of the eldest. "Can't ye hould yere silly tongues, an' not be draggin' sowl and body apart wi' yere clamer?"

The youngster thus suddenly attacked, sought refuge under the table — which being rather totter- ing, finding support, in the absence of a fourth leg, against the wall, suddenly up-turned, scattering tin and earthen dishes to the farthest corner of the · room. In a moment a cold potato was seized by one, the tongue of another applied to a molasses-dish, the baby's cries increasing with the vociferous noises.

Bernard, almost unconscious of the scene around him, had seated himself on an old stool, and was bathing the temples of his precious charge with cold water from a tin cup which he had seized on enter- ing. An occasional moan manifested some sign of returning life.

The woman, whose warm temper was now thor- oughly roused, sprang· from the corner, and was about wreaking her wrath upon the first object she might encounter, when her eye, for the first time, fell upon the new-comers. For a moment she stood mute with astonishment and rage, then placing her hands upon her sides, she made a sudden descent upon them.

"And wha may ye be?" she inquired, with clenched teeth, "a-makin' sac frac·in the house of anither?"

"Lave the lad brathin'-room, woman," exclaimed Bernard, passionately, as she attempted to push them both toward the door. A low moan and slight

6

movement arrested him. " Misther Lochiel," he said, gently. A hand was partially lifted, then all was again still. " Will you kill the lad — the son of the good ministher, too, you old hag ? " he inquired, fiercely. " His life shall be laid at your door if you stir a step toward the harmin' of him."

" And do you trow I care *that*," snapping her fingers, " for a' yer preachments an' ministers a'thegither ? An' wi' ye scare awa the Benshee the night at the bringin' of death among us ? Allan MacLoughlin ! " she vociferated, opening a small back window.

The sound of the chopping of wood ceased, the axe fell heavily, the door opened, and a young man entered. His kind, benevolent countenance at once attracted Bernard.

" I nade some help here, young man," he remarked. " Can you get any conveyance to the manse, at once ? "

Hesitatingly the door was opened, and a very small room appeared to view, in which was a wooden settee with some old clothes lying upon it. Casting a doubtful look at the woman, he inquired,—

" Could n't he lay here for a wee time ? "

" Out upon ye ! " she exclaimed. " It's nae i' my house he 'll find a footin'."

" Ye dinna ken mickle of the gude Book," he replied, sadly, " or ye wuld hae mair kindliness in yere heart, Katy."

" And lose my sowl by turnin' heretic, like yersel', ye fou' ! Ye'd mickle better git the priest to shrive the heathen, and nae stan' parlyin' 'bout naethin'."

There was no reply, but the young man disappearing for a moment, returned bearing the little cot, upon which were arranged smoothly two small, soiled blankets — the sole bed-clothing he possessed. Over this the cloak of Bernard was laid, and a tattered plaid belonging to Allan arranged for a pillow.

" I 'll aid you wi' him mysel'," he said, as Bernard, with a heart-felt " God bless you," lifted his charge upon it. Allan passed his arm carefully under it, to raise it more steadily.

" And wha 'll be cuttin' the wood in the time?" inquired the woman, angrily.

" Get your cuttin' done by some of your own stamp, who are worth nothin' betther," Bernard replied, impatiently, throwing a piece of silver toward her.

Silently pocketing the money, somewhat mollified at the sight of it, she permitted them to leave the house without further molestation.

" A warm house there, I guess, without the nade of asking," Bernard remarked with a shrug, pointing his thumb backward in the direction of the lot, as they carefully picked their way toward the manse.

" I look far awa', " he replied, meekly.

" Far awa' ! " exclaimed Bernard ; " I should think your wits would be naded nare home, to kape your head upon your shoulders, grantin' any may be left in such a brawl."

" It is n't my hame. I sit content at the Maister's feet, an' he points *there*," (raising his forefinger impressively,) " to anither an' a better hame. Eye hae nae seen, nor ear heard, nor heart conceived the glories —" Overcome with timidity, the words died upon his lips.

Bernard's heart was touched; he made no reply, but glancing toward his companion, he saw his countenance beaming with a heavenly radiance. Silently they proceeded until they drew near the manse. Bernard paused.

"I'm just a-thinkin', Allan," he remarked, "there's trouble enough at the minister's for one day, so we'll take Misther Lochiel to the Hedge. The lady has a big heart, and we'll be sartin of a kindly gratin'."

"Wha' is the trouble at the manse, sair?"

"No sair for me, if you plase; I am plain Bernard O'Dougherty, no better — no, nor half so good as yourself; but our kind leddy at the manse has gone to her long home."

An involuntary start shook the hand of Bernard; he turned inquiringly. Every feature in his companion's face was convulsed, and the heaving bosom told that a chord had been struck of which he had not the slightest apprehension. A gush of feeling followed, and uncontrolled sobs and tears relieved his pent-up anguish.

"Then you knew Mistress Graeme, Allan?" his friend inquired, kindly.

"She ha made me all I am. Twa year since, she took me by the hand, and led me right to Christ my Saviour; and he said, 'Come unto me,' and I came right awa', and since that time, on the eve of every holy Sabbath, wi' three other puir lads nae better than mysel', she gie us an hour's blessed counsel at the manse."

A fresh gush of tears followed.

"And a good cup of tay in the bargain?" Bernard inquired, desirous to divert the current.

"Ah, Kathleen's kindness was gude to think upon; alway a hearty welcome and good cheer i' the kitchen afore we parted."

The house now stood full in view, the closed windows mournfully telling that death had set its seal upon it. There was a shudder passed through the frame of Allan.

Bernard turned, and leading the way to a side door of the neighboring house, entered without asking permission.

A tall, dignified, sad-looking lady was sitting in the dining-room. She started and advanced, pale with alarm. "Not Dr. McMillan, Bernard? He left here only a few moments since."

"Misther Lochiel, Mrs. Cameron. Thenking there was grafe enough at the ministher's, I made frae —"

"Hold, good Bernard; no words are necessary; the sufferer will always find a welcome here."

The door to a small apartment, nicely warmed, was thrown open, and after freeing him from useless clothing, and wrapping him in a flannel morning-gown, Lochiel was placed in a comfortable couch.

"The Doctor, Bernard, immediately," said Mrs. Cameron. "Then return for refreshment, with your friend, in the kitchen. But the poor lad is pale from exhaustion," she remarked, as for the first time she glanced toward Allan. Bringing a cup of warm coffee, she bade him take it, and be

6 *   E

seated. With a grateful and a full heart, Allan partook of the beverage, and with feelings such as none could appreciate but those who knew not the name of comfort, in a very few moments sunk into the soundest slumber.

CHAPTER III.

" He stealeth all goodly names,
As wealth, as value, and substance."

DARK and gloomy as had been the ushering in of the morning, at noon, in all his glory and brilliancy, the sun burst forth over the hills and lochs of Glennair and its surroundings. Loch Leighton, bound in a coat of mail, reflected glitteringly every ray, while the tall firs and caves, heavily hung with icicles, in allegiance to the King of Day, offered no quarter to the unfortunate wayfarer. Thus far, the only exhibition of the power of his majesty was to throw a shower of crystal drops, pendent upon each point, upon the old cap of John MacLoughlin, as he beat with his heavy stick against the kitchen-door of the dwelling of Dr. Graeme.

"Can ye nae tap mair gently at the house of mournin', friend?" asked Kathleen, opening the door, and still holding the ladle with which she was dipping the fritters she was preparing for dinner.

"If ye kenned the news I hae fetched yer mistress, ye wud gie me room to come in, and gie me summat to eat, too, for I hae tramped mony miles to tell it to the parson, and am starvin' as a crow for carrion."

"If ye ken anything of our missing anes, tell us in maircy, for our hearts are sair to their core, and the minister is wellnigh spirit-broken."

"Nae, I will tell nain but the parson or his woman; to them I be sent, and ye can gae fetch them, mistress."

"Our minister is wi' his younger son at the hall, nae far frae this; the lad is mickle hurt; we fear he maun follow his mother."

"His mother!" echoed MacLoughlin; "Mistress Graeme hae nae gane, is she?"

"Our leddy hae gane where nae tidings will vex her mair. The body is still waiting the gathering of the bairns."

"Weel, weel," returned the man, lifting up the cap he had thrown down between his feet, and moving nervously upon his chair, "she wa' delicate, an' summut gane in years; sic maun expect to die; she is nae near, is she, mistress?"

"In the ither room; would ye look on her? She is like to life."

"Nae! nae!" he exclaimed, arresting Kathleen by the dress. "I hae nae fondness for seeing sic sights; there was nae need for the ither woman tae gang for Dr. Graeme. I wull tak a mouthfu', and gae to the hall mysel'."

At this juncture, Margaritte burst into the apart-

ment, and, almost breathless from haste, delivered
the direction from the minister, that the messenger
from Duncan and his sister should come to Mrs.
Cameron's, as he could not leave Lochiel.

"I wud hae been the ane to have fetched him,
but Bernard O'Dougherty sent me for the ithers. I
maun say I hae ben the savin' of them a'. I hope
the parson's purse-strings 'ill nae be tied in knots,"
he added, while he diligently manifested his approval of Kathleen's fritters. "Rough journeys helps a
mon's appetite," he remarked, pushing his plate to
be replenished the fifth time.

"I wull gie ye a steak frae this mutton venison
and some bread, friend, for Dr. McMillan, and maybe ithers," she sighed, "will be here to dine, an'
my fritters will nae hold out."

Without a reply he devoured the slice of meat
and several rounds from a loaf, not sparingly but-
tered. Margaritte, who had been serving him,
thought proper to wrap up the remainder, remarking as he passed out of the door, in an undertone of
disgust, "I will leave *ye* to scald and scour the
plates and things, Kathleen; I maun run and fetch
you what he kens."

Margaritte followed the man to the hall of Mrs.
Cameron. On reaching there, she passed in before,
and noiselessly opened the door of the little room
where was Lochiel, and the father, with Allan, anxiously watching.

"The mon hae come," she was whispering, when
John MacLoughlin caught a glimpse of his brother.

"Allan MacLoughlin," he surlily demanded in a

loud voice,—"why are ye nae at yer ain work, instead of wha ye are nae wanted, ye idle poltroon? Ye hae left yer wages wi' yer choppin, I can tell ye, Allan MacLoughlin." Before he could say more, or all of this, Mr. Graeme had come out of the room and Margaritte had prudently closed the door.

"Ye wull undo all the gude ye brag of, if ye wake our lad frae the sweet sleep we hope in —"

"Hold, Margaritte," interposed her master, "there is no harm done. We will go with this friend into the north room, and when he tells us all we shall love to learn, amends shall be made for all he has lost in our service." In this apartment were found Mrs. Cameron, a little, delicate-looking child coiled up in a large chair, and Edith Lincoln. Even the obdurate spirit of John MacLoughlin seemed subdued; his muscles relaxed into something like an inclination of the body, as he entered and stood before this family. Edith arose from a reclining position on a sofa, passed her fingers over her slightly disarranged hair, settled her comb, but the color suffused her usually pale cheek as she met and re-met the earnest, continued gaze of the stranger.

"I know'd her mither when I wa' a youngster, and all of us ca'd her 'Angel Helen o' the Hall;' as like are ye as gulls twa wings; yere een are blacker, and trouble hae taen awa' the dance frae them; ye *be* Hugh Lincoln, the Robber's daughter, beant ye?"

"We acknowledge no such appendage to that name, John MacLoughlin." Dr. McMillan had entered unobserved, and had heard the last sentence. Drawing the large chair between the sofa and Mac-

Loughlin, he lifted the little girl from it into his lap, and continued:

"Now, out with what brought you, man, and nothing false. Be speedy; where are, and what do you know of the son and daughter of Mr. Graeme?"

The man quailed for a moment before the steady, honest eye of his querist, and answered, — "Safely harbored in the Castle of Glennair; the young man would hae come in my boat, but the Laird forbade the risk."

"He said he tramped all the distance, when he came to the manse," Margaritte quietly remarked.

"The truth, John," rejoined the Doctor; "no truthtelling, no pay."

"We would know all you know, friend," said the pastor, "and please be speedy."

"All I ken is that they started for hame this morn, but the wagon stove an' the beasts wad nae haul, an' they are baith waitin' for anither chance, an' I wa' sent to see arter ye all, and if all wa' well."

The head of Mr. Graeme fell upon his clasped hands; Mrs. Cameron, beckoning to Margaritte, withdrew. The Doctor, without appearing to notice the anguish of his sorely bereaved pastor, said, — "Go prepare your boat, MacLaughlin; in five minutes I will be ready to go with you to Glennair, and, according to your deserts, you shall be recompensed," he added, seeing the man hesitated.

"Are you going away, too?" asked the little Helen, with earnestly appealing eyes.

"Not long, tiny Fawn," he replied, caressing her tenderly; "only to bring Duncan and Amy back to their father. Cannot you and cousin Edith take care of him while I am gone?"

Clinging to him, she waved her curls from side to side, to testify her inability and unwillingness. "Sister, maybe, can, but how can little Helen talk to Mr. Graeme?" she whispered.

"Will you try if I tell you?" the Doctor whispered in return.

She nodded a reluctant consent, while the tears gathered in her eyes.

"Well, then, when I have gone, you go and sit on the small cushion near him, and lay your hand upon his knee; *that* will soothe him."

Rising, the Doctor placed her in the large chair, and after a few comforting words to Miss Lincoln, left the three alone. Soon after, Helen, slipping from the seat and looking timidly toward Mr. Graeme, said softly to her cousin, — "Sister, will I go stand by him?"

"Do, precious, if you wish," she answered, releasing the little hand she had linked in hers. Softly the child approached the mourner and sat down upon the cushion. Not only the hand, but the cheek, was laid against his knee before Mr. Graeme was aware of her presence.

At length, raising his eyes and perceiving her, he stroked the fair hair, and murmured, — "Dear little one, you have but just entered upon a world of sorrow; may you be kept from the coming evils. Edith! do *you* find strength equal to your trying day, my child?"

"Would I *could* ever trust the blessed promises,

Mr. Graeme," she answered, vainly attempting to restrain the gushing tears. "My agonized spirit often cries loudly for relief, and rebelliously prescribes the method. The mercies of the last hour *must* help our unbelief, and we *shall* find his grace sufficient hereafter, — yet —"

" Heavy have been your trials, Edith," interrupted Mr. Graeme, " and unmitigated by the voice of kindness or affection. Keenly have *we* all felt our unavoidable (as we supposed) desertion, in this your hour of sore trial. That our course toward you has been erroneous, the providences of the last two days have clearly witnessed. To you, whom we have all, save Duncan, deserted in your sorrow, are we brought for succor in our extremity, and thus taught that we are henceforth to aid you in bearing your burden. We have acted from expediency — not scripturally, Edith ; a heavy chastisement has shown me *my* duty."

" I could scarcely receive sympathy, Mr. Graeme, from those who believe *him* culpable." Miss Lincoln moved to give the minister the seat beside her, which he had advanced to take.

" It is very difficult to give it credence, Edith ; and his *daughter* could not support the supposition. Leaving that subject, my love, I claim for Amy your former sisterly affection, and sue for forgiveness for all our delinquencies."

" Will heaven ever espouse the cause of other than the innocent ? " inquired the weeping girl.

" Never ! my child ; and how obvious the divine interference to prevent your suffering from the alien-

ation of your earliest friends and nearest neighbors;
yet, Edith, how generally, —

'Behind a frowning Providence,
He hides a smiling face.'

My Lochiel is recovering, his sister and brother are
returning home, and you, and your aunt — "

"We 'll forget the past, Mr. Graeme ; most keenly
have we felt your withdrawal."

Mr. Graeme laid his hand upon her head, as he
fervently and humbly besought Heaven's blessing
upon that household ; then, raising the little Helen
in his arms, from Miss Lincoln's side, where she had
been closely nestled during the while, he blessed
her ; also beseeching that "this lamb of the fold
might be. the light of the family, their prop in declining years, their aid in the Christian life ; that
light might be brought out of darkness, and their
latter days be bright."

It was enough for the child to know her cousin
was in tears. When Mr. Graeme put her down,
throwing her arms around her, she begged her not
to cry, saying in her childish innocence, that nobody
should hurt her, and that *she* would always be good
and mind everybody. Her cousin held her in a close
embrace and endeavored to wipe away the tears.
Mr. Graeme smiled on the little girl, and said he
and Allan were now to convey Lochiel to the room
Kathleen, and some of his parishioners, who had
been unremitting in their attentions, had prepared
for him.

"Edith," the minister spoke hesitatingly—"Edith,

7

is it too much to ask that you would be at the manse
to receive my Amy? You would have more power
to comfort her in the bereavement than any other
being in the world."

Edith made an effort to say she would be there,
but the words died upon the lip; she bowed an assent. Pressing her hand gratefully, Dr. Graeme left
the room.

"You look so tired, dear," said Miss Lincoln, "I
would like you to lie here and sleep while I go to
the manse; but first, I must kiss away every tear
from these cheeks. Dr. McMillan must not see his
'tiny Fawn' grieved."

"Sister, my Doctor says he has not room in his
heart for Aggie MacAlpin, I take up so much
space," sighing heavily, while her cousin kissed and
dried away the tears.

"I think you might move a little and let her in,
she is such a nice little girl."

"I would, sister, but the Doctor says his heart is
so crowded up, nobody else can creep in."

"He knows differently, Helen; his heart will hold
all the people in the world who deserve a place there.
Aggie, dear little Aggie, will not be left outside; so
now go to sleep and dream she is safely there."
Edith arranged her comfortably, remained long
enough to give a parting kiss to the sleeping child,
and then sought Mrs. Cameron to advise her of her
promise to Mr. Graeme.

"I decidedly disapprove of your going, my dear,
as would your father," Mrs. Cameron replied with
some asperity, when Edith had finished her report,

" and am more than a little surprised, Edith, that
you are willing to enter the manse, while the pastor
is *unwilling* to recognize you as the daughter of an
injured, honorable man. You have been commend-
ably prudent hitherto, and why would you *now* hazard meeting many who are the declared foes of your
father ? Indeed, Edith, I cannot permit this undig-
nified step." Rising quickly and taking from a
bureau-drawer a large shawl, she unfolded and threw
it around her shoulders. " I will go myself," she said
emphatically; " Edith Cameron Lincoln shall be
guilty of no act derogatory to her own or her father's
name, defamed as his may be by others. The grief
of Amy Graeme will be terrible ; none will be able
to check it for a time ; better, too, *you* should not
encounter that, dear ; you can hardly bear your own,
sweet bairn."

Tears started as Mrs. Cameron looked up and saw
the face of her niece covered with both hands.
" Surely, you will prefer not to see them just now,
Edith, my child ? " she asked, softly.

Withdrawing her hands from a face bathed in
tears, she said bitterly, — " Nothing, no, nothing
could add to my sorrow ; I might possibly mitigate
theirs ; I might be able to soothe Amy, aunt ; and
perhaps," she added, hesitatingly, after another
pause, " Duncan may think me unkind, and that
will give poignancy to his grief. Aunt Edith, *father*
would almost confront the people himself to comfort
Duncan Graeme ; but I will be satisfied with your
decision, and Duncan will with my reasons."

She said no more, and Mrs. Cameron was silent

until, when about to leave the room, attired for the visit, she kindly laid her hand on Edith's as they lay clasped over the back of a chair, and said tenderly, — " *I* know this is the wisest course, dearest, and Duncan will acknowledge its propriety. I am sure he would suffer any privations rather than have you subjected to the invidious remarks of those who will collect on this occasion, — and so would I. My Edith is as the apple of my eye." She folded her to her heart and left her.

Placid and beautiful in death reposed the clay tenement of Mrs. Graeme in the darkened room where sat the minister, when Mrs. Cameron entered. The watchers had retired, leaving the mourner alone with his dead. Without speaking, he clasped her proffered hand and led her to the side of the sleeper. Mrs. Cameron, bending over the face, wept for a time uninterruptedly.

"In the slumbers of the grave there are no dreams of evil, no heart-burnings; in death there are no divisions, we sepulchre no separations; beyond it, alienated friends all are reunited." Thus murmured the pastor, in a hushed, broken voice.

"She was universally beloved, and dearly prized by her friends, — by none more than the family at Thistle Hedge; nor were we requited by her ungratefully," replied Mrs. Cameron.

"Circumstances have separated us for a little while," responded the pastor. "I have been severely rebuked, my friend; I have sinned, I have been chastened, I repeat. God has in mercy withdrawn his wrath, and restored my children. He has again lifted upon me the light of his countenance, here, beside — "

"Believe me," interrupted Mrs. Cameron, " I cherish no enmity, Mr. Graeme, and am rejoiced to be able to befriend you, and deeply have sympathized in your sorrows ; yet I cannot feel entire friendliness with him who does not recognize or acknowledge his belief in the rectitude of Mr. Lincoln ; but this is not the spot for discussion, nor the advocacy of my brother, Mr. Graeme. We shall all soon be where there is no controversy, no root of bitterness, but where there is one love-cemented circle."

" Yes, oh ! yes, my dear friend, how insignificant do the affairs of such vast earthly importance appear, when we have a glimpse of an eternal home. May we all henceforth hold transitory things more loosely."

" I have frequently observed," Mrs. Cameron was about resuming, when she was interrupted by Margaritte, who whispered, as she passed through the room greatly excited, to open the front door, " Dr. McMillan's carriage is coming up from Fir Grove."

" Precious bairns ! " she exclaimed, as the Doctor lifted Amy from the chaise, and Duncan, passing his arm around her, almost carried her into the house.

" Take me, take me to her ! " she cried in anguish, as Mrs. Cameron received her from him. " Why, why was I separated from her ? Dear, dear mother !"

" Be composed, my love," Mrs. Cameron whispered. " Try to be calm before you meet your father. *Your* grief will be more than he can bear."

7 *

Amy raised her eyes, looked earnestly at Mrs.
Cameron, then at Margaritte, who was in tears;
turning to the Doctor, whose countenance could not
conceal the truth, she shrieked, — "Mother is dead!
Mother *is* dead?" she reiterated inquiringly. The
averted faces of the others, and the bowed head of
the Doctor, told all she dreaded to hear. With a
deep groan, she fell senseless into the arms of Mrs.
Cameron. Every effort to restore consciousness was
for a long time unavailing, and even then her eyes
wandered listlessly from face to face, her fingers occasionally creeping over or resting upon her forehead,
as though she would recall her roving thoughts.
"Daughter, dear daughter," said her father, tenderly
drawing her head against his bosom and kissing her.

She raised her head, and, shrinking back, surveyed
him earnestly. "Amy, my own Amy, do you not
know your father?" he asked softly.

"Yes," was the laconic answer, and she laid her
head with apparent confidence upon his bosom.

"Do not disturb her," said the Doctor, as her
father was about to speak again, "the restoration
will be very gradual — present scenes are unfavorable; the mind must be led back to earlier and happier hours to restore its tone; she neither recog-
nizes nor realizes anything yet."

"Hark!" she murmured, "hark! Lochiel is singing Lochabar; it is so sweet, — hark!" and she
lifted her head in an attitude of listening. "Edith,
call him back to sing again; I love to hear Lochabar —"

With grateful emotion the little group listened

with Amy to the deep, musical voice of Dr. Mc-
Millan, as he sang the exquisite stanzas to encourage
the delusion. She was obviously soothed; a sad
smile overspread her countenance, and the big tear
stood in her eye. Again the voice of the singer fell
upon her ear; the rich melody of the Psalm selected
told upon the heart of Amy: there was not that
unearthly brightness in the eye that met his own,
as the Doctor resumed his seat near her, when he
had finished.

"Praise, praise, it is all praise — that beautiful
Psalm," she said, placing her hand in his, "and 'we
will praise Him again as we pass over Jordan.' Sing
that, James; I always love to hear you sing; — but
where is Lochiel?"

"Not very far away; shall I sing, Amy?" But
the eyes of Amy were closed, and her head had
sought its resting-place against her father.

At a pleading look from Mr. Graeme, the mellowed
notes once more flowed from the lips of the Doctor,
but it was only to lead; Mrs. Cameron united with
him, and the sweet blending of the voices reached
the fountain of grief. Amy Graeme, when the
music ceased, was weeping. The father's countenance bespoke his gratitude; of utterance he was
incapable. Silence reigned; there was not a sound
in the house of death and mourning.

The door of the apartment was opened by Kathleen. Mrs. Cameron touched the arm of the Doctor,
who was sitting abstractedly, his head resting upon
his hand, and both upon his knee, "Kathleen says
Lochiel requires you," she whispered. "I know he

has been in impatient expectancy for the return of Duncan and his sister."

"We must endeavor to keep Miss Amy tranquil," he replied, in the same subdued voice; "and unless very urgent, it is decidedly better to keep her from the study until to-morrow."

"Far better, Doctor; but I doubt if she will be prevented. There is need of special influence to dissuade a Graeme."

"The genuine Highlander, Mrs. Cameron," was the response. "I will go to Lochiel;—what of Duncan?"

"He went immediately to the study, and is probably still there; he was overwhelmed to find *her* no more."

"Heavily, heavily stricken," sighed the kind physician, as he repaired to the chamber of his patient.

"What now!" he exclaimed, on entering the room. "Margaritte, what are you doing with this clothing? Not for Lochiel's present use, certainly?"

"I am trying what I *can* do, Doctor."

"Trying what you *cannot* do, rather. Insane boy, I had credited Margaritte with more sense. Lie down quietly and patiently, and wait the movements of others wiser than yourself. Death, my dear Lochiel, would probably result in an incautious physical effort; for the sake of those who are tenderly fearful of exciting you, be satisfied to remain alone until your sister is prepared to meet you. Great prudence is required in telling her the condition of her beloved brother."

"It was to Duncan I desired to go, Doctor; they told me he was alone with mother. The watchers had left him to grieve alone. I wanted to tell him I would try to be to our father the son he had been to both. She gave me her blessing, Doctor; but her blessings upon Duncan were for the past. Duncan was all her heart desired; but I, how often I have grieved our mother's heart. Help me, oh! help me, my mother's God, to be all my mother would have asked."

His head sank wearily upon the pillow, the long, dark lashes laid upon the pale cheek; any other than the practised finger that touched that pulse, would have supposed the spirit had passed away. Such was the thought that startled Duncan on entering the chamber; but the hastily extended hand and smile of the Doctor reassured him. Silently he bent over his brother, kissed his forehead, and for a long time stood sadly gazing upon the much changed face. "He is very, very ill, Doctor," he said, huskily.

"He has been, Duncan; but this is prostration; he will live. Your Epaphroditus will not be taken."

The lip of Duncan quivered, and he walked to the window to conceal his emotion. When he returned to the bedside, the Doctor remarked:

"I know of no more potent elixir than your presence. When Lochiel revives, Duncan, take my seat; hold his hand; speak when he speaks, not sooner. I will leave you now; Amy may need my services."

Laying the hand of Lochiel gently down, and

F

warmly clasping that of his brother, the Doctor withdrew. There had been no moment for explanation, anxiously as the heart of Duncan yearned to learn the circumstances attending his mother's last hours, and the wherefore his brother was in this condition, if either had occasioned the other. From Margaritte he could obtain no satisfactory information; with wringing hands she told him of the foreshadowings of evil; she perplexed and annoyed him by her recountings of Benshee cries, and other omens, to *her* mind certainly portentous of great calamity. There had been little opportunity of communicating with Dr. McMillan—then only in the presence of his sister; in their last interview, inquiry was impossible. He at times conjectured what might have been, and as often vainly imagined the very contrary. The clock told one hour—his anxiety, several, before his brother manifested any symptoms of returning consciousness. Opening his eyes languidly, he turned his head slightly, but did not at first notice Duncan; once again he turned, sighed heavily, and rested his eyes upon his brother; his lips moved, and a faint smile spread over his pale features.

"It is best to be very quiet now," Duncan whispered, bending over, and caressingly laying his face against his forehead.

"The boat—tell me of the boat—of Amy," he faltered.

"Amy is safe, and our boat was in no danger; when you are well, all shall be explained."

Lochiel looked satisfied, and lay quietly for a

long while, with his brother's hand clasped tightly between his own. "Duncan," he murmured.

"What is it, Lochiel?"

"Mother forgave me in all that I had grieved her — freely forgave, and left me her blessing, Duncan; you also have a large debt of waywardness against me, Duncan. I remembered all — bitterly remembered all, when the billows rose over the boat, Duncan."

"Let us both forget every past unpleasantness, Lochiel. I can recall instances in which *I*, not you, might be the forgiven. Lochiel, shall my page of grievances be cancelled also?"

"*You*, Duncan," he feebly ejaculated. "Mother distinguished me by 'my erring boy;' I hate myself, that I ever could have grieved my mother or my precious brother."

"Let by-gones be as though they were not, Lochiel; you are nervously alive to all your frailties. I never thought your 'terrible misdeeds' merited a harsher name. My affection for you now is the same I felt for that baby-boy I was called to see lying in Amy's cradle; I could not have loved anything more, and I love you no less now, my brother."

The tears coursed over the pale cheeks, as Duncan again and again stroked back his hair, and pressed his lips to his forehead.

"When is mother to be carried away, Duncan?" he whispered.

"The ground is unfit to-day; therefore, to-morrow noon is named."

"Is Edith with Amy, Duncan?"

"Better she should not be, Lochiel;—shall I bring Amy to you?"

"I have often distressed Amy also; can—"

"Let that subject rest, Lochiel: comfort me with the promise you will discuss the past no more; you would greatly pain our sister by any reference to former misdoings. She views them in the same trifling light I do. Our field is the future; you and I are to be the support, the staff of our father and sister. Let us endeavor to vie with each other in our kindness and attention to them; we are indebted to them both a weighty debt of gratitude. Rest now, Lochiel; if you are worse, Doctor will accuse me as the cause. So soon as you can bear it, you shall hear the occasion of our absence, and I will gladly listen to an account of the incidents of home during the time."

"Mother—"

"Nay, Lochiel, nay, no more now, or I must leave you."

"Duncan, I would like Amy to come to me," he said, after a very long interval of entire silence. Without replying, the brother left the apartment. He found Amy where he had anticipated. She was not weeping, but as calm and placid as the form before her. She was supported by Mrs. Cameron, who was soothing her by repeating appropriate texts of Scripture in the gentlest tone, mingling them with the praises of the friend she had always highly respected. Duncan entered unobserved, and stood by his sister. Mr. Graeme had thrown himself upon a couch, entirely overcome; he had been sustained by excitement, and the reaction was great. As one after another came into the room, Duncan suggested to Mrs. Cameron *they* should withdraw, and after speaking a few words with his father, gently forcing Amy from the side of their mother, retreated to the chamber of Lochiel, accompanied by Mrs. Cameron. Mr. Graeme very soon followed his children, leaving the unconscious sleeper to the care and watchfulness of endeared friends and sympathizing parishioners.

"It is lang syne Mistress Cameron ha' graced the manse," was the remark of Mrs. Finley, after the family had retired.

"*Death* gives a check to all dissensions," was the reply, "yet I mistake if there has been any between these neighbors; the inmates of Thistle Hedge avoid all their former friends, unless they are quite confident of their belief in the innocence of Hugh Lincoln."

"They will number a select remnant in that case," responded another. "Few doubt his guilt, who are acquainted with the facts; even Doctor McMillan, who always speaks the best he can for his fellowmortals, is silent about this villain. I am sure his daughter herself must believe him one, — for you know it was *she* found the papers confirming his guilt."

"I *ken* only what I *do* ken," returned Mrs. Finley, "and I ken Mr. Lincoln maun hae been sorely tempted by Satan himsel', to hae fallen frae his piety in sic a strange way, — sae sudden, and sae far."

8

"No, no, Mrs. Finley," replied her auditor, "the fall of Lincoln was not so sudden. Robert Traquair had suspicions of wrong doings, and had been narrowly regarding his movements months back; he warned the president, who was slow to credit any reports against Lincoln's honor and honesty. If ever the hypocrite is taken, there will be astounding developments. The proofs of his guilt are too glaring to be dimmed, or the Doctor would find his tongue in his defence."

"Yet, Fariss, did not McMillan once rebuke your abuse of him?"

"Not exactly, Mrs. Finley; he only said, 'Leave that to the court; better not anticipate what cannot be averted then;' but the court that tries Hugh Lincoln will wait long for the sitting. He is far enough from these parts, and some say the bankers have helped him off."

"Weel, weel, the Doctor's was good advice for us all, an' I for ane will nae condemn him till the judge pronounces his sentence; an' for all I ken it is nae right to aid the wicked to flee from justice, I rejoice Hugh Lincoln is gane, for the sake of his puir bairn, puir Miss Edith. She is sometimes seen wandering among the rocks, carrying a little basket over her arm. How canny she is, and how bright she used to be; but she never sings or laughs more. Some say," she added, lowering her voice, "Edith is daft."

"Nae doubt of that, an' nae marvel either, Mistress Finley; the child hae been followed round the lower bridge, an' seen fra the distance crossing the rickety bridge on wizard's stream."

"Mairey, mairey, gude Mistress MacClain, ye dinna say Elfin Bridge! Puir chiel, she maun be clean daft; it may be she wi' take her ain life some day — the canny, canny bairn: she maun be well guarded. My heart sored to look on her yester-morn, just when the big clouds were clusterin', an' the heavy storm comin' on — she wa' standin' lookin' out far over the distance for somethin', or some one to come: I could nae but stop, she looked sae like ane of anither world — sae pale, sae pitiful, yet sae heavenly. The wind had tossed off her mantle, and her throat, sae white, was bared; her dark hair, too, was blawn back, an' I ne'er saw her een sae bright, but nae wild at all. I said aloud, and did nae ken it, 'Angel of the hall!' It wa that they ca'd her mither. She heard me, and sae sweet she turned, an' in her ane auld winsome way she said, 'Come in, or hasten home, friend Finley, or the storm will overtake you.' I did nae say ane word; I went awa, and my heart just broke, an' my een told the tale when I got hame. Yes, I do hope he will escape the findin'."

"Miss Lincoln has been much admired. Her beauty and her character are quite in unison, I believe, although I never was acquainted with the family," observed Mr. Fariss.

"Evans Traquair wa' her humble servant till *now;* he has withdrawn his suit."

"Evans Traquair! — don't tell *me,* Mistress Finley. Hugh Lincoln came near blowing him into the channel, on the mention of his views to him. A Cameron listen to the overtures of a Traquair!

A McMillan, a MacAlpin, or the young Laird, it may be, might get a hearing; but such a proposition from a Traquair made the proud blood of Lincoln boil in his veins. But now, good lack, his bairn is weak, and her beauty marred."

"Her beauty marred!—nae, nae, not a whit; she is as queenly and beautiful as Venus herself, Mr. Fariss."

"Hoot awa'," joined in an old man, who had been an attentive listener. "The beauty of the bairn will deaf the voice of justice, I trow; it vexes mony to see how ye and ithers are overreached, an' how ye let this Lincoln gie ye the partin', cause of the canny face of the lassie."

"Ye ne'er heard hard word agin ither, neighbor Mitchell, afore the robbin' of the bank, an' few 'll forget the mony gude deeds of Hugh Lincoln and Miss Edith," responded Mrs. Finley.

"Weel, I say again, Mrs. Finley, it vexes me that all sic men, ither high-born, or in lofty stations, when they act the wrang, they are holpen off, or the gettin' awa' is connived at. On'y a puir fellow who steals a shillen, finds his way to the lock-up; ye canna' gie the nae to that, Mrs. Finley, or ony of ye, neighbors."

"We are aware you are right, Mr. Mitchell, and the principle wrong, yet Mrs. Finley has been misinformed in this instance. Hugh Lincoln has not been befriended: we all are so well convinced of his frauds, and the multitude so roused against him, that let who will have compassion for his daughter, he will be brought to justice and the gibbet, and I for one —"

The face of Dr. McMillan appeared at the door. He bowed gravely to the group, yet was evidently seeking some one not there.

"Doctor," said Mr. Fariss, "if disengaged, I would speak with you."

He came forward, and stood before Mr. Fariss, with his hat in his hand.

"Doctor," continued that gentleman, "there will be watchers required to-night, and I promised my wife to return after dinner. Who will remain?"

"Mrs. Cameron, myself, and one of Mr. Graeme's family, who is now taking rest to facilitate that intention. No other friends will be requisite."

A young man, whom the Doctor had not noticed, and who had taken no part in the previous conversation, then arose. Lifting his cap, he stood a few moments reverently beside the dead, then followed the Doctor from the room. Again he raised his cap, as Dr. McMillan turned at the call of his name, and revealed the head and features of Norval Neilson.

"Venturesome, truly, young man," remarked the Doctor, sternly.

"I would take the place of Maister Duncan this night; he had little rest the last."

"He will not watch, and the one who designs so to do, will not permit a substitute. Be assured, young man, this hour or spot would be no security, if this temerity lead to the discovery of the haunt of your father. Will you not be advised to leave here without delay?"

"Hardly worth the hindrance," returned the

8 *

youth, bitterly; "it is but a living death they lead there."

There was compassion in the eye that met Norval's, as he said: "Go over to the hall; Miss Edith will advise you what is best. I am of those who believe one of your name has done much mischief; yet fear nothing from me; I have been hitherto — and will remain — neutral."

The cap was lifted, and the head bent low, as the youth passed the Doctor, who closed the door after him. Never thereafter was Edith Lincoln seen among the rocks, or upon Elfin Bridge.

"At what hour will be the gathering," inquired Mr. Fariss of the Doctor, when he reappeared in the study.

"Noon had been suggested," he replied; "but Lochiel has inadvertently been told, therefore it is thought best it should take place at early morning, without his knowledge."

"Will Lochiel's mind ever be restored, think you, Doctor?"

"The slight aberration was produced by fever. He is perfectly himself at present, and will be in his usual health in a few days, unless unduly excited."

"And Miss Amy?" continued the querist. "She was distressed to derangement when she first came home; is she more resigned?"

"Miss Graeme," replied the Doctor, "is powerfully sustained by grace: she is quite calm, and has been ministering consolation to her father and brothers."

"I always kenned she wa' pairfect," said Mrs.

Finley. "She and Edith Lincoln seemed born for sisters."

To this Dr. McMillan made no answer. Calling the attention to the life-like appearance of Mrs. Graeme, he descanted upon her loveliness and her Christian character. When the current of conversation turned upon the Bank and Lincoln, he excused himself, and withdrew.

CHAPTER IV

AT the dawn of the following morning, Mrs. Graeme was silently and solemnly committed to the tomb, to await the resurrection of the just, by a few friends who deeply mourned their loss, and sincerely sympathized with the bereaved pastor and his children. The sound of footfalls, at this unusual hour, attracted Lochiel. "Look from the eastern window, Duncan," he called to his brother, who had remained with him during the night, and was still sitting by the side of his couch. "I have been listening to the continued tread of feet upon the frosted ground ; — a sound I had not anticipated till noon."

"Other arrangements were made since your inquiry, Lochiel."

There was no other question, no other remark; the grief of the brothers was noiseless. It was their first bereavement: they mourned their mother. The sound of footsteps ceased ; all was still.

"Who is with father, Duncan?" murmured his brother ; "I am selfish to keep you from him."

"Father is in Amy's room, with her and Mrs. Cameron."

"Strange that Edith Lincoln absents herself, Duncan: she would be a comfort to sister, and need encounter no others."

"I will go over for her myself, this evening. I would not have Edith compromise her dignity, even to comfort our sister, Lochiel."

"Mother loved her, Duncan."

"Did mother name her in her parting remembrances, Lochiel?"

"She did. The evening before she directed a keepsake to be made for Edith similar to Amy's,—a brooch with her hair, and name engraved on the counter side."

"Was there no message?—no wish?" he asked, with a quivering lip.

"Yes, Duncan; but father requested it might not be repeated to *you.*'

"Do not, then, I enjoin you, Lochiel: I conjecture the purport — dear mother —"

"Dear! dear mother!" was reiterated from the lips of the invalid, and a long silence ensued.

Mrs. Cameron opened the communicating door, and, with an effort to appear calm, beckoned Duncan to her.

"I have a note from Edith, my dear," she faltered; "something dreadful has occurred." He glanced over its contents.

"Can Duncan come? Oh, no, he cannot. Come, aunt, quickly.—Not Helen, no, no —   E. C. L."

Duncan hurriedly passed back the paper; throwing his camlet around him, he seized the nearest hat, and rushing down the stairs, was half-way to

the hall before Mrs. Cameron had time to declare
her intention to accompany him. His heart sank,
and a groan escaped him, as a new-made grave, in
a small enclosure, rose suddenly before him. "My
mother! my precious mother!" he murmured;
"would that thy last blessing might have rested
upon thy *eldest* boy also."

In the hall, Miss Lincoln was anxiously awaiting
him. "My Edith!" he exclaimed, encircling her
in his arms, "what new sorrow has been added to
your woes?" He kissed the brow of the agonized
girl, and led her to a sofa in the parlor; then bending down to the proffered lips of the little Helen,
raised her upon his knee, as he drew a chair near
Edith.

"Duncan," she gasped, after several efforts to
speak; "oh! Duncan, Duncan, hope is buried forever."

He only looked an imploring inquiry.

"The Fawn and Jessie MacAlpin found some
printed papers in the garret while playing there,
Jessie filling her little pocket with them. In wash-
ing the skirt, the servant drew them out, and at
the request of John Daley—who was making a visit
in the kitchen at the time—gave them to him.
They were given to Mr. Traquair as entirely cor-
roborative of father's guilt, and somehow impli-
cating Norval Neilson—and—and Norval is—
taken!" she shrieked, throwing her head upon his
shoulder.

"Impossible, Edith," replied the youth, in as
composed a voice as he could command; "Norval is

at their retreat: you are misinformed, depend upon
it, and nothing additional would give greater con-
firmation to their guilt in the community."

"No, no, Duncan; Norval is here—is in custody,
and the officers have come to examine for other
proofs."

"Did you see any of the papers the children
found, Edith?"

She drew from her pocket a small roll, and with
a trembling hand resting upon his arm, she anxiously watched the countenance of Duncan Graeme,
as he unfolded the first paper.

"This is preposterous, Edith,—a check to the
order of Norval, signed by Traquair! Who will be
next implicated?" he said, bitterly — staggered
himself to recognize the familiar scrawl of Norval
Neilson on the counter side.

"It cannot, *cannot* be!" She asked beseechingly,
"*You* do not doubt, dear Duncan — you still believe
them —"

"What a net is woven about them! No, my
Edith, I will never believe otherwise. I must see
the officers; where is Norval? Helen will remain
with you," he continued; "and your aunt will not
be long absent."

Edith bowed her face upon her hands; the child
stood by her, one arm thrown around her neck, and
her head resting against her cousin's cheek. Casting a sorrowing glance upon them, Duncan left the
room.

In an ante-chamber — the reception-room of former
days — days of happiness and of gayety — he was

introduced to the two officers from the bank, with authority to examine the house for papers similar to those sent to Mr. Traquair, which he perceived were like that shown him by Edith.

"We have secured the young forger in one of the outbuildings, and will take him with us to the city," the elder officer remarked, to which young Graeme made no reply.

"I had, perhaps, better conduct you," he said, coldly; "there are some windings in this house, with which I am more familiar."

There were no further discoveries, nothing more revealed, and the gentlemen, thanking Mr. Graeme for his attention, intimated their design to take Norval. To this Duncan merely bowed.

Returning to the parlor, he found Mrs. Cameron weeping, with her niece, over her recital. It was pitiable to witness the tearful earnestness of Helen, as she entreated her "sister to forgive her for finding the wicked papers, and giving any of them to Jessie."

"Is the search completed, my dear?" Mrs. Cameron inquired.

"Yes, without any more developments. Norval Neilson is their captive: I might not interfere, dared not rescue, and could not endure to witness the conflict."

The words had scarcely passed his lips, when a tap and the hasty opening of the door announced the presence of one of the officers. "Young Neilson has escaped, sir," he said, touching his hat to the ladies; "have we permission to go through the cellars, where he is probably secreted?"

"The power with which you are invested will meet no opposition," replied young Graeme, closing the door rather uncivilly and quickly upon him.

"This is an hour of deep sorrow, my children," Mrs. Cameron groaned, rather than expressed. "We may rejoice for those who slumber beneath the turf, unconscious of the trials of those they have left."

"Forgive me, Duncan," whispered Edith; "I had almost forgotten your sorrow in my own anguish. You know I sympathize—mourn for you; but I envy the undisturbed rest of the sleepers there—my own mother and yours. Would—"

"Check the wish, Edith, for your father's sake at least—"

"For your sake, Duncan, I would suppress all such selfish desires; my interest in living had nearly left me when *you* were missing: indeed, I will try to be a comfort to you all—to dear Aunt Edith. Attribute all I say, all I do wrong, to a whirling brain."

Mrs. Cameron, drawing her more closely to her, endeavored to soothe her by endearing words.

"This is a dark hour, my Edith," Duncan whispered, as he bent over her. "There is brightness in the future. He who sees the end from the beginning will bring light out of darkness."

"We are forsaken—forsaken of God, Duncan," she cried. "I cannot—I never pray—"

For some time there was no interruption to the convulsive sobbing of the despairing Edith. Duncan sat with his eyes resting upon the floor, holding

9   G

her cold hand between his. The little Helen, slipping down, had clasped her arms about her cousin, hiding her face against her.

At length, most tenderly, and in tones of deep humiliation, the voice of young Graeme arose in prayer: —

"Call back, O God! thy wandering, erring child. She has thrown away her buckler, her shield; she has turned from the hills whence cometh our help; she has gone aside from her rock, her refuge; she has restrained prayer; she has forsaken her God, and thy chastisement is upon her. Stay thine hand, thine anger: let her hear the still, small voice of love and mercy, recalling her to thy throne of grace, and to Thee; for the sake of Him thou gavest for us, lift upon her the light of thy countenance, O our Father."

Gently laying down the hand he held, he said a few words to Mrs. Cameron, and raising the child, he carried her with him from the room.

"Where are we going, Mr. Duncan?" she inquired, returning fondly his caress, as they passed through the back entry.

"To ask if there are any tidings of our friend Norval. Did you see him here, Fawn?"

"Only a minute; sister sent me to Nanny, while she talked with him: he always makes sister cry so when he comes; yet sister is always glad to see him, too."

As they entered the kitchen, the officers came in at an opposite door. Nanny was absorbed in her baking; she had taken out some cakes, and was just drawing out a large loaf; turning to look at her visitors, she incautiously took the bread in her hands; instantly letting it fall, she uttered an exclamation of pain — blowing her fingers violently, until the heat had somewhat abated.

"Ye wald hae handled it mickle better wi' a cloth, mestress," laughed old Willy.

"Haud yer tongue, or be civil," she muttered, with chagrin; "ye might hae given me a leetle help, in place of grinnin'. Ye hae made the oven sae ragin hot — ye hae nae wit sometimes."

"I trow ye would hae growled mair if it hae been too cauld for the large cake, Nanny."

"Weel, true; the large cake maun bake a leetle longer. Gang and fetch me some cauld water for my fingers, Wully."

The man, with a provoking laugh, obeyed, and the officers proceeded in their search in the cellars of the main building. Duncan, with Helen, stayed to learn the result.

"Entirely unsuccessful," one of them observed on their reappearance; "the fellow must be a wizard to elude us."

"Swifter feet to him than to his hunters," ejaculated old Nanny. "He is a bonnie lad; blessings, and nae harm, come to him or his."

"We did not expect much aid in our search, old woman," replied one of the men; "and very little doubt he has had help in his flight."

"That accusation must be well founded before it becomes actionable, sir," rejoined young Graeme; "there has been no barrier to your official proceedings, and nothing observable to warrant your suggestion. It is due to this family you should express yourselves satisfied they have in no way thwarted or frustrated your designs. *I* for one was not aware Norval Neilson was about the premises."

The gentlemen declared themselves wholly convinced "the youth had himself planned and executed his deliverance, and was probably hidden away among the fisher's huts."

"Ye wa' long fetchin' the water, Wully," said Nanny, after a nervous look from the windows after their guests.

"Cauld loaves misses the sting, and nae need the water, Nanny?" returned the old man, holding his side, and suppressing the mirth he could scarcely control. "Do look out, Maister Graeme; see if they be out of hearing; I canna hauld in muckle langer."

The first impulse of Duncan was to check his untimely gayety; but Nanny, respectfully touching his arm, whispered, "Tarry a wee bit, an' ye will laugh, too, for gladness, Maister Graeme. Maun the tiny Fawn tarry, too, Wully dear?"

"Helen's lips are sealed, if needs be," answered young Graeme, rather sternly. "Our little girl never will tell tales, will she?" he added, turning kindly to the child in his arms.

"No, Mr. Duncan," she said, softly, nestling her head closely upon his shoulder.

"We will trust the bonny bairn," replied Willy, now giving way to a burst of laughter in which Nanny joined. "I tell ye," he exclaimed, opening the oven-door which Nanny had closed upon the large cake, "Norval Neilson is the only fuel and fire that has been here to-day; the burning bread was baked yesterday."

The astonishment and gratification of young Graeme was only equalled by the gratitude of Norval. Little Helen was allowed to carry the pleasant tidings to her mother and cousin, and many were the praises and thanks bestowed upon Willy and Nanny.

"I shall be expected home to breakfast," said Duncan, in reply to the invitation of Mrs. Cameron. "We need not anticipate any further trouble; I will report, myself, from the cave this evening. Meanwhile, Edith must take nourishment and rest; and endeavor to be comforted from my source, dearest," he whispered, kissing her pale cheek. "It is the only, the living fountain." Her hands were instantly pressed over her eyes, to suppress or conceal the tears. Young Graeme stood a few moments irresolute; he sighed as he gave his hand to Mrs. Cameron; gently caressing the little Helen, he was about to leave the room, when Edith looked up with glistening eye, and called softly, — "Duncan — "

"What will you, my Edith?"

"I would love to go with you to father, to-day, and remain with him until to-morrow. Why will *I* not be permitted, Duncan? Norval told me Amy Graeme passed the night there."

"The stay of my sister was obligatory. Norval Neilson was aware of that."

"He said she was storm-bound, and his father conveyed you away by sea; that was all he knew.

Will Amy ever — Amy will never —" Tears choked further utterance.

"Amy is bound to secrecy, dear Edith. Edith, your grief breaks my heart," he said, sitting down once again by her side. "*I* have no words of consolation, but there is balm in Gilead; will you not seek the Physician there? Will you promise me you will make the effort?"

"I will — I will, Duncan. Oh, that I should add to your sorrow! Indeed, I will try to do all you desire. May I accompany you to the Grotto, Duncan?"

"The bridge must be replaced before you can venture. I will see you on my return."

She made an effort to repeat his farewell, but the sound died upon her lips.

"Dear," called Mrs. Cameron, in a hushed voice, following him out and closing the door, "what shall be done with this roll of papers? I do not like the responsibility of destroying them — neither to retain them in the house."

"Most inexplicable tissue of discoveries," he replied, placing them in his coat-pocket without further examination.

"Is your confidence disturbed, Duncan? Could Norval —"

"No, no," he interrupted, bitterly, "Norval could not, would not, dare not, so deceive us. Poor fellow, it is sinful to harbor a suspicion against him. Reputation seems no safeguard, Mrs. Cameron; we know not who may be the next suspected. I cannot expect you to return to my sister to-day. Edith needs you. She requires constant soothing; her cup of misery is overflowing. Amy and she might be a mutual comfort."

" You will see my brother, dear ; existing circumstances would lessen his objections."

" I shall not crave the visit as a boon, Mrs. Cameron ; it must be voluntary and proffered."

" A Graeme to the heart's core," said Mrs. Cameron to herself, after the exchange of " good morning," " yet the death of the mother does, in a degree, alter the position of the two girls."

Duncan retraced his steps homeward.

" What had occurred at the Hall, brother," inquired Amy, when left with him after breakfast ; " your replies were unsatisfactory, — I supposed owing to the presence of the Doctor."

" Dr. McMillan is not the only one inimical to the inmates of the cave ; some reserve is necessary in the hearing of father ; and I rather conjecture my sister is among the disaffected. I do not condemn you, Amy ; I only grieve that you and Edith Lincoln are so effectually disunited. I had a hope that the void made in our family and the advances made by Mrs. Cameron, after her kindness to Lochiel, would have healed the breach."

" The opinion of the world is to be regarded, brother, and the restrictions of a parent to be obeyed ; yet neither has, in the least, estranged me from Edith Lincoln ; my spirit longs for communion with her. Duncan, I had expected that our dear mother's death, under such aggravated circumstances, would have brought Edith to me."

" I exert no influence there, Amy ; the withdrawal

was not of her seeking ;—I judge the reconciliation must be of yours."

" The estrangement was grievous to mother, Duncan ; but father could hardly be censured ; his standing in the parish demanded all he did."

" His reasons and his actions were no doubt governed by his peculiar position, Amy ; he never submitted either to my judgment: I have acted according to my own, without opposition."

" Will you say to Edith, so soon as I have physical capacity to do so, I will return to her without the slightest abatement of my attachment. Will you, brother ?"

" With father's acquiescence ; without it, I dare not, Amy."

"The unprecedented kindness and forbearance of Mrs. Cameron, and her Christian sympathy, cannot but obtain *that*, Duncan. You may safely bear my message."

" I will bring Edith here this evening, dear Amy," he said, in subdued tones. " I am now going to the cave ; has my sister no soothing words to gladden its inmates ?"

There was more than a slight tremulousness in the voice of Amy Graeme, as she raised her tearful eyes and replied, — " From my heart, I wish them a full acquittal from all they are accused, and a sequent redress of all their wrongs."

"This, from you, will fall like balm upon their crushed heads, my sister," he replied, kissing the very words from her lips. She parted with him at the front door ; he took the path toward the sea ; Amy repaired to the couch of Lochiel.

CHAPTER V.

" The poor man counteth not the cost
   At which wealth has been purchased;
   He would be on the mountain's top,
   Without the toil and travail of the climbing."

THERE was a short, quick step in the hall of the Castle, and a servant ushered Mr. Robertson immediately into the library, where the Laird was sitting.

" My call has met a prompt response," he said, shaking him warmly by the hand, and placing a chair opposite to himself, at a small table.

" Where duty and pleasure combine, there is slight temptation to procrastinate," he replied, bowing upon the hand of his friend. " A visit to Lord Glennair, under any circumstances, I should always consider a privilege."

" And a greeting from the house of Dunbar will always be tendered sincerely to my best friend. But I have communications of a thrilling nature, Mungo, and in you only can I repose confidence, being conscious there will be no betrayal of the trust. Hugh Lincoln is treading the same shore with ourselves. No marvel you start and pale at such intelligence. Unfettered, yet almost within the borders of my own domain. Our only hope of the capture of the villain is in proceeding with the utmost caution."

" It is not possible, Robert ; Australia is now his

home, — if a guilty conscience, fearing detection, may find a resting-place. Who is your informant?"

"John MacLoughlin, the fisherman, — a source by no means reliable."

"MacLoughlin! He has twice perjured himself in a court of justice. His testimony is valueless."

"Not worth a sous; but self-interest alone gives him the temerity to seek my presence. He knows my opinion of him, and would not form a falsehood and brave my vengeance. He saw the powerful arm of Roger Neilson, which none could mistake, plying the oar in the storm of the past week; and he succeeded in landing at MacLean's inlet. Where Roger is, his master will not be wanting."

"Ah! Roger's home. His clan would follow him to the death. I doubt they would ever credit an evil report of Neilson."

"How difficult for any to view him in the light of a villain," the Laird replied sadly. "I regarded him as an humble friend, and trusted him with untold gold. It remains for us to ferret out their place of concealment, and let justice overtake them."

"He was but the tool of another, my Lord, and succumbed to strong temptation. I would scarcely wish to see *him* suffer the penalty of the law. Let foreign lands cover their shame. The remorse of guilty consciences will be sufficient punishment."

"Your mercy is poor, sickly sentimentalism, Mungo Robertson," his friend replied, impatiently, "You are a better friend than citizen."

"It was a moment of weak compassion, I confess, Robert. I am ready to aid you in any measures for their apprehension; but a retrospect of former days almost unmanned me; yet I always considered his standard of excellence too high for mortals."

"Prior to this defection, a finger could not be laid upon the first flaw in his character," the Laird replied. "The fall of the minister of our Kirk would not have been more astounding."

"Let temptation but beset *his* path," Mr. Robertson returned, sneeringly, "*I* hold that every man has his price."

"I would scorn to place so low an estimate upon my fellow-beings, Mungo; and *you* cannot speak from experience on this subject. Has opportunity ever seduced *you* from the path of duty? I trow not. Has not Providence smiled on every honest effort, prospering speculation upon speculation, permitting you to live in princely luxury, and not a whisper ever sullied your fair fame? With your high sense of honor, I marvel to hear so absurd a sentiment. Excuse my frankness."

A smile of gratified vanity played upon the face of his friend. "Without boasting, my Lord, my honesty has been pretty thoroughly tested; but the fall of our dear friend Lincoln has weakened my faith in mortals, yea, has made me weary of life, and ready to shun the face of man."

"Then while you are preparing a hemtage, I will seek more efficient aid. I boast no more stoicism than yourself; but before we grant all villains freedom because they once assumed the angelic garb, before justice succumbs to mercy — let every ensign of our isle be laid low, and our beautiful thistle, our national emblem, be erased forever."

"You misunderstand me, Robert; the law shall not fall powerless on the guilty, if in my power to prevent it. The sudden disappearance of Hugh Lincoln, independent of our clear proof, would be sufficient evidence of his guilt."

"To that step he was driven. Clamorous creditors of the Bank, you are aware, demanded immediate redress, and his life would have been the forfeit had he not sought refuge in flight."

"It was, indeed, a moral tempest; with difficulty, my hand stayed the tumult — and no marvel; simple trust abused, and earthly hopes blighted. But why, if innocent, did he not subsequently cast himself upon the protection of the law? But I detain and weary you with idle words. Your plans, my Lord?"

"Simply these: — Several officers, in the garb of citizens, may be stationed in the forest bordering the home of the clan of Neilson, to report any seditious movement, while you and I, accustomed to brave the weather, may, in the shades of evening, lend an observing eye also."

"Feasible and simple. Shall we this evening wend our way to the forest?"

At the close of that day, after partaking of a hasty and simple meal, the two gentlemen, equipped to defy the cold northern blast, set out on their mournful errand. Few words passed; but the strained ear was startled at the sound of their own footstep, and in every falling shadow the form of Lincoln was almost visible. Each twilight, for several succeeding days, found them the same vigilant watchers, at times approaching within the very precincts of the far-famed, and no less dreaded, haunt of the Elves, with feelings of undefined though unacknowledged awe; but all effort at discovery was unavailing.

"A whisper of suspicion has driven him from these shores," Mr. Robertson remarked, as with wearied step they retraced their way homeward. "The search may as well be relinquished."

"Feeling would prompt a ready assent to your proposition," the Laird returned, huskily, "and I confess I have almost feared his apprehension, when I have imagined him within the pale, — a culprit, a felon, a forger, — his life a forfeit to his country's laws. His winning manners, his benign countenance, his independence, his mild reproof, humbling without displeasing, notwithstanding every effort, stand out so prominently to view, that it dims my sense of right more than you can imagine."

"Hold! Robert, hold! my heart beats so much in unison, and vibrates with every chord you strike, that I cannot endure it. Shall we at once withdraw the officers, and leave him to his conscience and his offended Maker?"

"I fear we are acting hastily. An accusing conscience might be our meed for misjudged mercy. Let us on to-morrow's eve seek concealment among the clump of fir-trees bordering the mouth of the Elfin's cave. I have sometimes imagined something more than the whistling of the wind within."

Mr. Robertson was silent. A faint smile played

10

around the mouth of his friend as he inquired, — "Have you succumbed to popular superstition? If so, we must cast salt in our path to guarantee our safety."

"Not for a moment," he replied, with a haughty curl of the lip; "I believe philosophically we may account for every unnatural sound there. The officers will be stationed in the vicinity, of course?"

"Within sound of our watchword."

The sun had fallen far below the horizon, and darkness was gathering rapidly around, when a slight rustling from footsteps upon a few frozen leaves might be heard; then all was silent, as the two gentlemen nestled closely behind a clump of firs and a jutting rock, which aided in their concealment. The hand of each (unknown to the other) was clasped closely upon a pistol within his bosom, as their eyes wandered fearfully around. Silence reigned. A dark mass of barren rock and leafless trees alone stood before them.

An hour passed; not a word was interchanged. The moon arose, casting a lurid light upon all around, rendering the scene still more dreary. Suddenly there was a rustling sound; it drew nearer. Was it wrought imagination? Was it the beating of each heart become audible to the other? The eye and ear were strained to the utmost, but not a breath escaped them. Nearer and nearer it approached; human footsteps and suppressed voices were heard. A female form leaning upon the arm of a young man, was now visible. A low sob broke upon their ear.

"Speak not of blasted hopes, my Edith," her companion returned, in the lowest tone; "a dark cloud now covers your father's path, but the sun will burst forth in all its glory and scatter it forever."

It was the voice of Duncan Graeme, — his well-known voice, not to be mistaken. A clasp of the hand alone told both recognized it. Duncan Graeme, the friend, perhaps the accomplice of the robber. The big drops stood upon the forehead of the Laird, as he listened eagerly. The young man proceeded,—

"But, my darling Edith, listen to my plea. You need a protector in this dark hour; let my arm shield you. For the present, your father must absent himself until his character is proved to be unsullied. Let a tie be formed which will give me the right to say,— She is mine!"

"My father's consent to such a step could never be obtained, Duncan; on that point he is firm. Hark! I hear his step. He will convince you that you err in the proposal."

Another footstep was heard; — Hugh Lincoln stood before them. Was it indeed Hugh Lincoln? the erect, the robust, the bright Hugh Lincoln? Had the short space of a month wrought such a change? In return to the salute of Duncan, with his usual grace the cap was lifted, bringing to view a furrowed brow, over which some silver hairs were now scattered in place of the dark chestnut locks, which a short time since graced the polished forehead that had scarce seen forty years.

There was a wild burst of anguish as Miss Lincoln

threw herself upon the neck of her father. A warm kiss was imprinted upon her brow, as he ejaculated, — "May the Great Shepherd guard my lonely one in my wanderings, and keep her safely from all evil."

"Let me accompany you, dearest father," she expostulated, "you cannot go alone. Who, oh, who will care for you? Who will soothe your lonely hours? and I — I cannot live separated from you," she added, throwing herself again convulsively upon his bosom.

Placing his arm gently around her, she was permitted to weep in silence, until nature resumed its sway and she was comparatively calm.

"Your father needs you as a solace, Edith," he at length whispered; "you are only adding to his cup of sorrow."

"Forgive me, dearest father," she said, as he placed her beside him upon a jutting rock, " I was selfish, supremely selfish."

" I shall not be alone, as you suppose; friends will be raised in foreign lands. Were I guilty, I should at once deliver myself to justice to pay the penalty of my crime; but, innocent of every charge alleged, and apparently proved, I must elsewhere seek shelter until the storm be overpast, and my non-participation in any deed of infamy clearly proved. God can bring light out of darkness."

"Grant but my request, Mr. Lincoln: — let Edith be mine," urged Duncan. "At my father's hearthstone she will find a peaceful retreat, until we together hail your return to our beloved isle."

"None will be found to harm this bairn, Duncan, under the shelter of her aunt; and," he added, bitterly, "my dishonored name shall never sully the escutcheon of the family of Graeme."

"The gratitude my father feels to Mrs. Cameron, and the love he bears our Edith —"

"Say no more, Duncan. When Edith can resume her place among her peers, as the daughter of Hugh Lincoln, this hand is yours. Until that time arrives, she remains Edith Lincoln." ·

"Would that your determination could be moved, Mr. Lincoln," returned the youth, rising; "but your will shall be our law. Shall the first hour of your glad return hail the union of Edith and Duncan Graeme?"

"She is as yours now, Duncan. Watch over her; guard her as the apple of your eye. Let no evil befall her, and may the Cross be the refuge of both my children. But we must now part," he added, clasping the hand of Duncan warmly. "You will surely be required at the manse, my son. Your absence might lead to some suspicion; we must be wary. MacLoughlin is prowling around, and a missing oar of Roger's is supposed to be in his keeping. Even the watchful care of Allan will scarcely protect us from his wily snares."

"Suffer me to be with you, dearest father, through this night and to-morrow," urged the weeping girl; "it will be an unspeakable comfort to me. Within the cave we cannot be observed:"

"Be it so, daughter,— my darling one. We will now retire, and commend ourselves to Him who

10*   H

doeth all things well. It is time Duncan had departed."

The unsteady foot of Lord Glennair, as he and his friend arose from their place of concealment, and in silence issued from the forest, told of excited feeling somewhat unusual. No word was spoken, and at the gate of the castle a pressure of the hand was the only farewell passed between them.

At once seeking the privacy of his chamber, when the door was closed upon him, he endeavored to collect his scattered thoughts. Was he in a dream?—or was it indeed a dread reality? Had Lincoln stood before him? Had he witnessed the strong man bowed with sorrow, yet the same calm, dignified, uncompromising Lincoln? The most minute events of the evening passed vividly before him. His parental affection and the filial love returned. And Duncan — the chosen one of the forger's daughter! Duncan Graeme — the bosom-friend of Percy. Was *he* aware? Never!—not a thought but was in unison with his own. A doubt arose: — Was Lincoln guilty? Could such a hypocrite mar the fair face of this fair earth? And am I about to rend with agony that daughter's heart? Her throes of anguish, her despairing eye,— all, all were depicted upon his wrought imagination. His breath became hot and stifled, his bosom heaved, and he sought to recover himself at the open window. Throwing off his overcoat, which, in the tumult of his thoughts he had forgotten, he endeavored to obtain calmness. Suddenly there was a revulsion of feeling. The forged papers,— the same writing as those found in the overcoat of Lincoln; notes in his hand, hinting darkly at the deed; three hundred thousand pounds gone — and without his knowledge? — impossible! He is the guilty one, the hypocrite, the deceiver; only playing upon the kindly heart of Duncan. His deeds shall be brought to light," he exclaimed aloud; "and his guilt or innocence clearly proved." The morning light broke; and, forgetful that his head had not pressed the pillow through that night, the Laird of Glennair, as was his wont, descended to his library.

"I fear you are not well, dear papa," Miss Dunbar remarked, as she opened the door to announce a waiting breakfast. "It is full an hour beyond your customary time for joining us, and Kenneth has tapped repeatedly."

The Laird listlessly arose, and followed her to the breakfast-room. A scrutinizing glance was cast upon Percy, but his bright smile reassured him.

"No oaten cake, papa," exclaimed his younger daughter, as she caressingly threw her arm about his neck, and kissed his cheek,—"your own penalty, you know, for lazy folks; yet, for the first offence, I will show clemency this morning. If in power, I fear my want of firmness would weaken the arm of the law, as papa says all pardons have that tendency."

"For a first misdemeanor, papa would be lenient also," her sister replied, pleasantly; "but your infringement of rules was so frequent, that it was necessary to enforce them."

"But in a court of justice, papa," inquired Miss

Ellen, "when there is something more than an imaginary offence, should not the previous character be considered?"

"If sinning against light and knowledge, daughter, greater should be the punishment," the Laird returned, as he pushed from him his yet untasted cake, and rested his eye upon Percy. "Is not that your view also, my son?" he inquired.

"Certainly, father: the servant who knew his Lord's will, and did it not, should be beaten with many stripes," he replied, as his eye fell before the steady gaze of his father; "but there may be cases in which no proof could shake my confidence in the honor of those suspected."

"Were you ever called to pass such judgment, my son?" the Laird inquired, his eye still fixed anxiously and intently upon him.

The color mounted to the temples of the youth as he returned, "As I have no power, father, my private opinion is of little moment."

"Your reply is indefinite and unsatisfactory, Percy. Does your mind revert to any condemned by the community, with full proof of guilt existing, yet possessing high-souled, high-toned honor, in your estimation?"

Percy was silent. There was evidently a struggle between native independence and filial respect. The compressed, quivering lip, the change from ashy paleness to the deepest hue, showed the strife within.

"Papa, permit *me* to explain," interposed Miss Dunbar. "Percy is the soul of truth, and —"

"Daughter," her father interrupted almost sternly, "I cannot permit my question to remain unanswered. Percy Dunbar, do you consider the former Cashier of Glennair Bank among the honorable?"

The eye of his son was slowly raised; it met that of his excited father. Determination only was now visible in the countenance. In a low, but firm and decided tone, he replied: — "Were he upon the scaffold, I would believe him innocent; and," he added, raising one hand toward heaven, and looking upward, "I am confident it would only bring him nearer to the portals of heaven, where angels would await his spirit, to bear it to his Master, whom he has served so faithfully."

The face of his father was blanched with amazement. "And to whom are you indebted, young man, for your novel estimate of this high-handed villain," he inquired, his voice tremulous with anger. "Has other than he become the object of your censure? Has your father, or Robertson, MacAlpin, or Monteith committed this deed of infamy?"

"Pardon, my dear father," the youth returned, laying his hand gently upon his arm; "you are excited,— unduly so, perhaps. Would that my father could view the matter in the same light with his son."

"Would that your father were a dotard! Would that his vision were through so false a medium, that high-handed villains might be considered martyrs!"

"Not so, my father. Let me —"

"Enough, Percy Dunbar," the Laird peremptorily interrupted, as he arose to leave the apartment; "my patience is exhausted. May you have some little judgment ere we again touch upon the subject."

The door was closed. Percy resumed the seat from which he had arisen. "Would that I were arbiter," he murmured; "the just, the innocent, the injured, should be distinguished from the guilty."

"I cannot imagine, Percy," his sister remarked, "on what premises you found your opinion of Mr. Lincoln."

"And before Lochiel was the professed admirer and humble servant of Miss Lincoln," Miss Ellen observed, with a slight toss of the head; "before he was 'nursed so tenderly and so faithfully,' as he expresses it, he confessed to me that his father was so persuaded of the guilt of Mr. Lincoln, that his illness was altogether caused by the shock produced on his nervous system. Now his lips are sealed in regard to him, and I really tire of the praises of little Helen and *Miss Edith*."

"A youthful admirer, truly," Percy returned, glancing archly at his elder sister. "And does Miss Lincoln smile upon her young and devoted suitor?"

"I am not the *confidante* of either party," she retorted quickly; "but my story only goes to prove that others, beside Percy Dunbar, may be governed by feeling, in the place of conviction."

"And the force of such an example may well cause me to tremble. Poor, vacillating Lochiel,—

his mood is seldom the same for two successive days."

"*My* perception must be obtuse, indeed," she returned, with an offended air, "as I have never observed this fitfulness."

"What of his transfer to Miss Edith?" inquired her brother, playfully drawing her toward him. "What of that faithless step, my little sister?"

"Transfer — of what?"

"Of admiration to Miss Lincoln, of course, ascribed to *tenderness*. That tingles in my ear as a tender word, Miss Ellen."

"Let his admiration — yes, and 'tenderness' also," she returned, with a curl of the lip not to be misapprehended, — "be bestowed on whom he will; it is not of the slightest moment to me; he is free as air to seek his pleasure and bestow his attention on whom he will. Why do you suppose I would cast a thought upon the subject?"

"Only apprehensive of his good citizenship; fearful that his *tender* nursing would entice him from his allegiance to — his first lady-love," he whispered in her ear, as he laughingly snatched a kiss and made a hasty retreat.

On that night Laird Glennair entered the forest alone, a pressing engagement preventing his friend bearing him company. The same silence reigned as on the preceding evening. Hour after hour passed heavily along, but the stillness remained unbroken. Was the Grotto indeed untenanted? Notwithstanding all their vigilance, had Lincoln escaped when almost within the arm of justice ? There was a sensation of relief, and buoyancy of spirit, which an accusing conscience could not control. . He was startled by the falling of a stone. There was a feeling of sore disappointment as the form of Edith was distinguished issuing from the cave. "Remain within, father," she said, " the air is keen, and your breast will scarcely bear this exposure. Good night again, dear father," she added, " Duncan will see me safely home ; I hear his footsteps in the distance."

" Good night, beloved ; may Heaven protect you from all evil," was the return.

In a few moments a figure was seen approaching. As it drew near, Lord Glennair endeavored in vain to recognize in the shadow the slight form of Duncan Graeme. At this moment a heavy cloud obscuring the moon, cast all around in darkness. A quick step caught his ear ; light, yet bold and confident. It was not the step of Duncan. No — was it ? He listened eagerly, breathlessly ; a film passed over his sight, and a deep groan escaped him as the voice of Percy reached his ear.

Miss Lincoln started.

" It was the mere whistling of the wind," Percy remarked, " or a tendril disengaging itself."

His father, recalled to his wonted presence of mind, drew back into the recess of the rock.

" Mr. Dunbar ! " exclaimed Miss Lincoln, " I supposed it was the step of Duncan. I am surprised to meet *you* at this hour. Is Allan with you ? "

" At the foot of the bridge, awaiting us. Mr. Robertson claimed the services of Duncan this evening to examine with him some accounts at his dwelling. A most reluctant assent was given, as we intended visiting the cave together. A word in the ear of your father, Edith; I will then return and see you through this gloomy glen."

"Shall I enter with you, Percy?"

"As you please, Edith; from you no secret need be withheld."

For a few moments they disappeared; then the sound of voices low and earnest, at the mouth of the cave, was heard, and a low "good night" followed. Again ascending the steps, Miss Lincoln took the proffered arm, and silently they left the forest, each retreating footstep striking as a death-knell upon the ear of his father. Who can picture the tumultuous passions that raged within the bosom of Lord Glennair? Was his ingenuous, his confiding, his simple-hearted boy ensnared by the wiles of this insidious deceiver? "Face to face, I will charge him with this foul deed!" he exclaimed, starting to his feet and rushing toward the cave. "His guilty conscience must quail before one whom he is seeking to injure so irreparably." The mouth was reached, the steps descended, and his hand upon the rugged stone that impeded his entrance, when the voice of prayer fell upon his ear. Clear, calm, confident; pleading humbly in this dark hour for grace and strength to lay firm hold upon things eternal; pleading all the promises of God to the stricken in spirit.

"Thou, Lord, knowest the heart;—my heart," the voice murmured,—"free from every stain alleged by man; but wandering, and prone to wander far

11

from the fold of the Redeemer. Recall me by thy
love, and, as thy servant Moses of old, let thy goodness pass before *me*, and cheer me with the certain
assurance that I am thine — thine entirely — and
that a crown of rejoicing is awaiting thy sorrowing
servant." The Lord's Prayer was then repeated, in
which the broad Scotch accent of Roger Neilson,
accompanying the first speaker, was distinctly heard.
Then all was silent, calm, and hushed, as though no
being had found entrance there; calm and hushed
as the bosom that a moment since had breathed only
vengeance against its inmates. A voice seemed to
whisper, — "You are within holy precincts."

Falling upon his face, he lay almost unconscious
of surrounding things. At length, startled by a
slight movement within the cave, he arose, and
pursued with difficulty his way toward his home.
As he slowly ascended the steps, a voice pleasantly
remarked, — "This is an unusual hour for my Lord
Glennair to desert his own fireside; the occasion
must have been indeed pressing."

He turned; the same bright smile of the morning
met his view.

"Have you been with Mr. Robinson this evening?" Percy inquired, as in the hall he took his
father's hat and cloak, and, with his own, handed
them to Kenneth.

"I had private business in a contrary direction,"
he replied. The tone was such as forbade all further
inquiry, and in silence he followed his father to the
library, where the two young ladies were awaiting
them. A large arm-chair was wheeled by Kenneth

before a blazing hearth, and the heavy boots exchanged for a pair of slippers, carefully warmed by Ellen.

"You look worn, papa," she remarked, as she placed a stool closely beside him, "as though your journey this evening had been wearisome."

"And the rose will not long remain upon the cheek of my little daughter if she seek no rest until the midnight hour," he returned, stroking her hair affectionately.

"Her vigils have not been painful, papa," Miss Dunbar remarked, laughing; "a pleasant slumber has been enjoyed upon the couch since ten o'clock. Lochiel was with us until that hour."

"And are the engagements of Percy Dunbar of so pressing a nature," his father inquired, sternly, "that the dawn must so nearly anticipate him, 'ere he is enabled to free himself from their demands?"

There was evident confusion in the manner of Percy, as he endeavored to reply pleasantly. "The hand of the old faithful timepiece only pointed to eleven, father, when I returned; but, learning from Kenneth that you were still absent, and supposing you were transacting some business with the Bank directors, I desired to relieve the loneliness of your walk home, and have spent the last hour in making fruitless inquiry for you."

The eye of his father glanced toward Percy as he spoke. He was about replying, but, checking himself — with a knit brow and deeply sad countenance, with one palm placed upon the back of the other hand as they lay upon his knee — his head sank upon his bosom — he remained perfectly silent. Percy slowly walked the floor, evidently ill at ease, occasionally stealing a glance toward him. The silence was becoming painful, when Miss Dunbar suddenly inquired, —

" Did you hear the absurd report relative to the Elfin, Percy ?"

" Reports regarding it are many, Gertrude," he replied, carelessly ; " but little credence is given by any but the vulgar herd."

" In regard to the past, it has been so, brother, and the amount of salt strewn for defence, considerable ; but Lochiel tells us there is some sensation among the more intelligent classes of the community."

" And what are the wonderful new developments to cause the excitement ?" Percy inquired.

" No developments whatever ; but some fishermen are ready to make an affirmation that they were eye-witnesses to a phantom-boat, issuing from the cave, guided by a figure of blue flame, the profile of which bore an exact resemblance to the grandfather of Roger Neilson. Beside him sat a youthful female, of the same ethereal appearance, upon whom he cast dark and malignant glances ; a third form was also visible, but could not be sufficiently distinguished to be identified. Although in that terrific storm, it skimmed the waves lightly, and reached the Glennair inlet in safety, notwithstanding it had been apparently engulfed a few rods distant."

" And why so tardy in recording their wonderful vision ?" Percy inquired with a sneer.

" They were outward bound when it occurred,

were delayed — fishing, and did not return until yesterday."

" The present gloomy cast of Lochiel's feelings induces a belief in the supernatural that, if in health, he would spurn at once, as unworthy the first thought," Percy returned.

" It must have made its due impression upon the mind of his paragon," Miss Ellen remarked, " as she most strenuously advised him not to venture near the cave, and to forbear making any inquiry relative to it."

" I suppose she feared his natural love of adventure would lead him into danger," her brother returned, " for if he were carried away by some submarine fairy, her loss would be irreparable."

" Lochiel remarked this evening it was strange the Elfin's cave had not been termed Elves' cave, — the plural form. Why is it, Percy?"

" It was named by the *unlearned* gentry, centuries since," he replied, " and has, I suppose, become a technic among us."

" I always thought some interest was manifested by Duncan for the lady in question," Miss Dunbar remarked.

" Only the highest esteem and regard, natural to their close intimacy from childhood, I assure you," Percy returned quickly, as the color slightly mounted. " He has often told me he knew little difference between Amy and Edith. Of late, we have not touched upon the subject."

" You are certainly mistaken, sister," said Miss Ellen; " report gives Miss MacAlpin the palm over all others, in the estimation of Duncan Graeme."

11 *

" Report speaks goldenly of her," returned Percy;
" he could scarcely make a more judicious selection.
Does she smile upon him?"

" Smile upon Duncan! Let him but bend his powers to win, success is certain."

" It is time my children were retiring," the Laird
remarked, rising.

" Let me see you to your chamber, father," said
Percy, playfully proffering his arm.

It was gravely, very gravely, taken, and after bidding the young ladies good night, in silence they
proceeded to the chamber.

" My son," Lord Glennair inquired, as he closed
the door upon them, " do you remember aught of
that dreary morning when we laid your mother in
yon vault which this window now overlooks?"

" But faintly, father. It is full sixteen years since
that sad event. I numbered but four summers; but
I do well remember," he added, affectionately, " that
the duty of both parents has been fulfilled by you.
What do I not owe you, father?"

" Yes, Percy, I have devoted my life to the welfare
of my children; and in my only son, my pride, the
inheritor of my name, I have reposed the most implicit trust. Has my confidence ever been misplaced,
my son?"

" Never wittingly, father; I have conscientiously
endeavored to fulfil my duty toward one who has
stood in the light of no common parent."

"And has confidence never been withheld, Percy?"
he inquired, as he gently laid his hand upon his arm.

For a moment the youth was silent, then firmly

replied, — " Not in any manner that would bring disgrace upon my name or involve my conscience. My father's happiness is mine, and may my head be.pillowed in the grave ere I willingly bring a blight upon it."

" Then beware, my son; your too confiding nature may be overreached. Your assertion this morning has filled my mind with dread lest some temptation should overtake you; lest that villain may obtain access to you, and yet silver my hair, not with age, but sorrow."

The eyes of the youth fell, but he replied not.

" Leave me now, Percy," said his father, unclasping the hand which he had firmly grasped, " and remember that it is your father's desire — not command, (I trust that is needless) — that no communication be held with any one bearing the name of Lincoln."

" Father!"

" No more, my son; retire to your chamber; ponder the question whether your father has ever enjoined upon his son any but wholesome precepts. Good night, my boy."

The door closed, and Percy retired to his own apartment; but the morning broke ere either had found, or even sought, repose.

CHAPTER VI.

"To be pained for a minute, to fear for an hour,
To hope for a week — how long and weary!"

TIME rolled on, and daily, yea, hourly, the thoughts of Lord Glennair wandered to Elfin Grotto, and his memory lingered on the scenes witnessed there. The past became again present to him, and with his arm linked once more in that of his once much-loved friend, he strolled along conversing of by-gone days, or perhaps of the future — the world of rest. How written upon his memory, and how vividly could he recall the very words,— the look, the eye gradually lighting with his subject, until his whole soul beamed forth as he described the glories of heaven, the peace, the joy, the purity of that abode. "Can — oh! can he be the guilty one — the hypocrite?" he would often murmur, as with clasped hands he would hurriedly pace his chamber. Then the proofs, one by one, would stand in glaring array before him, shutting out every avenue to hope in the possibility of his innocence.

Several weeks elapsed. Rumors alone reached the castle, of wonderful sights and marvellous doings at the Elfin Cave; but rumor whispered not the true cause of the disturbance of the silence of the Grotto; and, notwithstanding every effort to suppress so improper a feeling, the desire was becoming more and

128

more intense that justice, in this instance, might not overtake the guilty. To none could he unbosom every feeling. His friend Robertson had left his home, to seek a more congenial climate for an invalid daughter. To his son his lips were sealed; doubt and distrust had taken the place of the most unbounded confidence, and the name of Lincoln, so fraught with interest, was never whispered.

A conversation between Duncan and Percy, in the chamber of the latter, was accidentally overheard by Lord Glennair. Seeking some papers in the room adjoining, the voice of his son, in earnest conversation, met his ear; his own name was repeatedly pronounced. His· high sense of honor would have induced an immediate withdrawal, but paternal solicitude deterred him, and he listened with breathless anxiety to catch the words of Percy.

"My mind is racked with torture, Duncan," he remarked; " do not render me more wretched."

"Your duty is plain, Percy; the Lord prefers mercy to sacrifice, and how can you ask his blessing while withholding aid and sympathy, in its utmost need, from his own chosen one, who is drinking sorrow to its dregs."

"But my father's prohibition. Is not the fifth command of equal force with other portions of Scripture?"

"And are you not following merely the letter of the law? Is it with his approval the wants of the inmates of the cave are supplied from his abundance?"

"My father gives direction to feed the hungry,

I

whatever be their moral delinquencies. But of that
matter I have taken little cognizance. Kenneth
being a warm friend of Norval, and one of the Mac-
Lean clan, leaves me small need to act."

"Yes, and if Lord Glennair were not blinded by
the misapprehension of the community, *he* would be
the last to hunt to the death such a man as Mr.
Lincoln."

"Has Mr. Lincoln made any mention of my withdrawal?"

"Some time since he inquired for you with much
interest, but my reply being vague, and my manner
probably embarrassed, he only remarked, with a
sigh, 'Dear boy, his past sympathy has been indeed
precious. I shall never be able to repay the debt of
gratitude!' There was a flush upon the face of
Edith, who was present, but she made no remark."

"Edith was not wounded?" he inquired, as his
eye bent anxiously upon his friend. "With Mrs.
Cameron I have had almost daily intercourse.
Edith surely cannot suppose me indifferent? How
is it, Duncan, *you* were received, even before the
sickness of Lochiel, and I denied?"

"Almost brotherly intercourse, from early childhood, gave me a claim which I at once asserted.
But time is waning, Percy; the perilous situation
of our friends demands immediate action. Suspicion is evidently abroad. Report of policemen occasionally seen by Norval, almost in the vicinity of
the Grotto, tells upon the prostrate and nervous
frame of the poor sufferer. The *Orion* is now lying
out, ready to sail to-morrow. I have made every

arrangement with the Captain,—a true friend of Roger,—and at dawn the effort will be made to reach her. The state of Mr. Lincoln is pitiable in the extreme. Debilitated and wretched, he can afford no consolation to Edith, who is agonized with the apprehension of her father's danger, and inconsolable at the anticipation of the separation. A word of solace from your lips to Mr. Lincoln would be as manna in the desert. You refuse it at your peril."

"I will see him this night, cost what it may, Duncan. Will Edith remain with him until the morning?"

"She pleads to be permitted to do so, and her father cannot deny her. She will probably await his departure."

"And who will accompany her on her return home?"

"Allan and Norval. She firmly declines my services, fearing to excite suspicion at the manse."

"Without permission, *I* will see her home. She might refuse me the gratification, if I proffered. None will be aware of my absence; I will return ere my father has arisen."

"There is one circumstance I withheld, Percy, fearing it would excite pain and indignation. MacLoughlin has closely watched the movements of Norval, and his thefts have frequently produced want within the walls of the Grotto. The coward was bold because he was aware there could be no redress."

"Wretch! miscreant!" exclaimed Percy; "Providence will yet bring that fellow to condign punishment. Shall I go with you to the cave this evening?"

"Not until nine; before that hour, some evil spirit might observe us: there is no moon now to tell a tale."

There was a warm grasp of the hand, as with some agitation Percy whispered, "Pray that I may be forgiven for this first act of disobedience to my only parent."

"A light conscience may follow this deed of mercy," was the reply.

The door closed, and Lord Glennair retired to his chamber.

"Miserable delusion — misguided boy!" he murmured; "would that the grave had closed over him ere his too confiding nature had been ensnared by such foul spirits as Lincoln and Duncan Graeme. Can *he* be an accomplice? No, never —" Such a suggestion he would not harbor for a moment; yet it had arisen, and gained a prominence he could not repel. "My noble, darling boy," he exclaimed, "you shall not fall a sacrifice to your own kindly feelings. I will anticipate the dawn, and, if necessary, unmask the villain who would be the destroyer of your fair fame. But no —" he said, rising hastily, "I will see him now, I will tell him all my conflicts, confess to him all my apprehensions, and, if driven to extremity, I will *command* that all intercourse be suspended, even with Duncan Graeme."

On his way to the apartment of his son, Kenneth met him. "Maister Paircy bid me say, my Laird, that he would nae return tae dinner, as he had an engagement."

"Did he say where he would dine, Kenneth?"

"I believe a' the manse. I heard Mr. Duncan tell him the hour for dinner."

Long and heavily passed the day with the Laird. In the most agonized suspense, he in vain awaited the return of his beloved boy, and, sick with disappointment, when the evening was far advanced, he retired to his chamber.

The hand of the old clock pointed to eleven, ere Percy returned home. The weary spirit of the Laird sought to obtain some rest: at length he sank into a dreamy forgetfulness of the present, but his slumbers were disturbed and broken. Lost in the intricate mazes of a thick forest, he saw in the distance three figures: in the outline of one he dimly recognized Hugh Lincoln. A female form was walking beside him, with the arm of a youth encircling her waist,—his ear bent low in the act of listening.

"My boy—my Percy!" he shrieked. The effort aroused him, and, springing from the bed, he, with a trembling hand, hastily stirred the embers that were just expiring upon the hearth-stone.

"It cannot, will not, shall not be!" he exclaimed. "Pshaw! It is only the vagaries of a disturbed imagination." Throwing himself into an old arm-chair, he endeavored to recall the truth:—the vision stood prominently before him.

"May not this be a warning?" he inquired. "No—absurd fantasy;—my boy would not dare,—

not wish, — not — I cannot tell. Why his evident anxiety for her this morning? Nay, — he is safe. The daughter of the robber is the betrothed of the unfortunate Duncan. My name and house will still remain unsullied. But should he proffer! Might she not yield to strong temptation? His house and lineage, his expectations, — the Laird, the owner of these broad lands. Never! never!" he exclaimed, springing from his seat, and striking the table vehemently. "I will arrest the evil; — I swear it, solemnly." His head sank upon his bosom, as he added, whisperingly, "Or will renounce my boy, my son, my loved one."

The parish clock struck five. Hurriedly arranging his toilet, and enveloping himself in a large cloak and slouched hat, he bent his steps toward the cave. Starting at every passing sound, fearing observation, he at length reached the place, and, almost spent with fatigue and excitement, he seated himself in the crevice of a rugged rock, entirely concealed from view. An hour passed, — another, and another. There was felt silence here: not a movement, save the quick beating of the heart, in unison with the heavy pulsations throughout the frame. His eye was not once lifted from the entrance to the cave, and the strained ear intently sought the first advancing footsteps. Suddenly there is a movement of the rude stone at the entrance; the blood recedes from his heart, a shiver passes through the whole frame, and the Laird sank upon the ground almost deprived of motion, but his eye still intently watching.

The next moment Percy appeared, leading a young lady, whose face was buried in her hands. For some time a low sob only reached his ear. The countenance of his son manifested the deepest sympathy. "Endeavor to regain some composure, Edith, ere we proceed further," he said. Taking a large shawl, which was thrown carelessly across his arm, and placing it upon a stone, he drew her gently to it, and seated himself beside her. "The Lord reigns, Edith; he doeth all things well."

"I know it, I know it, Percy," returned the agonized girl; "yet I am tempted sometimes to feel *he* is forsaken."

"Say not forsaken, Edith. He is tried in the furnace of affliction, but will escape unscathed."

"May the Lord forgive my distrust, Percy. He has vouchsafed his presence peculiarly to father since his misfortune, and his gratitude to you and Duncan is unbounded. What does he not owe you, Percy?"

"And why has the daughter of Mr. Lincoln declined all intercourse with her father's tried friend?" he inquired, laying his hand gently upon her own.

"Is not Lord Glennair's opinion of my father a sufficient reason, Percy? Would not intercourse with his daughter be inimical to his wishes?"

"With a common friend there might be some plausibility in your argument; but, previous to this sore calamity, was I esteemed so lightly that a breath — an idle tale, would drive me from your remembrance?"

"No, Percy, believe me, my mind often reverts

to you, and other esteemed friends, with whom I once held pleasant intercourse in days, perhaps, never to return."

. "And was I, and am I still, regarded but as a pleasant friend?" he inquired, sadly. "For years you have been dearer to me than life, Edith, and I longingly desired to lay my wealth, my honors, my all at your feet. Without you, the world's a blank: say this hand is mine, I am the most blest of men."

For a moment embarrassment and surprise held her silent; but the hand he had clasped within his own she gently endeavored to withdraw.

"You have noticed, certainly, my marked attention, Edith? Have you not given me encouragement to hope, — and will pride, self-respect — call it what you may — lead you to dash from me the cup of happiness?"

"I am distressed, dear Percy," she at length replied, tremblingly, "that you should so entirely have mistaken me. As a kind friend, you will permit me always to regard you; but I should be unworthy of your friendship, did I trifle with your frank and kindly nature, and "—sinking her voice almost to a whisper, she added — "my hand is pledged to Duncan."

"Pledged!—and to Duncan Graeme?" exclaimed the youth. "Edith, do I comprehend you? Is this the kind return for years of entire devotedness? Have I not lived for you — and would I not have died for you? And Duncan — my friend — my dearest friend as I supposed, recklessly has he deceived me."

"Duncan is incapable of duplicity, Percy, and from our childhood he —" She hesitated.

"I supposed it only brotherly affection," he returned, in a softened tone. "I have often heard him speak of all his early associations being connected with Thistle Hedge and Edith Lincoln."

"And he has often spoken gratefully of the kind attentions of Percy to Amy and myself. We neither felt you had any preference. Permit me again to ask that the friendship that has always existed may be continued."

"I thank you for your regard, Edith, but fear I could scarcely sympathize with Duncan in his happiness. On the Continent, I will seek forgetfulness of the past, and at the same time gratify my father's earnest wish that I should visit other lands. You alone have fettered me to my native shore."

"It is time, Percy, I was on my way homeward," she remarked, rising and placing her arm within his. "I feel, too painfully, I have unwittingly led you into error."

They left the forest.

"Noble girl," murmured Lord Glennair. "A powerful temptation offered and resisted, and my dear boy spared a foul blot upon his escutcheon."

12 *

"And if error cometh in like a flood,
    It mixeth with streams of truth ;
And the adversary loveth to have it so,
    For thereby many are decoyed."

IT was early morn, — the sun had scarcely risen
upon the hill-tops, and the wind was whistling
drearily, when a dark, ill-looking man appeared,
skulking along a ledge of rocks overhanging the
ocean, carefully picking his way from stone to stone,
and stealthily peering around, as though fearful of
being detected. Succeeding in reaching a point
which opened on a sandy beach, he was proceeding
toward another ledge, when a voice accosted him : —

"Wha ho there, MacLoughlin, and wha's the
errand o' maircy that ha brought ye to cool yere
fingers this mornin'?"

MacLoughlin started, but seeing his badge of
office, he forbore reply.

"It may be yere good conscience made too warm
a pillow for ye," he added, sneeringly, "or ye feared
the chilling the feet o' Allan by this exposure."

There was a scowl passed over his countenance as
he replied, "Ye maun inquire at the manse for that
gentleman ; he 's nae longer a fit companion for John
MacLoughlin. He 's nae use to me or mine since his
head was turned by his betters."

"Yere memory is somewhat treacherous, if my
138

eyes and ears are not. Does a' the help in cleaving
boards for fuel count for naething?—and wha's the
first to lend a helping hand to yere gude wife, when
food for the bairns is wanted frae the Castle, and
she kens she darn't sae much as shew her nose
there? Wha's the mon to do a' this? Tell me
that, John MacLoughlin."

. "And suppose ye the fine clothes· cast off by the
Doctor and Maister Duncan ha' naething to do wi'
the call at the Castle? Was he so frae to gang
afore he could hauld a sound cap, and jingle some
little siller to make himsel' welcome to the house-
maids? Nae, nae,—he is nae the same lad, or nae
the same use in the cabin, since the gentry and the
kin o' Hugh Lincoln the robber took him up, and
since he shared the bed and the breakfast of that
Bernard O'Dougherty. Hae ye any news o' *him*,
Maister MacFin?"

"News of wha? Of Bernard O'Dougherty, who
rides wi' that fine young gentleman, Dr. McMillan? '

"Nae, nae," he returned, hesitatingly, and looking fearfully around,—" the t'other—the first missing mon, ye ken."

"And wha hae ye or I to do wi' missin' men or
missing women? We'd better mind our ain affairs,
John MacLoughlin, and nae trouble our consciences
wi' men, mayhap, four thousand miles across the
waters. Yere nae sae sharp-sighted, are ye?"

"A short line would measure the distance, I
trow."

"The length of an oar, think ye?" asked Mac-
Fin.

"An' what of an oar?" he inquired, fiercely.

"Naethin';—I only guessed it was yere measurin' pole, when it and the boat parted company."

"An wha calls John MacLoughlin a thief? Let the owner of the oar come face to face, an' I'll gie him the lie, direct."

"Take the short line, and measure the distance wi' him; mayhap he's wi' in the hearin'."

MacLoughlin started. "Wha's wi' in hearin'?" he inquired, with a face of terror. "Be Roger Neilson in these parts?" he whisperingly asked. "Why would I touch an oar belongin' to anither?" he said, more loudly.

"To mend yere fortine, an' make a little should ye find a purchaser. Was the oar marked wi' the name o' Neilson?"

"An' if it wa'. It wa' cast away, wi' ain end in the ocean."

He was interrupted by the sound of oars. A boat drew near, and two men, also with the badge of office, jumped on shore. There were some words, in a low tone, passed between them, and some meaning glances cast toward MacLoughlin. Whistling with an air of pretended carelessness, with a hand thrust into either pocket, he seated himself upon a rock at some distance, carefully noting, however, every word that reached him.

"Wha was the first to make the discovery?" MacFin inquired, with an arch glance toward Mac-Loughlin. "Did ye say tae the Laird, Maister Lincoln wa' here?"

Turnbull hesitated. "Wha is the reward?" he inquired.

"Nae, nae!" exclaimed MacLoughlin, starting from his seat, "I hae the Laird's word, an' nain ither 'ill ha the right tae a pound o' the siller."

"An' wha hae ye tae do wi' the matter?" inquired MacFin, sternly. "Would the word o' sic as ye be ta'en by my Laird Glennair?"

"In a cauld morn I braved the storm, an' the report I bare him led tae all the sairch, an' I'm the mon for the profit, if profit there be a his ta'en."

"And may the siller airned in sic a deed," returned MacFin, seizing him roughly by the collar, "be a curse an' not a blessing tae ye. May yere bairns prove false to ye, as ye ha' played false to yere friend Roger Neilson."

At this sudden and unexpected ebullition, the face of the fisherman was blanched with terror.

"Loose your grasp, Mr. MacFin," he cried, endeavoring vainly to free himself. "It wa' for the Laird I did it, meanin' nae harm to Roger."

"It wa' a dirty business, ye craven, mak' the best of it. When ye were hungry, wha fed ye? an' when ye were naked, wha clothed ye?"

"I warn't naked nither, an' his auld duds warn't o' mickle account."

"An' when ye came near bein' houseless, wha put it into the heart of Maister Lincoln tae stand for ye? Wha but Roger Neilson?"

"Allan hae tauld ye lies, an' I'll mak' him suffer fa' his fine tales o' me."

"Ye hae but little rule o'er Allan; but if ye touch but a hair o' his head, I'll skin ye alive, an' hang ye up in the mountain for a terror tae all the like o' ye. Now tak yoursel' frae these parts, and ne'er show yere nose among us, or I'll teach ye better manners than yere had o' late."

So saying, with a hearty shake of the collar, he relinquished his grasp, and MacLoughlin, with a low growl and a defiant scowl, slowly retraced his steps, and was soon hidden from view. Crouching down in the recess of a rock, he closely watched the movements of two boats below.

"Would that my tairm of sairvice had expired, Turnbull," MacFin remarked, "ere I'd been on this hard duty."

"An' were it not I was sworn to do justice, I wud now frae my hand from this unwelcome business," returned his friend; "but the law wull nae punish the innocent. At any rate, we are nae the responsible anes."

"We could nae save him if we would," replied MacFin; "the twa boats below are filled wi' determined spirits, loth to credit good o' Lincoln or Neilson. They'd follow them to the death wi' good consciences. Would that Maister Lincoln had an inklin' o' the truth; our skirts wud then be clean tae our country, and "—lowering his voice—"our ain friend safe."

"May there be a sore blight upon the man Mac-Loughlin," his companion returned, "an' may his ill-gotten siller be a curse, rather than a blessin' tae him."

"Amen to that, Turnbull;—but, hark," he whispered, as the sound of a heavy oar struck upon the water; "it's nae ither than the oar o' Neilson.

The die is cast — may heaven shield them from the impending storm."

Pale and excited, he sprang into the boat at a signal from those already on the water, and was immediately followed by his two companions.

The measured sound of the oar drew nearer. The lowering brow of MacFin checked the exultant looks of the remainder of the party. Every ear was bent to listen, as suppressed voices were heard.

"The vigilant eye of the fisherman would soon detect us, and the Laird of Glennair would not long be wanting information," was almost whispered.

"The head o' MacLoughlin is scarce ta'en frae his pillow, in this raw, airly mórn," was the reply, in a louder and more confident tone. It was the voice, the well-remembered voice, of Roger Neilson.

The compressed lip and flushed cheek told the tumultuous feeling within the bosom of his friend MacFin.

"We will soon be within hailin' distance of the *Orion*," continued Neilson, "and on her deck we are in safety."

"May it be the will of the Lord we should reach it," ejaculated Mr. Lincoln, despondingly.

The face of Mr. Lincoln was hidden, his head resting upon his bosom, as they suddenly drew within sight of the boats. The exclamation of Neilson startled him. Springing to his feet, he at once realized the certainty of their fate, and falling back upon the seat, he murmured, — "The will of the Lord be done."

"Slack yere hold of the oar," cried one of the

men insultingly, as he seized the prow of the boat, " an' we will save you the trouble of rowing so fast or so far. Will ye halt and bear us company the while ? "

The collar of the speaker was seized instantly, and the next moment he was struggling with the waves and fierce passion.

The oar of Neilson was immediately extended, and the man, clinging to it, was released by one of his comrades, who put out in his boat to rescue him. A scene of confusion would have ensued had not the quiet dignity of Mr. Lincoln, and the stern, uncompromising countenances of the two officers, held them in check.

" Ye richly desairved yer duckin'," said Turnbull, as he stepped into the boat of the prisoner, " an' yere shiverin' an' shakin' is of your ain seekin'."

"I have an extra cloak here," Mr. Lincoln remarked to MacFin. " Let the man make use of it, or his death may lay heavily upon your conscience."

It was slowly and reluctantly taken by Turnbull, who, tossing it to the man, remarked, — " Mr. Lincoln offers ye his cloak in return for all yer kindness. Shame on ye ; shame, shame."

A flush of confusion crossed the man's face, as, receiving it, he muttered, — " On'y a bit of a joke, no harm."

" Then keep your jokes for them that understand them, and lairn to haud yer tongue when yer betters are concerned."

" Haud yer ain tongue, Turnbull," he returned ; " I tell ye I thank him for his cloak, an' wad na do the like agin tae the gentleman."

The concession was, however, lost upon Mr. Lincoln, who, having resigned the oar to MacFin, had again seated himself, his head resting upon one hand, apparently absorbed in thought.

"Mr. Turnbull an' I will take charge of the boat," MacFin observed to his comrades; "the sairvices of nane ither will be required till we reach the landing."

A nod of assent was given, and all resuming their oars, silently accompanied the boat of Neilson.

The boat stopped, and for some moments the officers rested upon their oars, irresolute how to proceed, Mr. Lincoln still retaining the same motionless position, the eye of Neilson resting intently and anxiously upon him.

"Wi' ye take the carriage, Maister Lincoln?" Turnbull at length inquired, respectfully.

There was a quiver upon the lips of Roger, as Mr. Lincoln calmly arose and prepared to follow the officers. The boats being all secured, Turnbull and MacFin entered the carriage with the prisoners, the guard following at a respectful distance.

"A painfu' part we have performed this day, Mr. Lincoln," MacFin observed, with much feeling. "We would fain hae bid ye 'God speed' to the *Orion*. Ye hae been a kind friend to me an' mine, and it seems a strange retairn for all yer kindness."

"You have proved yourself faithful in the post assigned you, David," Mr. Lincoln returned; "there is no reflection on my part, I assure you."

"Nae, nae, Mr. Lincoln, my vigilance was nae so commendable, an' the deck of the *Orion* would hae received ye had my faithfulness alone been put to the test ; but there were eyes keen an' sharp, an' hearts nae open tae trouble, that gave nae rest tae their evil spirits till the evil wark was accomplished. Would they had yere clear conscience, Mr. Lincoln."

"May I mak sae bold," observed Turnbull, " the law must an' will make a' good tae ye, or it's nae law that a mon can trust."

" Human tribunals cannot always shelter the oppressed, my friend ; but there is a judgment where all will obtain the just reward for every action, and a Judge who will by no means clear the guilty. May you and your warm-hearted friend seek to have consciences void of offence, before you are called to that dread bar."

"May the enemies of my Lord, and of my dear Maister, a' be scattered," murmured Neilson, as the carriage stopped before the jail-door.

" Amen, an' amen to that," returned both the officers, earnestly.

A hand of Mr. Lincoln was kindly proffered ere he alighted. " You may know the preciousness of the religion of Jesus," he said, " when I tell you that even while this dark cloud is resting over. my head, ready to burst upon me, — even while this terrific storm is pending, — the Lord has vouchsafed me his presence, and I have found a peace which passeth all understanding, of which the world knows nothing."

A tear was hastily brushed from the eye of Mac-Fin, as he held in a close grasp the hand of his prisoner. Mr. Lincoln, taking two small Bibles from his pocket, and presenting one to each, said, — " Receive this parting remembrance from one perhaps on the borders of eternity. That we may all meet in that better land, will be my constant prayer."

" I thank ye frae my heart, Maister Lincoln," said MacFin, " an' will try tae seek the way ye hae sae kindly pointed out, an' when I hae lairned to pray, I 'll ne'er stop for ye till yere out of all this trouble."

There was a warm shake of the hand, a fervent " God bless you," and the doors closed upon them.

Every sound had died away along the shore, save a single footfall, jumping from rock to rock, loosening in its way, at times, some stone from its restingplace, as the foot slipped on the rugged and steep mountain, producing a slight ripple as it disappeared in the water. The Glennair inlet was at length reached, and a figure might be seen approaching the gate of the castle. " The siller is mine, and I ha' the Laird's promise o' it," he muttered, as he knocked hesitatingly, " an' I 'll nae gie it up, for a' I 'm caud a puir craven an' the like."

. The gate was opened by Kenneth, who sullenly demanded his errand.

" I maun see the Laird, at once," he replied ; " I hae news for his ear tae please him."

" Ye can tell yer message, an' I 'll carry it if it 's worth the trouble."

" Nae, nae, Maister Kenneth, it 's for the Laird's ain ear, an' he tauld me tae come an' tell him."

" Well, I dinna ken how the like o' ye can hae a matter with my Laird, but tumble into the hall wi'

ye, an' dinna keep me starvin' wi' the cauld o' this
raw mornin', an' I 'll ask if ye 'll have a hearin'.''

The tap of the door was answered by Percy. He
was alone; and his heavy, soiled boots, not yet removed, showed that his step had been bent somewhat beyond the precincts of the manor on that
morning.

"The mon MacLoughlin hae a message tae my
Laird. Is he risen, Maister Pairey?"

"Send the man immediately to me," said young
Dunbar, "and, Kenneth, have some policemen in
readiness, should I need their service."

The arch and pleased countenance of Kenneth, as
he bowed a ready assent, showed there was no need
of a repetition of the order; and with the utmost
alacrity, the next moment MacLoughlin was ushered
into the presence of his young master. Starting
back, as he was about entering, he said, hesitatingly:

" It 's nae the young Laird; my message is tae my
Laird Glennair.''

" The Laird cannot yet be seen," young Dunbar
returned, rising as he spoke and placing a chair
within the door, " but to me you can confide the
object of your visit this morning."

" An' it please ye, Maister Dunbar," he returned,
looking timidly around and lowering his voice to a
whisper, " I 'm the mon that's ta'en him, and nane
ither.''

" Taken who, or what?" inquired Percy, quickly.

" Why the mon, Maister Lincoln, an' Roger wi'
him.''

The youth started from the seat he had resumed,
exclaiming, " Taken! How? By whom?"

"By the Bobbies, but wi' my assistance," Mac-Loughlin replied, rubbing his hands with glee at the anticipation of the promised reward. "They wad nae hae done the business but for me, tho' they ca'd all the curses on my head, for my treachery, as they ca'd it."

The young man, making great effort to conceal his agitation, when able to command his voice, inquired with assumed pleasantry: "And in many ways you were able to annoy him, were you not?"

"Never fear me, Maister Paircy," he returned, thrown entirely off his guard. "Never fear a mon wi' his wits at work all the time. Yes, yes, I well kenned his doin's, an' mony's the nice meal my bairns hae feasted on, meant for ither hands than mine."

"Ah!" replied Percy. "Well, now tell me how you managed matters? It must have required a close lookout."

"Close, indeed; but the dyes an' masks of Norval did n't hide his pretty face frae me, an' mony a basket brought frae the castle — "

"What! Stolen from the manor here?"

"The same thing, Maister Paircy, — begged for robbers. An' there wa' many a wee bit fixed by Mistress Cameron, that Mistress Cameron's brother neer had a grip on. Nae, nae, Maister Paircy," he continued, now thoroughly excited by the interest manifested by young Dunbar, "there's scarce a mon o' the country's side cauld hae managed matters sae nicely; for nane o' the group, nae ane o' them, dare tell the tale."

A loud ring of the library-bell by Percy, startled

13 *

him.   The summons was answered by a hurried rap
at the door.

"Weel, I maun be goin'," MacLoughlin remarked,
rising hastily as Kenneth entered.   "I canna be
longer wanted a' the cabin by the gude wife an' the
bairns.   Wi' I ca' again tae see the Laird, Maister
Paircy?"

The eye of Percy glanced toward the door as several figures appeared there.

"You will be some time wanted ere you will reach
them," he returned, coolly.   "Kenneth, let the
police enter."

"Maister Paircy!" exclaimed the terrified man,
"ye're nae surely goin' tae take hard all the words
o' an innocent mon?   I did it a' in the Laird's sairvice, an' nae for any ane else.   Yet the mon's caught,
an' maun I gang tae the prison for a'?"

"Your thefts have been suspected, but could
scarcely be proved until now.   You are condemned
from your own mouth.   Commit him at once, my
men; and in default of other evidence, I will myself
appear and bear witness to his guilt."

The officers came forward, and, notwithstanding
his protestations of innocence, secured him between
them.

"Alack! alack.!" he exclaimed, wringing his
hands, "wha' wi' the gude wife think o' a' this?"

"Do not trouble yourself on her account.   For
her petty thefts on our grounds she will this day
meet the same reward."

"But the bairns, — the bairns, — wha' wi' become
o' them?"

"Placed under much-better influence than ever before, where they will be taught to respect the laws, if, springing from such an impure fountain, they can ever be brought to any moral sense."

With countenances in which there was little commiseration, the officers led away their disconsolate prisoner, and young Dunbar, without awaiting breakfast, sought an interview with Duncan.

His ring at the manse was answered by young Graeme, who seeing him from his chamber-window, and alarmed at the untimely visit, hastily descended to meet him.

"No tidings of evil, I trust?" he inquired, seeing the disturbed countenance of his friend.

Percy shook his head mournfully.

"You are the bearer of evil, Percy;—of that I am assured; but you have not yet heard from Mr. Lincoln."

"All is lost, Duncan," he replied, as he threw himself into a chair in the study.

"How!—what!" exclaimed his friend. "Have they not reached the *Orion?*"

"They are taken—betrayed,—through the wiles of that crafty fisherman."

"MacLoughlin?—Has he dared—"

"He has dared nothing. I conjecture the police have made use of him as a tool. I know nothing, Duncan, save that they are taken captive, and immured within the prison-walls."

"I must at once see them, if practicable," said Duncan, hastily seizing his hat. "But Edith, Edith, how will the sad tidings be conveyed to her? *I* cannot, Percy—I cannot witness her anguish."

"I will see her, if you desire it; but would *you* not be more fitted to assuage her grief?"

"No, no, I have no words of consolation to offer; my own spirit is seared as the yellow leaf;—I am crushed, withered, stricken. Go, Percy, go; and in your communication have the wisdom of the serpent, that she be not at once borne to the earth. But *you* need no counsel; your own kindly nature will prompt to the utmost tenderness and caution. Let Amy be sent for, to remain with her through the day," he added, as he turned and hastened down the road.

"'Crushed,—withered,—stricken,'" Percy murmured, almost bitterly, as he touched the bell at Mrs. Cameron's. "Gladly would I relinquish a diadem, to be even as Duncan Graeme."

Miss Lincoln came immediately into the dining-room on hearing his name, and Mrs. Cameron followed.

"Have tidings of my father yet reached you, Mr. Dunbar?" she inquired, with an anxious face. "Only say he is on board the *Orion*, I shall be comparatively happy."

"Such a nature as Mr. Lincoln's is not fitted to endure perpetual exile, Edith."

"Say not perpetual. When the community is made sensible of its error, it will recall him. I am confident the ocean will not long separate us. His home will be mine also. Is he safe in the *Orion*, Percy?"

Young Dunbar was silent.

"If aught has occurred, dear Percy," interposed Mrs. Cameron, "tell us,—let us know the worst."

No word escaped Miss Lincoln, and the bloodless lip and cheek alarmed Percy. Leading her to the sofa, he seated himself beside her. "The Lord reigns, Edith," he whispered; "your father's hairs are numbered as one of his chosen ones; He will assuredly guard him from all evil."

"Is he taken — taken?" she gasped, as her cold and clammy hand clung to Mrs. Cameron for support.

"If a particle of justice remain with us," was the reply, "he will be tried and honorably acquitted. Fear not, dear Edith, — despair not." But the words passed unheeded. Fixing a listless eye upon him, her head sank upon her bosom, and she would have fallen, had not an arm of Percy immediately encircled her. Her head was laid gently back, and she rested in a state of total and blessed unconsciousness. The youth stood gazing upon her lifeless form.

"Would that I were the one united in spirit," he thought, "linked in a closer bond than that of father, brother, — my idolized, the object of my fondest hopes. Would that I could soothe every pang, guard from every ill, and — But what am I in her estimation? One of ten thousand —" The thrill of agony was insupportable; he turned from the sofa as Miss Graeme entered, — to whom Nanny had given the alarm, — followed by her father and Lochiel. In a few moments Duncan returned, and Percy, finding his services no longer needed, silently left the house.

By the low, earnest tones of Duncan, entreating her to speak to him once more, Edith was aroused.

"Sister, dear sister," cried little Helen, as her cousin pleadingly cast her eyes around, "Uncle Hugh *will* come home, indeed he will, sister; Mr. Duncan will bring him home to us."

"I must go to father, Helen; I must go to him; I must save, or die with him. Oh my father! my father!"

"Stricken child," said Mr. Graeme, gently forcing her to the sofa from which she had arisen; "he shall be saved, if in the power of those who love him; justice will be done, Edith; the very stringency of our laws make them equitable."

"I know it, I know it; and his enemies have produced false testimony sufficient to — to —" She shrank back with a shriek of despair

"Try, Fawn," Lochiel whispered,—himself entirely unmanned,—"try to comfort your cousin; she will listen to you."

Again the head of the beautiful child was laid beside the cheek of Edith, and again she softly whispered, "Uncle Hugh will come back,—I know Lochiel will help Mr. Duncan to bring him back; don't cry, sister, any more: he shall come home, — Mr. Duncan says so."

The gentle accents of the child soothed her; she drew her little hand to her lips. "Uncle will soon be home, sister," again she whispered, throwing her arms fondly around her neck.

"Sweet Fawn," Edith murmured, "I will try to believe so. Where is Duncan?"

Without relinquishing the hand he had been holding, he bent toward her and answered, "We *all* hope so, and *I* fondly believe it, Edith."

" Did you see father, Duncan ? "

" I succeeded, after some difficulty. He is comfortable, and entreats you will endeavor to be resigned to this unexpected turn in his destiny. He has pencilled you these few lines, to assure you of his confidence in his release, although it may be deferred. His hope is in the avenger of the innocent." Duncan raised his head and his voice in uttering the last sentence.

" He who is with us in six troubles will not desert us in seven," said Mr. Graeme. " He can deliver the guiltless; he is a strong tower, a secure refuge. He can scatter all His and our enemies: to Him we will look for deliverance. We will remember, ' Vengeance belongeth unto God.'" He ceased speaking. The solemn interval of silence that ensued was interrupted by the entrance of Dr. McMillan.

The searching eye of Duncan Graeme met his as he advanced into the apartment. The return glance was evidently satisfactory, and a few guarded sentences passed between them when an opportunity offered. He stood a few minutes by the side of Edith, who recognized his presence by a return of the kind pressure of her hand.

" I called at the manse expecting to find you, Amy, as I understood you were indisposed," said the Doctor, placing a chair near Miss Graeme.

" Very slightly, Doctor ; — nothing to prevent my being here."

" And you will remain ? " he returned, in a low voice. " It will not be well to leave her ; your sympathy and society is not to be wanted here for a few days, Amy. Mrs. Cameron has great fortitude, yet she requires to be sustained in this depth of bitterness. You, Amy, are eminently calculated to soothe and comfort ; and as respects your father, Mrs. Rushbrook cheerfully consented to supply your place during your absence."

"How kind in aunt, and considerate in you, Doctor. That will remove the only impediment ; I can stay with entire convenience."

"Fawn," said the Doctor, pushing his chair toward the sofa without rising, and drawing her from Miss Lincoln toward himself, "I want you to ask Cousin Edith to walk with you in the garden every morning ; you are looking so pale." ·

"Is Helen sick ? " Edith asked, eagerly.

"No, Edith," replied the Doctor, stroking back the curls of the little child, — "but she needs fresh air, and her obtaining it will depend upon you ; she is your shadow."

"I certainly will make any sacrifice for Helen's sake," she replied, with moistening eyes, — "our sweet Fawn," — folding her arms about the child, who had returned to her position by the side of "sister dear."

"Doctor," resumed Miss Lincoln, after a short interval, "I suppose you will visit father professionally : — might not I be permitted to accompany you, sometimes ? "

The countenance and color of Dr. McMillan changed suddenly, yet instantly recovering himself, he answered, —

"I could not possibly be admitted as medical

adviser, Edith, even should I apply. The prison officers have appointed Logan, and he is the physician there now, I presume."

" Would I — could I — could I be denied the privilege of seeing my father? — of ministering to his comfort?" she asked, looking tearfully from one to another of the circle surrounding her.

" Interest and inquiry shall be made, Edith," replied Duncan; " meanwhile rest upon your father's own counsel, 'Be tranquil, and trust the issue will be all we hope.'"

" 'All we hope,'" she reiterated, clasping her hands together in utter hopelessness. " In whom are we to hope? In those who are wilfully plotting his destruction? — In the perjured, who will bring forward false testimony? — In whom are we to hope?"

" In an all-wise, almighty Avenger, my darling," Mrs. Cameron answered, weeping. " The orphan's God — our refuge and our strength; our very present help in time of need. Will Mr. Graeme guide us in prayer, before he leaves us?"

Rising, Mr. Graeme looked inquiringly at Edith; there was a slight inclination of the head, as the dark eyelashes fell upon her cheek. All knelt. Solemnly and fervently did petition after petition ascend for the smitten family and its absent head; sympathizingly did every heart respond.

When Mr. Graeme took leave of Edith, she said, " You have comforted me; your supplications sank into my heart. I will endeavor to be tranquil: — beseech for me at your own altar." .. . . . .

14

"It would be a false step, my son," said the min
ister to Duncan, who had followed his father to his
chamber after their home worship, — "and were
my permission granted, Lincoln's still would be
withheld. None can minister to a mind diseased.
Hers is a crushed spirit, Duncan; no change on
earth would lessen the poignancy of her suffering,
save the release of her father. Human power fails.
Meet her always with a Scripture promise, — there
is healing balm in the words of Jesus. My son,
yours is a sore, a heavy affliction; go, my Duncan,
go yourself to the great physician; you have need of
rest for your own soul. Good night, my son, — may
the Lord bless and keep you," he added, placing his
hand upon the head of Duncan, and his lips to his
forehead.

Slowly Duncan arose and lifted his lamp from the
table, — set it down, lifted it again, looked at his
father and to the floor, — hesitated once more at the
door, then only said, "Good night, father," and
closed it.

" I gave my harp to sorrow's hand,
  And she has ruled the chords so long,
  They will not speak at my command,
  They warble only to *her* song."

YE hae had a clean scape, Norval Neilson, Nanny tells me; but how did ye find out Maister Traquair wa' to sail in the *Windermere?*"

" I draw in as much as I blow out from my pipes, Willy," was the youth's reply, " and caught the news from himself as I was singing 'The Last of the Saxon Race' in his kitchen. I hear what ye could not dream, through these pipes, Willy, and I use them for that purpose as much as for disguise. As for the loss of passage in the packet, it matters nothing whether I stay, or leave this parish, or the country. My father, nor the father of the one who dwells in this Hall, will ever breathe the air of freedom; their fate is fixed — so much I know; so much I have heard through my pipes, Willy. Yes, yes, I heard it whispered again and again, by those who little knew the heart they crushed in the telling."

" Wha' wi' ye do, my lad? Ye canna bide here safely."

" Be advised by Maister Duncan, Nanny,—I care not what to do or whither to go."

" Ye maun try to keep a brave heart, Norval;— A' is nae lost tha's in danger."

159

"Mistress Cameron has quite a nice letter from Maister Robertson, from foreign parts," rejoined Willy; "it ha' cheered the gude leddy."

"Why, surely, he believed Mr. Lincoln the worst of villains," interrupted Norval; "what can he say?"

"I am sure I dinna ken; I only heered her say for a' he blamed our Maister, he offered sic kind words for him and for a' the family,—he did nae taunt nor upbraid,—and they say he lost mickle siller."

"But little missed from *his* coffers, Nanny: but how does he know anything of our present circumstances?"

"Fra' the printed papers; and he says the young leddy Agnes is too ailin' tae be brought home shortly."

"Pity the grass of strange soil shall wave o'er her grave, bonnie lassie; and pity, too, he is nae here. He might do mickle for our Maister and yere father, Norval. Maister Mungo ha' nae been the same foe as our Laird of Glennair."

"And yet, but for his son, Mr. Lincoln and myself would have perished in the cave. Little did Mr. Ralph Rushbrook trow, and less the Laird, when orders were sent by Mr. Percy for coal, that it never reached the manor nor the manse."

"I ken a' that, Norval,—and how he and Maister Duncan bore the cots themselves, on the dark e'en. Why wa' it ye stayed carryin' the baskets, bairn?"

"So often stolen by the fishermen;—one, in particular, who knew I dared not complain to the police. Kenneth sometimes, but oftener Mr. Percy or Mr. Graeme, brought the provisions."

"Ye were weel cared for, Norval."

"Yes, we tested foes and friends in our dark, silent retreat, Nanny. We have left it now to the Elves forevermore. There is Maister Duncan coming up the path;—I must meet him."

"Have you seen Dr. McMillan, Mr. Duncan?" he inquired, after returning the friendly salute of the young Graeme.

"I have, Norval; the agreement has been withdrawn which was made with the captain of the *Windermere.* One packet is too narrow for a Traquair and a Neilson."

"All of the name are madly bitter against mine, sir; they may yet have cause to repent of their malice."

"It is unerringly written, Norval, Blessed are ye when accused falsely."

"Ye are greatly in advance of your pupil, Mr. Duncan, in these matters," he replied, bitterly. "Had I the half of your religion, I would welcome the summons to the sodded bed and dreamless sleep."

"And leave your father to breast the breakers alone, Norval?—You are selfish."

"My father is in the heart of a jail, and facts so well established against him, even his friends might think he enacted all. My father is all of earth left me, Mr. Duncan, and *you* would have me desert him. Oh, that I might deliver myself up, stand the trial, and share his fate." He leaned his head upon his hand, and his arm upon the railing that enclosed the cemetery of the two families.

14 *   L

"Norval Neilson," said Duncan, solemnly, "such a step would seal your father's condemnation and be Mr. Lincoln's death-warrant; there would be needed no further proof,—*your* tacit confession of guilt would decide judge and jury."

"I have no heart to seek concealment, or to act in self-defence," he murmured, without lifting his eyes, and unconsciously scraping the earth with the end of his boot.

"The *Nubia* leaves Glasgow in a fortnight for the Continent; passage can be taken for you:—and, Norval, under your assumed name, I promise, you shall be duly apprised of every occurrence. There is certainly great hazard in remaining here."

"I will follow your guidance, Mr. Duncan. Yet I think no disguise will be more effectual than that of the piper, and then I might learn all that transpires, without a medium. May it not be so?" he asked, raising his sadly expressive eyes to his friend.

"Your judgment may err, Norval," he replied, "but I cannot refuse your request; *I* could not be sent away under your circumstances."

"Oh, thank you, thank you,—I will be prudent. I can die with him, but existence would be unendurable separated from my father."

"Take your own way, Norval, but do not venture too far,—nor to the Traquairs too often: they may be curious to learn the why of so many visits of a piper. Farewell, Norval:—where will you be found?"

"Farewell, Mr. Duncan; my very best friends must be ignorant of my lodgings for the present."

After a little hesitation, Duncan said, "It is best, Norval. Farewell."

Miss Lincoln was reading, and did not notice the approach of young Graeme. He stood in quiet admiration; her head was bowed over the book, her cheek resting upon one hand, the other raised with a finger bent, ready to turn the leaf. The rays of the lamp fell upon the chiselled features; the dark eye seemed to be penetrating into some mystery; the subject was obviously pleasant, for the countenance was beaming, and the lips parted into an almost smile. Her attention was riveted. It was not until Duncan softly pronounced her name, and laid his hand upon her, that she was conscious of his presence.

"Sweet, and not bitter, is the stream my Edith has discovered this evening; I would drink from the same cheering fountain. I have never known it fail."

The startle sent a tinge over the face usually so pale, and Duncan felt, proudly felt, there could be nothing in nature so perfectly beautiful as "my Edith."

"What was the entrancing theme?" he again inquired.

"I had been reading the account of the three children in the fiery furnace, and comparing them with father. I found great consolation, Duncan. Their same companion is with father and Roger, and they have the same Omnipotent Deliverer. I felt so calm, so hopeful, so confident as I read —"

"Yes, dear Edith, to the decree that we shall have tribulation, He hath added, 'I will never leave nor forsake you; I am with you even unto the end of the world.'"

"I believe him;—I trust him: yet how weak is the flesh, despite the willingness of the spirit," she mournfully returned.

"So many rivulets from the same source, to meet all emergencies, Edith. 'Come unto me all ye that labor,' are words familiar to every afflicted pilgrim, and how comforting. If I mistake not, your attention was drawn to the *New* Testament when I interrupted you."

"When you came in, my thoughts had fallen on, and my drooping spirit was cheered by this passage in the Revelations, 'And God shall wipe away all tears from their eyes; and there shall be no more death, neither sorrow nor crying, neither shall there be any more pain.' Duncan, I felt it would be good to be in that peaceful, sinless, tearless home." She laid her clasped hands upon the book, her face upon her hands, and wept.

"My life's counsellor is beneath the clod, Edith; would you deprive me of the light of my eyes also? This heart would yearn for its idol; yet perhaps it is so to be;—I have worshipped you, my Edith."

Raising her head, and throwing it upon the arm that encircled her, she said vehemently, "Forgive me, Duncan; I will endure the tribulation of this world for your sake, and for father's. And Aunt Edith, with her own bruised heart, how she tries to uphold me; and our Fawn is a precious flower on life's desert."

"It is well to remember and recount our mercies, Edith: we will always find full measure, however mingled with woes.—Have you walked to-day? It was the Doctor's prescription a fortnight since."

"*Your* wish had quite as much, and more force with me, Duncan. I have not only regularly walked, but worked in the garden daily with Helen. She wondered to-day 'if Doctor wished us to get so *very* tired.' I was not aware until then I had overtaxed her."

"And insensibly fatigued yourself also, Edith?"

"Physical toil always operates beneficially on an overcharged mind, Duncan; any mental exertion is insupportable."

"Yes, it is difficult to fix the attention where the mind is estranged; Edith, this is the only volume which has that power. 'Wait on the Lord, be of good courage, and he shall strengthen thy heart.' But where is Helen? She is seldom missing from your side, Edith?"

"Gone very reluctantly home with Mrs. Rushbrook. She was convinced by her mother there was a propriety in her returning Mrs. Rushbrook's kindness to us, in remaining at the manse to permit Amy to stay here: I shall miss her sadly, but change is absolutely necessary for her; she is too much among sorrow."

"Helen is a very remarkable child, Edith."

"Only peculiar from circumstance, Duncan; she would not be so dissimilar to other children, if under the same influence: her mother's training and exclusiveness has formed our Fawn."

"Independent of original material, Edith?" he asked, standing still suddenly before her as he walked the floor. "Why, then, are Lochiel and I so different? Why my mother and Aunt Rushbrook? Why every member of every family, if training and influence create the character? I have known an unguarded expression affect most seriously, and a remark may make a man; yet, Edith, your argument is not tangible. Propensities may be met, characters may be changed by circumstances, but believe me, the inner is as different as the outer man in every human being."

"Perhaps so, Duncan; but I am not wholly convinced. I should have been far more worthy of your affection had I had a mother to love and instruct me. Aunt Edith's misguided indulgence has made me —"

"Faultless," interrupted the youth; "faultless in my eyes, Edith, and I am not to be persuaded to the contrary. The moonlight invites a ramble — shall we accept its call?"

"Not outside the grounds, please, Duncan.—Faultless," she murmured; "experience will teach you the absurdity of such language." Equipped in a few moments for an evening walk, after telling her intention to her aunt, Edith accompanied Duncan.

"How balmy the air is," Edith remarked; "how serene all nature, and that glorious orb seems pleading with man to commune with his God and his own heart. It appears to me hardly possible to act out a wicked design on such a night as this."

. "And yet the most atrocious deed ever enacted on our earth was on such an evening."

"True, Duncan. Oh, 'what is man that Thou art mindful of him?' may well be written. Shall we go further, Duncan? *My* steps always linger near our enclosure." They stood silently looking upon the mounds before them.

"Strange idea of Young's, that 'dreams infest the grave,'" Edith said softly.

"A question with him, Edith; but the spirits of these are doubtless praising around the eternal Throne; dreamless, their bodies are awaiting a re-union."

"Envy of these, dear Duncan, sometimes arises notwithstanding all my efforts to subdue it, when the dreadful phantom of what may occur troubles my lone thoughts. I would not, Duncan; the feeling rises uncalled."

"Earth's shadows encompass us just now, Edith; yet as surely as the dark clouds roll back to usher in the dawn, so will light be brought out of the moral darkness that surrounds us."

"Yet, Duncan; oh, dear Duncan,—what if it should not be? Should the sentence—how shall, how can I endure—" She leaned upon the railing for support.

"*I* could not, much less *you*," he replied. "The leaves of autumn and the winter's blasts would sweep over other graves than these, while our freed spirits would join with his in anthems of praise in that world 'where the wicked cease from troubling and the weary are at rest.'"

"Oh, blessed, blessed thought!" she exclaimed, raising her clasped hands and her eyes toward heaven.

"And a blessed truth, too, my Edith," whispered Duncan. "These afflictions will work out for us a far more exceeding and eternal weight of glory. Shall we return home?" he asked, drawing her hand gently through his arm.

Not a word was exchanged until they reached the door of the hall.

"Do you feel more hopeful, Edith?" he asked.

"More *trustful* — calm and passive, Duncan."

"Sheltered by the Rock that cannot be moved, Edith. Good night."

The 'good night' was returned, and Miss Lincoln repaired to the apartment of her aunt.

"I have made Norval very comfortable, with the assistance of Nanny. I was so glad Helen was away, dear; she might innocently have betrayed us to Duncan."

"It is Duncan's desire he may remain in ignorance that he may declare it, if needful. I would not have withheld it any more than Fawn, had Duncan not intimated his wish."

"Nor would I expect you to do so, dear; nor is your confidence misplaced in Duncan Graeme. I only wish all mankind were as stable."

"Is Norval in the house now, aunt?"

"Just come in, darling; he has been piping our health and situation to your father and his own."

There was a very long interval of silence broken at length by Mrs. Cameron. "Dr. McMillan came while you were away, dear, to borrow your side-saddle for the use of Gertrude Dunbar. He said it was idle, and hers was not nearly so comfortable, and he had promised to ride with her during the pleasant mornings. I regret it has become a daily business.'

"I suppose, aunt, Miss Gertrude is not well; and we all know the Doctor is always ready to proffer kindness."

"I should think so, Edith; but this morning he sent his man with the carriage to drive Amy, with Mrs. Rushbrook, to her home. Tobias said his master had engaged to ride with the Lady Gertrude."

"It certainly has a singular appearance; his attentions to Amy were very marked, and not discouraged. I shall be greatly disappointed to find him vulnerable to rank and fortune."

"I noticed at the time of the death of Mrs. Graeme, his devotedness to Amy,—which to me was perfectly evident,—did much to soothe and restore the dear girl's calmness. It will be terrible if he have gained her affection and cast it away for a noble name."

"So very unlike himself, aunt. I have heard him indorse all Mr. Graeme's opinions respecting unequal connections. Our minister holds that there must be equality of rank and some similarity in circumstances, to insure happiness; and he said he would never consent to his daughter entering a family to be *only* received, to the exclusion of her own relations. I remember Dr. McMillan replied, 'It was contemptible, and ought to be deprecated.' And, aunt, although the Dunbars are interesting,

15

and thought lovely, the Doctor would not have in Miss Gertrude a companion such as Amy; he has read so much with her, and always seemed so to really enjoy her society. How did she appear on the reception of the message?"

"She did not exhibit the least surprise, but was apparently indifferent to the apology. He had offered the carriage the night before, and, they supposed, himself with it. Norval was piping at the manor, and unwittingly told of his playing chess all the evening with Gertrude, and engaging to ride with her every morning before breakfast."

"I wish, aunt, you would make inquiry of the Laird; I fear he has trifled with Amy,—and I know she is attached to the Doctor."

"I cannot, dear; interference never helps or hinders. What is Duncan's opinion?"

"Duncan says his advances have not been discouraged by his sister; yet he thinks it more prudent to be silent until the hand has been actually proffered, which is not the case."

"Excellent judgment, dear; and we will act upon it. But you look wearied: I hope you will sleep peacefully. Good night, love. All will be well."

The saddest smile attended the return "Good night."

Edith did sleep, and awaked at early dawn sensible of an additional burden upon her heart; for her sister in affection, the friend of her childhood, she saw there was prospect of trouble; and the occasion,—Dr. McMillan,—he whom she had always almost reverenced; her beau-ideal of all that was

noble and excellent; he who had been the true friend
of Amy in deep sorrow, her counsellor in difficulty.
Could James McMillan be capable of duplicity? or
could his devotedness be attributable only to his
inherent sympathy with all suffering? The interest
of Edith for her dear friend for the time changed
the current of her thoughts into another channel.
With overwhelming force, it returned upon her heart
with uncontrollable emotion. She threw herself upon
the bed; ejaculating: "Amy has her father to love,
to protect, to shield her; oh! *my* father, my dear,
dear father!" When the paroxysm had subsided,
she arose; walking to the window, she stood gazing
with strange calmness on the little enclosure not far
from the house. "There is rest *there*," she murmured; "rest for the weary, the broken heart: —
Bless me, even me also, O my father," she exclaimed, raising her clasped hands, then dropping
them, and her head upon them, on the ledge of the
casement.

Nanny had entered unheard. She was much
moved by these expressions of grief from her young
mistress. "It has passed, Nanny; do not weep,"
she said, perceiving the old woman on raising her
head. "It was a moment of great darkness; I
thought my heart-strings would break. It has
passed, Nanny. Does aunt await me?"

"Yes, darling," replied Nanny, in vain trying to
wipe away her tears with the corner of her apron.
"The mighty trial is on us; it will a' pass soon, ane
way or the ither; the hame o' the gude is nae far
frae us a'. Will I fetch you summat here, or wi' ye
gang to the mistress, my sweet bairn?"

"I will go to aunt, Nanny,—she is alone?"

"No, Mistress Edith, our young Doctor is with her, and Norval hae lingered to hear summat the Doctor hae to say—"

"Of father, Nanny?" she asked, tremulously.

"Nae, nae, lassie; it is nae mickle he kens o' the maister; I hardly ken mysel' the matter o' the tidings; but the mistress bid me tell ye Miss Amy maun nae want ye or hersel' longer than ye can make ready to gang to her; summat hae come upon the pastor, I trow."

Intensely anxious, Edith descended to the breakfast-room, where she found the Doctor and Norval Neilson with her aunt.

"What is it, Norval?" she asked eagerly, struck with the pallor and anguish of his countenance:— "what of my father—and of yours?"

"The trouble is at the manse, my love," replied Mrs. Cameron; "we have nothing new of our absent ones. Amy pleads we will come immediately to her."

"I am ready, aunt; I do not care for breakfast." The cup Dr. McMillan was holding he placed before her. "Drink that, Edith," he said, "you will require it." She did as he desired. Not a word more was spoken. The eye of Edith turned from one to the other. Norval hurriedly left the room. Mrs. Cameron, pale as ashes, sat looking on vacancy, her cheek resting upon a closed hand; Dr. McMillan stood with compressed lip, apparently in deep thought.

"What has befallen Duncan Graeme?" Edith asked, starting from her seat. "I have drunk the cup of agony to the dregs; ye cannot add to its bitterness; I can but die; tell me, I beseech, I implore, — is Duncan dead?" she demanded more gently, laying her fingers upon the arm of the Doctor. "Aunt, is Duncan dead?"

"No, my precious one, Duncan lives; but ask no more, dear Edith; we will go to Amy."

Pleadingly, Amy looked toward the Doctor.

Taking her icy hands in his own, he led her unresistingly to his carriage. Mrs. Cameron followed. To Norval, who was leaning against the pillar of the hall-door, the Doctor said, — "To leave here at present would be very imprudent; be cautious, also, when you go with the pipes, my lad." Taking the reins, he himself drove to the manse.

The minister was alone when he entered. Rising to meet them, he said, in broken accents, "Woe, woe is indeed upon us all;" — folding Edith to his heart, he continued: "I have not one word of comfort for you, my daughter; we are engulfed together in the stormy billows; oh, my son, my boy, my Duncan!"

Dr. McMillan shuddered to see the rigid features of Edith. She spoke not; there was no outward manifestation of feeling; she seemed transfixed; she looked a breathing statue. She changed her position slightly on the entrance of Lochiel; he threw his arms around her and wept impetuously. "Lochiel, my son," implored his father, "remember the injunctions of our Duncan; he begged you would be our staff, our support until his return. Command yourself, my son."

15 *

" Return ! — where is he ? " she almost gasped.

" It was Duncan's request *sister* should communicate the circumstances to you, our Edith ; she knows all. Will you go to her ? "

She bowed her head, and vainly attempted to rise. The powerful arm of Dr. McMillan carried her to the apartment of Miss Graeme ; there he left her, and returned to the group in the study.

" How was the intelligence conveyed to Duncan ? " Mrs. Cameron inquired of Lochiel ; " the Doctor did not correctly know."

" The cashier dispatched a messenger with a writ for the magistrate last night, to say his presence was required on the instant. Duncan was about retiring ; Mr. Traquair sent a carriage for him ; we have not seen him since. He wrote a few lines ; Amy has them."

" I only heard," rejoined the Doctor, " that Duncan Graeme had been implicated in the transactions imputed to Mr. Lincoln, — had been arrested and imprisoned. Of other particulars my informant professed himself ignorant. What was the purport of the note of Duncan ? "

" *I* will get it, my son ; in your excited state you had better avoid Edith and your sister."

Mr. Graeme was little less agitated, but leaving the room, he returned a few moments after with a folded paper, which he handed to Dr. McMillan, directing him to read it aloud.

" In haste, my dear father, I tell you with infinite astonishment, suspicion rests upon me as the accom-

plice of Mr. Lincoln in the Bank fraud. Papers
and coins have been discovered in a secret drawer
of my desk, the existence of which I had no knowledge; the papers were written so exactly in my
handwriting, I suppose I shall be indicted for perjury for my persistence in the denial of them.
Lochiel will bring Edith to the manse, where it is
my earnest request she may remain: Amy can, better than any other, make this unprecedented communication to her. I would much desire our families could remain together until my return; perhaps
Mrs. Cameron may consent. The villanous, atrocious plot is deeply laid. Hope nothing, dear father,
fear nothing. I beg you will, with me, leave all
with Him with whom all things are possible. Beg
Lochiel to command himself, and be the staff of
you all. To our dear friend, James McMillan, I
commend you also: he will be a great solace. I
dare not trust myself to think of home. May you
be supported, and may I also. O father! humanly
speaking, this is a trial insupportable. Send immediately for Claybourne — I desire he should be my
counsel — father's early friend. D. G."

"Incredible! — this the handwriting of Duncan,
such a scrawl?" the Doctor remarked, folding the
paper, and returning it to Mr. Graeme.

"He wrote hurriedly and excitedly, poor boy,"
replied Mr. Graeme. "What can be the inducement to impugn his reputation? Who can harbor
hatred toward Duncan Graeme?"

"It may be one step too far, my dear sir," returned

the Doctor. "This may lead to the detection of the originator of the whole; perhaps providentially permitted."

Lochiel darted from the room.

"That boy," resumed the Doctor, "is almost beside himself; yet any effort to control him is unavailing: he is beyond restraint."

From the bosom of Mr. Graeme there was a deep groan.

"We have foes of no common bitterness," observed Mrs. Cameron. "Usually, there is mercenary motive: the object here is entirely unfathomable. What course is to be pursued, Doctor?"

"We are powerless, Mrs. Cameron,—we must await legal proceedings — how long, I am uninformed. The entire transactions must be to promote their own interests, whoever may be the villifiers of the characters of such men, subjecting them to this ordeal. The betrayers will be yet betrayed in their own net, I feel well assured."

"The plot has been subtilely devised, James, and unless overthrown by some mistake in their own proceedings, we have nothing to hope from our court or jury. Our sole reliance is upon Almighty power; man is impotent: but our confidence and trust is in Him. Prayer is prevailing, James."

After a long silence, Mrs. Cameron said she would see Edith and Amy. Shortly returning, she replied to the Doctor's inquiries for them that Edith was calm, *too* calm; Amy wept incessantly. "Lochiel is with them," she said, "endeavoring to instil his hope that the arraignment of his brother would lead to the acquittal of them all."

"*That* was his object in leaving us so suddenly," said Mr. Graeme. "Is Edith willing to comply with the wish of Duncan, Mrs. Cameron?"

"She seems to have no opposing wish or thought to any proposition; but how can I part with her, my dear friend? We must be a mutual support."

"This blow, Mrs. Cameron, falls severely upon us all: you listened to the further proposal of Duncan— would it not be possible to accede to it? We naturally cling to each other in affliction."

"Norval, Mr. Graeme, is the impediment to such an arrangement. He is withered, crushed;—he cannot be left."

"I feel he is sorely stricken with us, my dear friend, and it is fitting we should care for him; he can be accommodated with a cot in Lochiel's chamber; neither will object, and he will be more secure here."

"I would advise his present retreat for a short period. Similar investigations to those made at Thistle Hedge may be required at the manse— we—"

"Testimonials of my beloved son's guilt," faltered Mr. Graeme. "Can it—will such a search be asked of his father?" He wrung his hands in anguish.

"If demanded, dear sir," said the Doctor, gently forcing the Pastor into a seat, "it will, it *shall* be delicately executed: I only feared for Norval Neilson; his arrest would be certain, if here at such a time. Be assured, Mr. Graeme, I will defend you from all unnecessary intrusion."

"Of that I am very certain, James,—and may I

M

be strengthened to suffer his righteous will,—to receive the evil with the good in meekness. Ah! I thought it so desirable we should have our friend with us; I will endeavor to be submissive in this disappointment."

"You shall not be disappointed, my pastor; Norval can have shelter with *me* till the threatened danger is over; and this difficulty being removed, I will go over with Mrs. Cameron, and apprise Norval of our disposition of him for the time being."

"It is not possible to express my gratitude for your kindness, James; and Mrs. Cameron — how shall I thank you? I only wish Duncan had the comfort of knowing of your ready compliance with his wishes. We can mingle our prayers for our dear absent ones, and strengthen each other to bear our same sorrow. While you are absent, I will go to the children and communicate your intentions."

CHAPTER VIII

> " I 'm weary with thinking !
> With visions that pass
> So thickly and gloomily
> Over my brain."

A LACK!" exclaimed Kathleen, laying down her iron and hastily gathering up the article she was smoothing, "alack! I have scorched the frill of the Maister's shirt. I hardly ken the right frae the wrong o' anything o' late. The twa weeks Maister Duncan ha' been awa' is like as mony years. I ne'er had the dread o' sic days as these, Margaritte."

"The morrow wi' be the darkest o' a', Kathleen, for Willy says the search-men are comin'. He speers little and kens a'. The Maister and the leddies, wi' the Fawn, are ganging to Thistle Hedge the while; Lochiel and the Doctor wi' bide here wi' us."

"I maun gang wi' them, Margaritte; I fear I canna be still o' my speech."

"I trow ye wad mak the bad waur if ye open your lips; but the Maister wills that we baith bide here, and I trow ye winna do ither, nor I."

"As ye will, Margaritte; but wha comes here?"

"Some gooseberries from Mr. Traquair's garden, with his compliments," said the messenger, respectfully bowing and handing in a large dish of fruit.

179

"I mis ken if Miss Amy wi' ha' the berries; he is the same who sends the officers, Willy says," said Kathleen, as they stood gazing at each other in questioning wonder, after the exit of the man. "That fellow is Jim Daley; he gardens now for the Traquairs," Kathleen resumed. "He kept Maister Lincoln's horses ance; ye dinna forget him, do you, Margaritte? Mistress Cameron missed mair than a little auld wine, syne he wrought for her at springtide. I shall nae wonder if he try his wit a' Woody Glade."

"I ken him now, Kathleen. I tell ye, Jem wi' nae be sae daft as tae mak awa' wi' onything there. Rogues can be honest when it be safest."

"Well, carry in the berries, and take the minute to speak o' the closet for Maistress Cameron; she is sae cramped in the trunks, ane must take thought for the ither, nowadays." She sighed heavily and returned to her ironing.

"I trow ye wi' hae these sent awa', Miss Amy: they came in a present frae Maister Traquair," whispered the excited Margaritte, exhibiting the splendid specimens of Scottish culture.

"It is exceedingly kind in Mr. Traquair," observed Miss Graeme, without appearing to notice the import of Margaritte's query. "He is desirous of showing his friendliness to the family, while he acts only officially when averse to it; he is a very estimable man, and no doubt shrinks from the task necessarily imposed upon him."

"True, daughter," replied the Pastor, "Mr. Traquair has manifestly proved himself our friend; he has spared no trouble or expense in his efforts to obtain the best counsel from Edinburgh and Glasgow."

"Was he successful in his last endeavor? Was his offer accepted?" faltered Edith.

"No, love; the principal barristers in our chief cities suppose the facts too well established to be controverted, and severally decline all interference. Our hope at present is from Dundee. Arthur Claybourne, an old classmate of mine and of your father, is examining into the cause, at Duncan's request, and is willing to undertake for us. Claybourne is a man of sound judgment, an eloquent pleader, and, withal, a family friend."

Helen nestled closely to Mr. Graeme, upon whose knee she was sitting. "Then *he* will bring them all home, he will, will he, Mr. Graeme?" she asked, anxiously.

With a heaving heart and scarcely articulate voice, he answered, "God will bring them home, darling."

"My father," said Norval Neilson, "was so certain all would be against us, he spoke of a petition to King George for a pardon."

The eyes of Dr. McMillan turned almost fiercely upon him. "*That*," he remarked, "would be verily an admission of guilt; the suggestion had better be withheld."

"My father convinced Mr. Lincoln it would be a gude course, Doctor," pursued the young man.

The pained expression of his countenance was noticed by the Pastor, and *he* answered, —

"I suppose, Norval, your father and Mr. Lincoln

16

thought their future course would not only establish their innocence, but their freedom would enable them to pursue measures to discover the perpetrators of the frauds, and ultimately retrieve their characters."

"We can but see, Dr. Graeme," resumed Norval, without raising his eyes, "that an ignominious death would stay every doubt of their guilt — " A stifled groan from Edith arrested him.

" We cannot dread such a result," Mrs. Cameron responded quickly. " We may reasonably expect much from Mr. Claybourne's arguments, and also from Mr. Traquair's interest."

" To his Majesty, King George, I would reluctantly appeal," rejoined Mr. Graeme. " His exalted views of the supremacy of law would uphold a jury in any verdict, most probably."

"It is only to try, Doctor Graeme, if the only means left," said Norval, sadly.

Dr. McMillan arose. " As you pass the Glade, Doctor, will you do me the favor — "

" It would be difficult to find the *favor* James McMillan would not be proud to execute for Amy Graeme," interrupted the Doctor, extending his hand for the note she held. " You wish me to leave this at the office ? "

" If you will, I will be grateful to you," she replied.

There was a touch of reproach in the glance, as the Doctor bowed his good-bye.

" What will you with me, Kathleen ? " inquired Miss Graeme, perceiving the woman still standing, and evidently trying to engage her attention.

"A wee while wi' ye, my young leddy," she replied in a hushed voice. Amy followed her from the room.

"What is it, Kathleen? Has anything occurred?"

"Nae, nae, my bairn,—only Mistress Cameron is so crampit, Margaritte was sure if ye did trow, ye wad gie us the word tae lift the clothes fra' the closet. Will we do it, Miss Amy? The trunks o' the Mistress wi' hold them a'."

"Where is Mrs. Cameron?" she asked, excitedly.

"Gane wi' Miss Edith tae your room. Poor, dear child!" she added, her eyes moistening.

"I will attend to it *now*, then, Kathleen; prepare the trunks—I will refill them," she said with quivering lip. With a strange calmness, Amy Graeme lifted from the pegs and folded carefully each article of her brother's clothing. In the arrangement of an overcoat she had difficulty; the impediment was a roll of loose papers which she drew from the pocket. Her eye fell upon the outer fold; a paper directed to her brother in the handwriting of Norval Neilson, saying he had succeeded in drawing the money over Mr. Traquair's signature, to his order, in his absence from the bank, for £500; also many papers with abbreviated words, counselling great secrecy and caution,—some directed to Mr. Lincoln, evidently furnishing information and proving their guilt, while Duncan was doubtless implicated. She had too frequently seen the peculiar characters of Norval Neilson to be mistaken. Hastily she concealed the package about her person, hearing the step of Kathleen.

"I kenned it would gae hard wi' ye, puir bairn," said the kind old woman, attributing the increased pallor and agitation to the employment, — "will ye nae gang, Miss Amy? I will put a' smooth and right; canna ye trust me wi' the things?"

"Yes," she stammered, — "yes, — I must not be disturbed for the next hour, Kathleen. I will go to your room."

In an agony of mind indescribable, she rushed to the little attic of the domestics. Drawing the bolt of the door, she threw herself upon her knees at the side of their bed; for a short time she remained in silence. "Why — why have I lived to discover the just implication of my idolized brother?" she at length ejaculated. Then rising, she found the tinder-box belonging to the room. Wondering at her own strength, she succeeded in lighting a candle which stood there. With trembling hands and withered heart, she sat down on the floor near the little stove (never used excepting in time of sickness) to examine and destroy the papers.

There were several communications from Mr. Lincoln advising Norval how to proceed, — recommending extreme caution in presenting his checks. The heart-sickness on the recognition of his signature dimmed her sight. "This," she murmured, as she unfolded another, "is indisputably the handwriting of Roger Neilson." With a sensation of horror, she read, — "No fear of discovery, my son; Graeme will be your security; *he* will never be suspected."

Amy would have fainted — might have died, —

but this was an emergency where the nervous system seems superhumanly empowered; her strength was aroused for action. She had with intensity scrutinized each paper, examined each word, every signature; her heart revolted at the disclosures there made; it was undeniable. These atrocious men, hypocrites, villains, had degraded, had ruined, had murdered her brother. Her head reeled, yet again she rallied, and deliberately applying each paper to the candle, threw it into the stove; and with prudence inexplicable — with that extraordinary forethought often exercised when the mind is wrought to the verge of frenzy, she saw the one reduced to ashes before she ignited another. The last ember had died out; with it Amy's strength. She extinguished her light, and there remained no further occasion for energy or action. With a moan of bitter anguish, she fell prostrate on the floor where she had been sitting. It is written, "there is a joy with which none intermeddleth." There is such a sorrow. This sorrow filled the heart of Amy Graeme; she felt there could be no relief in communicating the cause of her grief to any being; she must bear it alone. "Oh, our Father!" she ejaculated, "preserve my reason, my shattered brain; Teach him of thy righteousness and of a judgment to come; teach *me* to say, 'Thy will be done.'" She arose after a long, long interval of silence. There was a hopeless calm upon her features; there was no further outbreak; she buried her discovery in her own heart, and, returning to the family, merely replied she "felt chilly," to her father's anxious inquiries. Her in-

16 *

creased dejection was thought the natural result of
circumstances ; yet Mrs. Cameron remarked to Dr.
McMillan, " There is a sternness in Amy's grief
entirely foreign to her character, and her aversion
to all society is quite alarming. That of Norval
Neilson seems peculiarly distasteful to her."

" Others have felt Amy's estranged manner," was
his reply, " which I think is independent of recent
occurrences. Amy Graeme has singularly changed
since the death of her mother; there is a capri-
ciousness never observable before ; she sometimes receives me with all her native urbanity and friendliness, — oftener with marked reserve, to me unaccountable."

" *I* have noticed no great peculiarity, Doctor. She
is entirely void of all hope regarding her brother.
She insisted on remaining, and followed the officers
employed to inspect the house from room to room.
Kathleen told me she had violent hysterics after
they had gone ; but she has not named them since,
and never speaks of Duncan. Indeed, she seldom
utters a word upon any subject. Edith is greatly
distressed for her ; *she*, poor child, endeavors to bear
up because her father so earnestly besought she
would for his sake. Amy appears to have no motive. Her father is himself crushed to the earth,
and the very life of Lochiel is ebbing away." Entirely overcome, Mrs. Cameron gave way to an uncontrollable gush of emotion. Dr. McMillan sat by
her, sympathizingly silent. After some time, Mrs.
Cameron having given vent to her feelings, resumed :
" My poor baby is the sole gleam of sunlight we

have, Doctor; Edith acknowledges she is a tie to existence, and she sometimes succeeds in beguiling Amy into a little talk."

"Sweet, tiny Fawn," said the Doctor, dropping his eyes to conceal the tears her words had occasioned; "her little pensive face reflects the sorrow surrounding her. Helen herself requires change of scene, Mrs. Cameron."

"I am sensible of that, Doctor; but Helen must not, cannot be wanted here. I do not think she could be persuaded again from her cousin; she is wrapt up in 'sister dear;' she is essential to Edith; she would never walk but for that child, and Amy is frequently induced by her persuasive manner to join them."

"Amy!—you surprise me," replied the Doctor; "*I* have tried every inducement and failed."

"It is her winning childishness; they cannot withstand her. 'Take me to walk, sweet Miss Amy,' or, 'Do, please, dear sister, I am so tired!' The child's confident expectation of seeing them 'all very soon' has a happy influence, too. She asked Mr. Traquair yesterday 'how many days before you will bring my uncle, and Mr. Duncan, and Norval's father, home?' He won her heart and her belief by telling her it would be done in a very few days, if he could do it himself; that he would willingly give half of all his money to bring all, or even one of them to her. She climbed instantly upon his knee, and kissing him eagerly, said in her earnest, plaintive voice,—'Go then, do go, Mr. Traquair; give every bit of all your money, and when I grow big I will pay you all of it back again. Will you?—will you?'"

"What could he answer?" asked the Doctor.

"'It would not be enough, little Helen.' The child looked anxiously and curiously into his face for a moment, and then so innocently inquired,— 'Hasn't anybody got some more?' I then called her away."

The Doctor sighed, "The directors and officers have exercised great forbearance, believing, as they do, Mrs. Cameron."

"Yes—excepting Robert Dunbar; he is implacable and quite angry at Mungo Robertson for advising leniency. He is convinced Duncan Graeme has been deluded. His family all differ from him, yet dare not express their opinion—the Laird is so exacting."

"A real Scotchman—firm and upright—showing no quarters to any other—with a heart to hold a world of such."

Mrs. Cameron remaining silent, the Doctor resumed: "I noticed the name of Claybourne among the coach-passengers from Dundee."

"Lochiel mentioned it, and we tremble for the result of his investigation, Doctor; an unfavorable decision will be death to my poor child."

Dr. McMillan walked toward the window.

"What is *your* expectation, Doctor?" Mrs. Cameron asked softly.

The Doctor turning, again stood before her. "None from Mr. Claybourne, Mrs. Cameron. The perpetrators did not forget to raise a barrier to all legal proceedings; proofs are too well authenticated to admit of controversy. Really, Mrs. Cameron, some of the notes purporting to be written by Mr. Lincoln might stagger his own sister."

"I imagine not, sir," she replied coldly; "and those in the handwriting of Duncan Graeme, would they disturb the faith of *his* sister, think you? I trow not; or would the belief of Edith be unsettled by witnessing them *all*, Dr. McMillan?"

"Pardon me, Mrs. Cameron," said the Doctor, "I spoke unguardedly; it is a mystery none can fathom."

"It is a plot of incomparable iniquity, indeed, Doctor. How the papers and coins could have been introduced into our house, has yet to be unravelled. There is, as you well know, no other than our ordinary mode of access. Poor, ignorant old Nanny, although possessing so much shrewdness, insists the fairies are the operatives. She 'hae heard fearfu' souns' and seen fearfu' sights o' nights o'erhead.'"

Dr. McMillan smiled gravely. Stroking his hands over his knees, and rising, he said he had several sick folks to visit, and would like to meet Mr. Claybourne in his interview with Traquair. "I will see you this evening, Mrs. Cameron," he said, after his 'good morning,' "and report his decision relative to his acceptance of the cause."

Dr. McMillan arrived at Woody Glade just in time to be introduced to the barrister from Dundee, at the hall-door, as he and Mr. Traquair were starting for the manor of Glennair.

"How opportune, McMillan," exclaimed the latter, cordially clasping his hand. "It is essential I should be at the Bank; will you do me the kindness to present Mr. Claybourne to his old friend, our Pastor?"

"Mr. Traquair informs me, very regretfully," observed the lawyer, as they walked through Firwood crags, — "yes, very regretfully, that the course of your Pastor's son has been rather downward of late, and from all the documents he has shown me, I fear his guilt is too palpable to admit of defence. It will require some time to examine into the affair."

There was a reluctant response to its truth in the mind of the Doctor, on account of Duncan's constant intercourse with Lincoln and knowledge of his retreat; but prudently checking his assent to its probability, answered, — "From all my intercourse with Duncan Graeme, I should judge him entirely unaltered; he is the same inimitable son and brother, and, until suspected in this matter, he held an elevated position in the public mind. Did Mr. Traquair mention in what way he had strayed, or how he had retrograded? He himself pronounced young Graeme the envied and enviable of the parish a few months since."

"Maister Traquair spake confidentially; he said he desired to be merciful, but he had ascertained of a truth that the youth had daily communication with Lincoln and Neilson before their imprisonment; that he knew and visited their place of concealment, and that his intercourse with them had led to the discovery of their retreat — Goblin Cavern, as we called the place in my boyhood. He also told me Graeme was seen bribing the doorkeeper, to permit him to say a few words to them after their capture."

"That, sir," returned the Doctor, "was in connection with his daughter, most probably. I recollect Duncan bringing a note from Mr. Lincoln to her the same evening — perhaps the bribe was a gratuitous addition: human nature is too ready to accelerate the ruin of the falling."

"And the same propensity to exalt the rising. This is a strange world, my friend, that he whom I judged of almost unexampled probity, with the highly esteemed gardener of a neighboring parish, and the model for all sons, Duncan Graeme, are charged with crimes of deepest dye, by those whose character for truth and honor are indisputable. The counsel *versus* the Bank will have little strength. What family has Hugh Lincoln, sir?"

"A sister and an only daughter, — now residents at the manse, — with a little child of Mrs. Cameron."

"I recollect the rumor of her extreme beauty reached Dundee with the downfall of the father."

"Mr. Graeme has observed, and is coming toward us, Mr. Claybourne."

The meeting of the friends was sad indeed. The numerous lines and deep furrows told of the sufferings of Glennair's minister. Although his early friend gave no expression to his thoughts, Mr. Graeme read them in his countenance.

"*Time* has left some traces, Arthur," he remarked, "but trouble has outstripped him, — such trouble as will soon close my pilgrimage."

"I hope I may be able to do more than sympathize with you, Malcolm, and we had better suspend our judgment in the case of our friends. As regards appearance, none of us realize time's inroads upon ourselves, Malcolm: *I* might very probably have passed with you for my father."

"Considering the long time we have been separated, Arthur, you have surprisingly little changed; yours has been a lot of uninterrupted comfort."

"His goodness and mairey have followed me so far, Malcolm, and I trust great mairey may be in store for you; but I shall prefer attending the first sitting of the court, to-morrow, before I pass any judgment. The bills are regularly filed, and will be brought out in their order. My whole interest is awakened, and so will be also any skill I may have, to overturn the opposing counsel." There was not very much more said during the visit of the lawyer, yet his words had laid the foundation for some little hope.

The morning came, and with it the bright sunshine of a cloudless, frosty spring day. Amy Graeme closed the blind; with clasped hands and throbbing heart she turned from the window. The family met at prayers, and at table few sentences were interchanged. Then each sought the solitude of her own chamber, while Mr. Graeme and Lochiel wended their way in silence to the Court-House. The face of the father was buried suddenly in his hands at sight of Duncan,—his own Duncan, a prisoner at the bar. For some moments he was unable to raise his eyes, but when they did meet those of his son, there was the same clear, calm expression of "not guilty" to be read there, as fell upon the ear when the question was demanded by the judge.

The gaze of Mr. Lincoln was upon vacancy when the solemn answer was required of him to "Guilty? or not guilty?" Quickly turning to the sound of his name, he replied deliberately, almost sternly, "*Guilty* would find a universal belief *here*, yet the tribunal will be set where my '*not guilty*' will be verified throughout eternity, and mine accusers put to shame and everlasting contempt."

The attention of Neilson had been wholly absorbed in his master; twice he was named before he listened to the question from the bench,—"Roger Neilson — guilty? or not guilty?"

"As guiltless as my fellow-prisoners," was his answer; "but as weel gather the drops from a sieve as plead innocent here; aye, ye may convict, ye may condemn, ye may sentence us all to the death; but for all, ye canna mak ane of us what ye think ye ken us to be. We are nae guilty of any of the charges ye have read; and ye will ane day all ken I speak naething but the truth."

Roger wiped the drops from his broad forehead, and turned again toward the object of his intense interest — Mr. Lincoln, who stood the very personification of sadness, his hand hanging over the shoulder of young Graeme.

There was some weariness manifested in the court, and Mr. Claybourne seemed quite restless, while Mr. Grant, counsel for the Bank, went leisurely

and tediously through even the structure of the
building, and all the arrangements of the banking
company. He at length mentioned the contriv-
ance of a safe within a closet, having a door of
narrower dimensions, to prevent it from being pur-
loined bodily, but which had been done through
the ingenuity of one or more of the prisoners now
at the bar.

"As counsel for the defence, I would ask," said
Mr. Claybourne, "by what imaginable method
could a box of greater magnitude than the aperture
be taken through?"

"By removing and replacing the surrounding
panels," replied Mr. Grant, with a shrug of contempt.

"With the leave of the bench, we will inquire if,
in the removal and replacing of said panels, the
residents of the dwellings convenient might not have
heard, and been curious to learn the occasion of the
unusual noise at that hour of the night?"

"There was no inquiry, and the safe was removed," returned the barrister; "*how*, we are not
bound to inquire; enough that it is no longer there.
After six weeks allowed the learned counsel for investigation, it might be supposed he had fully acquainted himself with all the details."

"It is scarcely needful to say to the able speaker
from Dundee," said Mr. Reid, "the absence of the
chest is conclusive evidence it was carried off; *how*,
is not the question, but by whom."

At this juncture a slip of paper was produced,
corresponding with that used by the Cashier of the

Bank. "This," resumed Mr. Grant, "is minus signature. It is giving directions to a man named
Roger, to be punctually at the eastern vault at 11
o'clock, P. M. The slip is fitted precisely to this
sheet, found, on investigation, in the desk of Hugh
Lincoln, the late Cashier; and who will dispute the
handwriting?"

Mr. Claybourne involuntarily started as he surveyed the paper in question; the characters were
perfectly familiar to him — he could not but recognize the hand of his early companion: yet, instantly
recovering self-command, he asked, "Could not
others have had access to the desk of Mr. Lincoln?"

"Our case does not rest upon so slight a basis,
sir; a brief examination of these more important
documents will substantiate in your, as in our
minds, the proofs of the guilt of the Cashier, the
porter, and his son. At a later date, others have
been discovered, leaving no room to doubt that the
eldest son of the most worthy, much-beloved pastor
of Glennair has forged very extensively. We refer
you to papers discovered, with a great number of
missing coins, in a secret drawer of his private desk
at the Bank since the sitting of the court. Loose
papers also, drawn from an old boot by some children at play, in a garret at Thistle Hedge, has revealed to you the enormity of Lincoln's duplicity,
and also that of Norval Neilson, who has so far
eluded justice."

There was a long period of painful silence. The
head of the distressed father had sunk upon his

knees; Lochiel stood beside him, his eyes earnestly fixed upon the countenance of Mr. Claybourne; *he* was obviously disquieted by the revelation in the papers before him; the occasional change of color and compressed lip, spoke the unfavorable result of his research.

It was a relief when his voice broke upon the stillness. "Upon more than one of these papers there are spots of whiting, and many of them are quite soiled; it would seem they had passed through other than the fingers of the supposed writers."

"That, sir," replied the opposing lawyer, "was noticed, discussed, and accounted for: the garret had been cleaned after their concealment,—the boots also were bespattered with the same wash. They had been the playthings of several children before presented to us;—*they*, no doubt, are accountable for the blemishes."

The cheek of the Dundee barrister blanched as he slowly arose from his seat by the table. Folding the numerous documents, one in the other, he placed them again in the hand from which he had received them.

"The court will be adjourned until to-morrow," was announced, "when the trial will be continued."

The carriage of Dr. McMillan was considerately sent to convey the Pastor home. Mr. Claybourne and the broken-hearted Lochiel attended him. There was a hush amid the crowd as Mr. Graeme left the court-room; subsequently, group after group filed off in different directions, discussing at large the downfall of Duncan Graeme.

"It was a sair pity," said one, "that ane so young would hae the ruin o' hisself, and sic a situation all maun ken would hae driven him daft."

Such was the *now* general opinion of the selection of young Graeme to this responsible position in the Bank. He of whom language was too meagre to find sufficient plaudits a little while since, was now the subject of universal scorn and reproach.

A tight grasp of the hand that had held his during the ride, was the only recognition of the presence of his friend by Mr. Graeme. He retired to his study immediately, whither Amy followed. Lochiel, rushing to his own chamber, gave vent to his overflowing grief.

"My sister, Mrs. MacAlpine, has desired me to insist upon your making your sojourn with her, Mr. Claybourne," said Dr. McMillan; "but in our Pastor's family you can hardly be wanted at this trying time: I would urge your remaining here, sir."

"Wherever you think best, Doctor; the only solace I can offer is my prayers."

"Is our cause then hopeless?" Mrs. Cameron inquired, with quivering lip.

"I have been *shown* no accusation against Mr. Lincoln meriting capital punishment, my dear madam," replied Mr. Claybourne. "He may be imprisoned for an indefinite period. The condemnation of the youth is inevitable."

The timely aid of Dr. McMillan prevented the fall of Edith to the floor. The swoon was deep, and baffled every effort to subdue it, and the Doctor almost desired she might never be restored to con-

17 *

sciousness; but she was, and to a sense of desolation
unendurable.

Mr. Claybourne, supposing, in the absence of Mr.
Graeme's family, he might make the communication, now assiduously endeavored to retrieve his
error. The attentions of the Doctor, too, were unremitting; it was his talent always to say and to do
the right thing at the right place. Fruit and flowers from the hot-house of Mr. Traquair were daily
offerings, with his kindly inquiries for their welfare.

The week previous to that of the decision of the
court, Mr. Traquair appeared in person, with an
especial request to see Miss Lincoln.

Before the servant had left the room, Miss Edith
lingered, looking toward her aunt for encouragement to decline the visit.

"You had better see him, dear," was Mrs. Cameron's reply; "it would seem ungrateful to refuse,
and he may have something important to say to
you."

Mr. Traquair, instantly rising on her entrance,
advanced to meet her. "You will pardon my apparent intrusion, my dear Miss Lincoln," he said,
leading her to a seat, and placing one beside it;
"the object of my visit is to prove the sincerity of
the interest I have taken in your welfare."

"We all have perfect confidence in your sincerity,
Mr. Traquair," she replied; "although your efforts
to befriend us have been unavailing, it has not in
the slightest diminished our gratitude."

"Your father, Miss Lincoln," he resumed, after
recognizing gracefully her polite reply, "has been

convicted of fraud *only*, as you well know, which we all feel subject of thankfulness." (Miss Lincoln looked bewildered.) "My kinsman, Otho Traquair," he continued, at the same time producing a folded paper, which he turned and twisted in his fingers, and then laid upon the table before her, — "this relative of mine holds this check over my head, declaring unless the amount he has lost by Mr. Lincoln is refunded, he will present this check, forged by Mr. Lincoln, before the court to-morrow; yet do not, I beseech you, be agitated, my dear Miss Lincoln. I have come to convey *comforting*, not exciting intelligence. My cousin Otho has consented to receive Woody Glade, with its improvements, in lieu of his losses, which I am ready to transfer to him this day, and not only save your father from the imputation of forgery, but secure him from any penalty whatever, — giving him immediate freedom and acquittal."

"Heaven bless you!" ejaculated Edith, "words cannot express my gratitude. How shall I thank you, our noble preserver?"

"*I* need no thanks, my dear Miss Edith; it remains with *you* to establish and confirm your father's freedom, or to shroud his destiny in deepest. darkness. That Hugh Lincoln is a free man, or dies upon the scaffold, is his daughter's fiat."

"In mercy explain yourself, Mr. Traquair," she gasped. "Why? — how? — how am *I*—how can *I* save or destroy? Keep me not in suspense, I implore, — my head reels."

"The obscurity of my name, my parentage, my

humble origin, Miss Edith, induced your father to
deny me the boon I once asked of him; the same
boon I entreat of his daughter herself. For the possession of your hand, Miss Edith, I am willing to
encounter poverty, to toil for my daily bread; I give
in exchange all my lands. Become my bride, and
you save your father from an ignominious death. I
am well aware, Miss Lincoln, although your father
has not been *falsely* accused, he is an honest man;
he has been deceived, deluded by Duncan Graeme
and —"

"Forbear!" she exclaimed, "in pity forbear.
Father in heaven, teach me how to act." She
buried her face in her hands. Mr. Traquair sat in
silence a long interval; at length he said, in very
subdued tones, "Will you that I show you the check
and the transfer deeds drawn, Miss Lincoln? I am
persuaded you will be directed to decide aright. My
life, my happiness, is dependent upon your yea; and
what possible good can be effected by your refusal?
I plead, I conjure you, Miss Edith, to give your assent. By the ardent love I bear you, — for the
acquittal of your beloved father, — speak the one
assenting word, and all is well." He held one hand
in a tight clasp, — with the other she covered her
eyes; drawing the one from his, and clasping her
hands together, she exclaimed, —

"Save me from perjury, O my Father! give me
entire submission to Thy will; give me strength of
purpose — strength to act." Her eyes fell upon the
parchment; Mr. Traquair remarked, as his eye followed hers, "That is the transfer to Otho Traquair;

this," he added, pointing to a smaller paper near her, " is the check in question. Decide, dearest Edith," he whispered,— " decide mercifully for me, mercifully for your father."

Her dark eye glittered ; her purpose was formed on the instant, and the check as suddenly grasped and committed to the flames.

" Edith Lincoln !" shouted Mr. Traquair, darting forward. He seized the paper and rescued it, scorched, and with scarcely a word legible. " That was a daring deed," he said ; " none other could have defied me."

Receding a few steps, she replied with haughty bitterness, — " A deed saving *me* from perjury, *you* from beggary, and the soul of your kinsman from the foul stain of murder !" Closing the door upon him, she rushed to the apartment and into the arms of her astonished aunt. Without awaiting any inquiries, Edith poured into that sympathizing bosom the details of her interview with the paying-teller of Glennair's Banking House.

" My darling child," said the weeping aunt, folding her closely to her, " you have verily been shielded from the weapons of the destroyer ; you have indeed resisted the great adversary."

" Oh, Aunt, — Aunt Edith, — he is not saved ; father is not saved. *I, I* have confirmed, I have sealed his ruin."

" My own Edith, our friend and counsellor saw only the papers condemning the one ; there was and is nothing lacking to sentence the other ; no propitiation can be found ; your self-sacrifice would have

availed nought; Providence interfered, my Edith;
in that Providence still trust."

" Aunt, *he* said the offence was defalcation, not
forgery."

" Mr. Claybourne is since differently informed; the
sacrifice of yourself would have embittered the remnant of his days, Edith; his life, no human power
that will be exerted can lengthen.   I say it, love, to
save you from any remorseful feeling with regard to
your conduct to-day; and moreover, Traquair cannot be ignorant of this.   I fear he is not all he rep-
resents himself toward us."

" Why did father so dislike him, aunt?   His unprecedented kindness since our misfortunes has dis-
posed me to think dear father was prejudiced."

" Until the proceedings of this day, my child, I
too have been induced to look upon him more favorably; yet I never knew your father to err in judgment with respect to character, and he always held
him at a distance as an evil-disposed person.   Circumstances unfold intentions; his have ever been to
supplant Duncan Graeme.   The obscurity of his origin might have had some weight with your father,
yet independent of it, and of Duncan's claim, he
believed Traquair to have acted dishonorably in
some business transactions, and he found him selfish
and untruthful.   He scorned the *man*, rather than
the name of Traquair; yet he has eminent talents,
superior intellect, is well-looking, and has a good
address, and withal, has amassed, somehow, great
wealth."

" Who is he, aunt? of what family, or clan? "

"Nobody knows,—not even himself,—though he says his possessions have come to him by collateral inheritance. It is said in Glennair, he is the nephew or grandson of a poor, worthy boatman from Windermere. I only know that Robert Dunbar, meeting with him and noticing his cleverness, resolved to educate him, which he did, and by his influence promoted him to the situation he holds in the Bank. I never felt or took any interest in, and have seen little of him till of late. His cloven foot was certainly quite visible to-day."

"Has he any power — any influence, dear aunt? Can he do us any injury?"

"It is not in the ability of a human being to add to our woes now, love." There was a dash of bitterness in the tone, unusual to Mrs. Cameron. Edith well understood the words and their bitterness; she bowed her head upon her aunt's knee.

CHAPTER IX

"Purity of motive and nobility of mind
 Shall rarely condescend
 To prove its rights and prate of wrongs,
 Or evidence its worth to others."

GOOD Kathleen surely will find Miss Amy's bonnet. The morning is so fine, you will ride with me, Amy; the air is invigorating — will you not oblige me at the request of your father?" All this Dr. McMillan urged coming into the kitchen, drawing his riding-whip through his fingers. "I know I have taken you unawares, but leave these operations and come try the benefit of exercise, Amy."

"Why do you or father ask me, Doctor?" she inquired, mournfully; "how can I go?"

"Very few persons are stirring yet, Amy; we will ride toward Tristy Loch and avoid any; the exercise will create the strength needful to sustain your father."

With Kathleen's assistance, in a few moments Amy was equipped, in pursuance of the wish of her father, and the desire to be strengthened for his service.

"Will I nae fetch a chair, Doctor?" inquired the old woman.

"No, Kathleen, no necessity," replied the Doctor, raising Amy between his hands with entire ease and seating her in the saddle. "I thought it better to bring the pony of Miss Dunbar; she will not need him, as she expects to make a few day's visit among the Peaks ; I am to accompany her at noon, and that will be fatigue enough for her. The saddle I borrowed for Miss Gertrude, from Edith ; so you see, Amy, how greatly you are indebted to James McMillan."

" The considerate kindness of Dr. McMillan would make him a universal creditor," replied Amy.

"I had hoped they would have been more especially appreciated where they were intended," he answered, slightly piqued.

" Do not believe me entirely insensible and thankless, Doctor," she said, raising her eyes to his for a moment and instantly dropping them ; " my emotions are all seared ; *gratitude* is perhaps the least so."

" I was not appealing for thankfulness, Amy ; it is enough to feel I may contribute to your comfort at all ; would I could in any way meet and lessen the poignancy of your sorrow, Amy. Do you consider the cause on trial so utterly hopeless ? Why do you, Amy, when some anticipate their acquittal ? May we not, in two weeks, controvert some of the schemes of the plotters ? A fortnight may reveal much now in darkness. Is the whole position cheerless to you ? Is there no single point of comfort — no ray of hope ? "

" None, — none, — unless by miracle, no — "

The girth slipping at this moment, turned Miss Graeme over on the horse. Dr. McMillan caught the reins, and, springing to the ground, exclaimed, " Are you hurt ? Are you hurt at all, dear Amy ? "

18

"No, only jarred, James; the fall was attributable to my own carelessness." The girth was adjusted, and they had proceeded a few paces only when Mr. Traquair came in sight. He bowed; they turned to avoid him.

"That is a singular person," the Doctor remarked, glad to escape to another topic, and lead Amy, if possible, from that so constantly absorbing her.

"Is he? Until lately, I have only thought of him as the wealthiest, handsomest, and most talented person in Glennair; his paintings are exquisite, judging from those sent to our house in a present to Mr. Claybourne."

"*They* are copies; Traquair draws from nature beautifully, and his handwriting resembles the finest copper-plate; he can imitate, too, any text or any character set before him. He excels in science, also; as a botanist, he is incomparable."

"Yet, Doctor, he is not generally admired in the parish; why is it?"

"There is nothing more true, Amy, than the proverb, 'Just as the twig is bent the tree's inclined.' Traquair lacks early, native refinement, — cradle culture, as Mr. Lincoln terms it. Educate, promote such a person, elevate him to the very pinnacle of political or literary eminence, he is unpolished still, and continually the lack of that which cannot be attained, nor is ever acquired, will be observable. The courtesy, suavity, and refinement taught in the nursery, will outshine and outlive great intellectual attainments; *they* gather strength with age, while mental honors decay. But we are home."

"Our Doctor combines all," Amy murmured, as she laid her habit and bonnet in their places. "How gently, how sweetly he tried to lead my thoughts from their constant theme." She repaired to the study, to her father, quite refreshed. Edith was with him. Lochiel and Mr. Claybourne were sitting with him also; Mrs. Cameron was walking.

"Where is Aunt Edith, Fawn?" inquired her cousin, as Mr. Claybourne drew her chair close to him at the breakfast-table.

"Mother said she would be home after a little time, but to excuse her from breakfast; she could not eat anything this morning. I left her by the hedge talking with Mr. Traquair." An ashy paleness succeeded the momentary flush occasioned by this information, unnoticed by any but the child, who inadvertently said, "I am sorry I told you, sister." Fortunately, at this juncture so embarrassing, Margaritte came in to say, "Dr. Graeme was required on the instant, to come to a dying man."

"I did hope, but without much expectation, that our good Pastor might be detained from court to-day; all the anxiety ever evinced by his son is for him and Lochiel," said Mr. Claybourne. "My dear boy, may we not miss you, also? Your absence will greatly tend to the composure of your brother."

"I comprehend Duncan better than you, sir. I will be found with him while suffered to remain. I may not be dissuaded, Mr. Claybourne."

The watchful ear of Miss Lincoln recognized the step of her aunt, and through the half-closed window she saw the grim smile that parted the lips of her companion, in his "Good morning, Mistress Cameron." Pouring out a cup of coffee, she followed her to her apartment.

"I have greatly feared, my dear Edith," observed the aunt, after partaking of the beverage, "and have now not a vestige of doubt, his whole bias has been against, while apparently befriending us. He made some expositions of his true character when exasperated because my influence with you was withheld. I declined all interference. My suspicions are quite settled that he has not been what he professed to your father; toward Duncan he has never made any pretence of friendship. Edith, love," she inquired, in a hushed voice, after a pause, "are you sure Duncan destroyed that roll of papers found in the garret?"

"Of course, aunt; their importance secured their immediate destruction; and the keen scrutiny of the investigating officers would have ferreted them out, had they been concealed, no matter how secretly. I have no fear from them, dear aunt," she added, while the increased pallor of her cheek belied the declaration. "Did Traquair allude to them, aunt?" she asked, softly.

"Only indirectly; his mention of documents brought them to my instant recollection. I feared they might be in existence, and would lead to untold trouble."

"Oh! no, no," replied Edith, nervously, "or they would have been produced long before this, aunt."

She opened the door in reply to a gentle tap. Lochiel came to the room to inquire for his sister.

"I am going now with Mr. Claybourne, Edith; if I have opportunity to deliver it, what message may I carry?" Lochiel spoke hurriedly.

"We are all *trust;* you cannot speak of *hope* with much truth, dear Lochiel."

"*It* shall be my own addition then, Edith; their support is our hope. Are you ill, Mrs. Cameron?" he asked, kindly.

"No, dear, only sorely vexed. I am in rich possession of that promise of 'tribulation in this world,' yet rest upon the annexed sentence, 'that the world has been overcome.'"

The eyes of the youth fell; he leaned over the couch of Mrs. Cameron. "The Lord bless and prosper you, dear boy," she whispered, laying her hand upon his head. Pausing a moment to kiss the pale cheek of Edith, he turned sadly and slowly away.

"Do not wait dinner for us," he returned to say. "Mr. Claybourne thinks they will have a lengthy sitting to-day."

Edith's lip quivered; Mrs. Cameron turned her face upon the cushion; neither answered.

"It would seem preferable, aunt," Edith remarked, recovering from an uncontrollable fit of weeping, "to be present during the proceedings; the suspense of each day is unendurable."

"Your father was very certain absence was the less evil, dear, or he would not so strictly have prohibited our being there; and how *could* we listen to an adverse counsel, Edith?"

A convulsive heaving of the heart was the answer.

18 *   O

"Dalcy was very communicative to-day," continued Mrs. Cameron; "no doubt to ingratiate himself with Kathleen to procure employment. He says Mr. Traquair threatens to use every influence against the Lincolns, which he has hitherto used in their favor; and Kathleen was somewhat amazed at his addition, 'Why, maistress, the mon hae nae power bigger tha' my thumb; I tell ye he'll nae miss the warp in the rope an he begins, I trow.'"

"What can the man mean, Aunt Edith?"

"Not more, I imagine, than to gain an end he will not reach now at the manse, or again at the Hedge; he appears very well to do in his present employ. Traquair surely deals very liberally by him, and he appears to have abundant time for gossip, and is not sparing of his master's reputation."

"Both Kathleen and Margaritte would discountenance such a person; and I am sure, aunt, he would meet with no quarter from Nanny."

"He has found favor among them by his attentions to Helen; he has laid out a plot in the garden for her, selected and planted choice roots and rare seed in it,—the very spot you and Duncan took so much pleasure in cultivating when children. He has won all the domestics by his assiduity in pleasing Helen, and I have felt grateful to him myself,—it is so desirable to have the ordinary current of our Fawn's life changed, even by such an agent. I suppose the expression of my thankfulness to him has encouraged the repetition of his visits here."

"Fawn has been telling me 'Jamie' had arranged her a garden, and I have promised to go with her to admire it; but I have not had resolution to look upon that spot, much as I desire to please her."

"Nor is it necessary, love. I have purposely said very little about it. The place will either pass from us forever, or be restored to us in happiness. Our child enjoys herself there; Kathleen takes her every morning. Nanny has always returned with her until this said 'Jamie' has undertaken to be her guide, which gives him the opportunity of conversing in the kitchen. I do not approve, but cannot see how to avoid it. Helen comes immediately to me, and is full of the praises of Jamie's kindness and gardening powers."

"I cannot divest myself of suspicious feeling, aunt. I connect that Dalcy with Mr. Traquair, and think all their good deeds are a mask to something evil."

"Yet it is hardly to be imagined, dear, that little Helen could be made a medium for any wrong action, and the arrangement of a garden-plot cannot be other than innocent."

"It is scarcely conceivable, I know, aunt; still the man's countenance engenders dislike, and repels any wish for intercourse."

There was a very uncomfortable expression on the face of Mrs. Cameron. Rising from the couch, and unrolling some linen, she handed part of it to Edith, saying, "The collars had better be finished; they might be needed." In uninterrupted quietness, they sat sewing until the entrance of Helen. She brought a note for "Miss Lincoln," marked "private."

"James Daley says," she exclaimed, throwing herself into her mother's lap, " that he is very sure Uncle Hugh will get orders to go home to-morrow or next day; but he does not think my flowers will be ready to cut, by then.   How glad we shall all be, mamma," she added, clapping her hands.

" Why does James think so, my child ? "

" I cannot tell, mamma; but James knows all about it.   I mean to stay home here to-morrow, to see uncle first — before you, sister."

" Yes, darling," her cousin replied, abstractedly, " will you see where Miss Amy is to be found, and ask her to come to me ? "

" Miss Amy is driving; I saw her ride by with Doctor."

" I did not see his chaise this morning, Helen."

" It was not here, — they went on horseback, mamma."

" That is a *ride*, not a drive, dear; but there is Lochiel — go talk to him until I call you, Fawn." The child instantly disappeared.

" Lochiel has returned unexpectedly early; — but the letter — what has Traquair to say further?   I judge it is from him."

With a trembling hand, yet with unaccountable calmness, Edith read : —

" ADORED MISS LINCOLN : — The crisis is at hand; to-morrow will be too late.   By one monosyllable you may avert the doom of your father; the sentence on the morrow decides it irretrievably.   If confirmatory evidence were necessary, the key of the chest stolen from the vault, found by Daley in digging in the Hedge Hall garden, would cast the die.   It is now in my possession; I am prepared to declare null and void many proofs adduced, and to withhold the last, which could not but destroy every vestige of belief in his innocence, even in his own counsel. My action will be governed by your reply.   T."

Her eyes met those of her aunt as the last word fell from her lip; she read indignation only and plainly there. "Return it in a clean, blank sheet, my dearest Edith," she said, huskily. "I have wept over the graves of five of my own children; — I can give to your tomb the same tribute, and far rather than behold you linked to consummate villany — to an embodiment of atrocity — no, not to save your father — my only brother." Mrs. Cameron sobbed uncontrollably.

Throwing her arms caressingly about her aunt, Edith succeeded in soothing her; then taking a pencil from a chain, she wrote: —

"Miss Lincoln can die with her father; but to avert the anticipated sentence of the court, she never, no, never, can doom herself to inexpressible misery; and she adds her belief that the power to change the decision, claimed by Mr. Traquair, is fabulous."

"You are home unexpectedly, my son," the Pastor remarked to Lochiel, as he passed the window, leading his sister's palfrey; "where is Mr. Claybourne?"

"I heard Mr. McMillan urge him to return with him to dine. The adjournment of the court was occasioned by the death of Mr. Benson; — he was drowned in Loch Dhu, — supposed to have been taken with cramp; and as he was one of the promi-

nent witnesses of the day, the court was dismissed.
Father," pursued Lochiel, drawing near the window,
and still holding the bridle, " the cave will not be
searched, for no two men could be found of bravery
sufficient for the undertaking: the fear of ghosts
appalls them."

" Stable the pony, my son, and come in ; the east
wind is chilling," said the Pastor, closing the casement.

Lochiel did as desired, and the family gathered
in the apartment of Mrs. Cameron until the dinner-
hour.

" To whom were you summoned so abruptly,
father ? " Amy inquired.

" To a thoughtless, prayerless man, daughter,
who, to the death, was deaf to every remonstrance,
insensible to all pleadings, — he would listen to no
entreaties.   It has seldom been my lot to see life
close upon so seared a conscience — so hardened a
heart.   Strange he was to have presented an overwhelming evidence against Duncan this morning."

"Amazing ! — Benson also was to have appeared
as —"

" The same, my son.   He was rescued last evening from a grave in Loch Dhu — a suicidal plunge,
I conjecture ; and I imagine he succeeded in another
mode of terminating his existence, though I am not
authorized to say it."

" How inscrutable," observed Mrs. Cameron.
" Benson had all that could invite the love of life,
and seemed so calculated to enjoy her offerings."

" He flourished as the green bay-tree, and was

cut down as a cumberer. Oh, Mrs. Cameron, friend of my early prosperity, and my companion in deep sorrow; oh, my children! I mused as I stood by the side of that bed of down, on the comparatively little importance in the mode of death. Whither had that spirit passed from its tenement, fed sumptuously every day, clothed in purple and fine linen? We shudderingly leave our query. We yearn in anguish over·those who, in all probability by false accusations, will be doomed to an ignominious death; but in a little while — yea, a very little while, we shall join, and spend with them an eternity of blessedness —"

As he continued, the countenance of Edith seemed illuminated, her dark eyes riveted upon the speaker. Amy Graeme fell fainting upon the bosom of her brother, who stood with clasped hands intently listening to the words of his father.

"Amy pleads to be left alone," Dr. McMillan observed, on returning from the room whence he had carried Miss Graeme. "She rejects all our consolatory ministerings; her entire hopelessness is remarkable, and unlike her natural disposition."

"True, Doctor, her temperament is hopeful; but from the beginning of these troubles, my poor child has been wholly despairing. Mrs. Cameron has remarked that effort to impart comfort was useless,— every avenue was closed: to be alone, is the one desire of Amy."

"And yet," returned Lochiel, "it could hardly be the tone of discouragement in father's remarks that induced sister's distress to-day; they were in perfect consonance with her own feelings."

"The prospect for this world is dark indeed," rejoined the Pastor; "words of encouragement have failed." He looked earnestly at Dr. McMillan.

"Earnest prayer and deep sympathy cannot fail for our friend and Pastor," replied the Doctor, moved to tears. "The Lord reigns, Mr. Graeme."

"And under his dominion we are safe, James. Yet the present chastening is grievous; may it produce the peaceable fruits of righteousness."

"Though he slay, let us trust in him," murmured Mrs. Cameron; "whom he loves he chastens."

Edith, who had withdrawn to Amy's room with the Doctor and returned with him, had been sitting looking on vacancy, apparently listless and indifferent to what was said, until the voice of her aunt attracted her. Raising her eyes, she gazed wildly around, then rising slowly, she advanced toward the group. "Tell me," she asked nervously, "will I live?" Duncan promised I should die with my father, and will I live without either? No! no! no!" she cried vehemently. "I must, I will — you cannot surely tell me I will not die. Aunt Edith, dear Aunt Edith," she continued in softened tones, "*you* said I might sleep in the grave. Will you call me back? Will you speak falsely to your orphan niece? Yes, my father, — yes, my Duncan, the sun that rises upon yours, will set upon the grave of your Edith."

Mrs. Cameron, unable to speak, held her in a close embrace; Lochiel, weeping impetuously, knelt on the floor by her, entreating her to be calm for his — for her aunt's — for her father's sake.

After this burst of agony had in a measure subsided, the Doctor begged she would retire, desiring Mrs. Cameron to remain with her; to permit nothing to induce her to leave her; adding that he himself would remain in the house until after the returns of the morrow's court.

"What will be the result of these outbreaks, Doctor?" Mrs. Cameron asked, weeping.

"Edith is in the judgment of to-morrow, my dear friend; with that sentence she lives or dies; she will not survive the decree we dread."

"And Amy?"

"Her *father's* life is dependent upon *hers*. Edith is very peculiarly stricken. Amy will form other ties," he added hurriedly, "Edith, never!"

Mrs. Cameron groaned bitterly, and repaired to the chamber of her niece.

"I will rest on this sofa, Margaritte," the Doctor answered to her.

"Ye'll find a lighted candle on the table when ye will like to gang to bed, Dr. James. There is mair than spare room syne the Maister hae gone wi' Lochiel to our dear ane to tarry the night. I trow there'll be light slumbers the night, and deep anes for some after the morrow. Doctor, will ye nae tak the room above?"

"No, Margaritte, I will remain here; should I be needed I am ready; no fear disturbing me."

"Weel then, gude night, Doctor; and a quiet ane to the Maistress and the lassies." Dr. McMillan kindly replied, and Margaritte withdrew.

An occasional quick step in an adjoining apart-

19

ment, which the Doctor knew to be that of Norval
Neilson, alone broke upon the deep silence of this
sad, sad night, to the inmates of the manse.   Dr.
McMillan, from the casement, watched the moon
and stars shedding their brightness over the parish
in solemn indifference to all its sorrows.   Just after
daybreak, the latch was raised, and Miss Graeme
came into the room.   Receding a step on seeing the
Doctor, she said with surprise, " Why down so early?
I thought all asleep but myself."

Waiving the question, he advanced, and leading
her gently toward the window, pointed to the eastern horizon, observing, " Let us endeavor to think
that emblematic of our prospect, Amy."

Shading her eyes, she murmured, " No, no ; the
retreating lights of the earlier morning were fitter
emblems of our fate, Doctor.   But I seek Norval ; I
supposed you were above stairs."

" I would dissuade you from an interview just
now, Amy ; the despondency of Norval would increase your own.   Suppose you suspend all intercourse with him until after to-day."

" Perhaps he could relieve my mind by answering
a few questions now burdening my heart, Doctor ;
to-morrow, they may need no reply," she added with
sadness.

" Mayhap, *I* may be as well, or better able to
meet your difficulty, Amy.   Shall I invite your confidence ?"

" No — oh, no ! James.   I could not intrust even
you ; yet Norval Neilson might delude me."

The purple veins filled upon her brow as she

pressed her hands over her face to shield it from observation. Doctor McMillan walked the floor, occasionally stopping before her with the hope she might raise her head from the table on which she was leaning, and again address him. After a long interval, seating himself by her, he said in a low, emphatic tone, "Amy." Without changing her position, she murmured, —

"What will you, James?"

"Amy," he said again, in the same subdued voice, "you believe in the entire guiltlessness of Edith's father, of Duncan, and the others?".

"What prompted that question, James?" she inquired vehemently, raising her eyes and pressing her hands together. "You know, saw, found nothing to induce a contrary opinion?"

"Never, dear child; how could my question have conveyed such an idea? You are morbidly nervous, Amy; do not harbor these evil surmisings. Since the arrest of Duncan, I have been all hope and trust; even at this late hour an acquittal will be the result. The scrutinizing judgment of Scotia's barristers and an overruling Providence, are strong fortresses, Amy. I own I once saw with the eyes of the condemning, but Duncan — "

A suppressed moan interrupted him; he noticed the shudder as he released her hand, and carefully avoided allusion to the subject again.

Mr. Graeme and Lochiel came home together. The father was silent, composed, and very, very sad. Lochiel had no command of himself; he wept incessantly. Deep grief forbade any questions, and

Mr. Graeme forbore the mention of their mournful visitation. Kathleen remarked afterward, "The salmon maun as weel ha nae been sairved, for it ganged nae tasted frae the kitchen as fra the faist table." The little clock in an upper room struck ten, as the carriage of Dr. McMillan drove to the door. The Pastor arose, glanced at his son, who immediately left the apartment, Mrs. Cameron following. "Dear boy," she sobbed, as he wrung her hand, "there is no hope?" "None!" he groaned, "that key—" Mrs. Cameron, in a state of mind bordering on frenzy, hastened to her own chamber. Lochiel moved toward the door.

Mr. Graeme laid his hand upon his daughter's head while she clung wildly to him. He tried to speak; no word was heard; the lips only moved. He approached Edith, who had thrown herself upon a sofa; bending over her, he made an unsuccessful effort once more to speak. Again embracing Amy, and gently forcing her into a seat, he hurried from thence to the carriage in waiting to convey them to the court-room, which was already crowded to suffocation.

There was no noisy demonstration on the entrance of the parish pastor; universal respect was expressed by the instant falling back to admit him, with the younger brother of the accused. A number of papers lay upon the table before the counsel; some opened, others rolled together; near Judge Scott was a small brass key, which he continually twisted in his fingers while listening to the summing-up of all and every evidence against the prisoners, by Judge

Carter. "Before the jury retire," remarked that gentleman, we would express our sincere regret that we have before our bar, three persons, whom we would have supposed the most improbable to be so circumstanced ; proving forcibly the truth of Scripture relative to the deceitfulness of the human heart ; and we who would fain have rejoiced in the reverse, have heard testimony far more than sufficient to condemn the accused under our law. To you, the jury, we commend them to your mercy ; duty is stern, is severe, and whatever the verdict, it will be just. Our *laws* demand justice ; our hearts recommend mercy."

Wiping the clustering drops from his forehead, Judge Carter sat down. The jury retired ; it was a mere nominal withdrawal. The unanimous verdict on their return was, "Guilty of Fraud, Forgery, and Perjury." There was a momentary buzz through the assembly ; all was hushed when Judge Scott arose. His face was of an ashen hue, and evidently with great effort he assumed his usual calmness. He was about pronouncing the sentence of death, when a piercing shriek proceeding from the box in which the prisoners were seated, fell with a startling sound upon every ear, and arrested the voice of the speaker. The next moment Lochiel sprang forward and threw himself at his feet. "Take *me*," he gasped, — "take *me*, — let *me* pay the ransom. Let *my* life be the forfeit, and let my father's stay — his first-born, his beloved, his heart's idol, still remain to be the prop of his declining years ! " Exhausted, he sank almost lifeless upon the floor. The Judge attempted to speak, but failed. Mr. MacAlpin gently raised him, and endeavored to lead him into the adjoining apartment, but resisting every effort, he again threw himself before the Judge, and in a plaintive, piteous tone pleaded for the life of his brother.

" Who will be the staff of the declining years of my dear father when his sun begins to set?" he inquired. " Who will watch over and pour balm into every wound, and be his counsellor in every difficulty? Let me be in the place of that dear brother, and send not the gray hairs of that precious father to an untimely grave."

" Remove the dear youth," Judge Scott whispered, with tremulous voice, in the ear of Mr. MacAlpin. " I cannot perform my duty."

" Grant, oh ! grant but my request !" he continued. " Duncan is innocent, — innocent as I, of every crime alleged ; and — " he suddenly arose and stood defiantly before him — " he must, he will, he shall go free, or may Heaven's heaviest curses for a wicked, unrighteous decision rest upon you and all concerned in this, this — "

He fell prostrate.

Lord Glennair, unable longer to endure the heart-rending scene, rushed from the court-house.

CHAPTER X.

"Behind him lowered the thunder-storm,
Which the caldron of his wickedness had brewed;
Before him was the smooth, steep cliff
Whose base is ruin and despair."

HE was about entering his carriage, which awaited him at the door, when a voice accosted him. He turned; a man in livery, whom he immediately recognized as a waiter of Mr. Robertson, stepped forward.

" What are the last tidings of Miss Agnes, John ? " he inquired.

" She 's nae better, my Laird, and Maister Robertson has left them baith i' the warm country tae recruit."

" Why ? He has not returned, surely ? "

" Yes, my Laird, on the last eve, and is now in the last agonies, and bade me bring ye speedily, if ye would see him alive."

" What do you mean, John ? Do I comprehend you ? Is Mr. Robertson ill ? "

" Scarcely be amang the living when ye reach his hame, my Laird."

Lord Glennair heard no more, but, giving directions to the coachman to follow, in a few moments he reached the palatial residence of Mr. Robertson. In the upper hall he was received by young Robertson — the only male inheritor of his broad lands.

223

Bowed with grief, he silently led the way to his father's apartment.

The magnificent and gorgeous furniture seemed to mock the anguish of the poor sufferer upon the couch. The only response to the warm clasp of the hand, and the heartfelt, "Dear, dear friend," was a deep groan.

The left arm lay splintered beside him; his shaven hair exposed a gash in his temple, pressed together by artificial means. In the lifeless eye and ghastly face there was not a trace of the bright and buoyant friend of whom he had taken leave so few months since. His physician sat beside him, and an old faithful housekeeper stood at his feet, with the deepest sadness depicted upon her countenance.

"Is there no hope?" the Laird whispered to the physician, as he pressed the throbbing pulse.

The Doctor's head was shaken sadly.

As he spoke, the eye of the sufferer turned upon him for a moment, but was immediately averted.

"Mungo," inquired the Laird, tenderly taking his hand, "have you no message, no kind word, nothing that I can do for you before — " He hesitated.

"Mr. Robertson," said the physician, "if you have any matters still unsettled, it would be well to arrange them and relieve your mind from care."

An expression of the utmost anguish passed over his countenance, as he inquired faintly, "Is life so rapidly waning? Must I so soon enter that world of — "

"Rest and peace," quickly added his friend. "Your high morality, your unexceptionable character — "

"Hold! Robert Dunbar, hold! The thought of a future judgment maddens me."

"For such a man as you, Mr. Robertson," interposed the physician, "there is little fear. Doubtless you have clothed the naked and fed the hungry. What more would be required of us?"

Throes of anguish and deep groans interrupted the speaker.

"My dearest Maister," exclaimed the woman, tears coursing rapidly down her cheeks, "might I mak' frae tae point ye tae Jesus, the sinner's friend; he'll wash away all sins, if they be as scarlet, and he tells us all tae come tae him. But the best of us canna gang wi'out him, for it's only through the cleansing of his bluid we ever approach the maircy-seat. Dear, dear Maister, gang tae him, and he'll save ye, and mak' yer dying bed saft and pleasant."

Overcome with her emotion, she covered her face with her apron and wept.

The lip of the physician curled, as he remarked, haughtily, "For such as your master, there is no need of this or any other atonement; his good deeds and blameless life will be a sufficient guarantee."

"Nae, sir, nae," she replied, "there is nane ither name gi'en under heaven by which any of us can be saved; and, on a bed of death, ye'll find your stronghold naething; but, oh! dear Maister, dinna listen to such teachings."

"Time is waning, and my dissolution rapidly approaching," said Mr. Robertson; "I would be alone with Lord Glennair for a short season."

The physician immediately arose; Katy reluc-

P

tantly followed, casting an anxious glance toward her master. The door was closed upon the two friends.

"Take paper from that escritoire, Robert," he said. "Pen and ink, — quickly. A few more running sands — a few moments, and time will be no longer with me. Robert, I am the most miserable, wretched being that has ever trodden God's world."

"Say not so, Mungo; your physical state has produced this morbid feeling. Say not the most miserable; *you* leave a stainless name. Compare yourself with Lincoln, and young Duncan Graeme; their blasted characters, their ignominious deaths."

A piercing shriek thrilled to the heart of the Laird. "Pardon, my dear friend," he said, soothingly. "I was rash in reverting to the sad reality; it has been too much for your sensitive and kindly nature."

There was an effort to reply, but utterance failed; the quiver of the lip, and the shudder which passed through the whole frame, alarmed the Laird, and he was about recalling the physician, when, by a strong effort, he seized his arm and pointed to the desk. The materials for writing were obtained, and the Laird again seated himself beside him.

"Robert," he at length said, in a low, deep, guttural tone that startled his friend, "do not hate, do not execrate my very name. Bear in mind that I shall be borne on the wings of time, to where the pangs of conscience will pierce this immortal frame, — immortal in sin, immortal in wretchedness, immortal in the home where the worm dieth not and the fire of conscience is never quenched."

Again there was a fearful shriek.

Lord Glennair started to his feet in terror, but the close grasp of the hand forbade all call for aid.

" I was not always so, believe me, Robert," he continued, after a short pause, — "my downward course was gradual ; success attended my first deed of villany ; would that I had been detected, and, in irons, brought to repentance."

" Your mind is surely wandering, Mungo. Why write bitter things against yourself ? "

" Hold ! Robert, — interrupt me not. The mysterious hand has appeared upon the wall, writing bitter things against me. See," he exclaimed, as, terror-stricken, he pointed upward, " it awaits me, ready to seal my doom. Deed after deed was committed until my coffers, filled to overflowing, permitted me to gratify the mad ambition of my proud heart. I lavished recklessly, accumulating wealth, not by patient industry, but by means from which my whole nature at first revolted.

" Taken from the lap of luxury, my income would not suffice my wife's expensive habits."

" Are you mad, Mungo ? " inquired his friend anxiously ; " or is this, indeed, sober reality ? "

" Reality," he repeated, while his brow knit as though in the deepest thought. " Reality — nay, it has been a dream — a nightmare — a delusion, from which I could awake, only to the consciousness of a mad career of wretchedness, of guilt, of ruin." His voice rose as he proceeded — "Of — of — Robert ! " he almost shrieked, "*Lincoln is innocent — guiltless — I* am the offender against the laws of God and man. *I* and my two accomplices have wrought all this ruin."

The paper fell from the hand of Lord Glennair, and he firmly grasped the bedpost for support. "And Duncan, what of the dear young Graeme?" he inquired, breathlessly.

"I had no part in that," he returned, quickly. "The dark plot to ruin that guiltless youth was laid during my absence. Through my name, they obtained access to private apartments in the Bank. I knew not, until the papers told of his arrest, that his name had been implicated. No, oh! no, Robert, the one false accusation drove me almost to frenzy. I was fully aware of the place of Hugh's resort, and expended large sums in veiling the eyes of justice. The officers would long since have effectually done their work but for bribery; and the master of the *Orion*, in view of an ample reward, promised protection. I have experienced what no tongue or pen could portray during this trial. Within the precincts of the eternally lost, no soul has ever endured a greater conflict of agonized feeling. Duty urged its claim; but the love of life and honor rose paramount, and bore down all better feeling. But He who sitteth in the heavens has hedged in my way, and forced me to make restitution. Let the paper at once be drawn out, which will place the innocent in their true light."

"Nay, Mungo, Neilson himself presented the check to the order of Lincoln, with your forged signature, and once again, to the same order, over mine. How was this? — how without immediate detection?"

" Robert! Robert! *I*, wretch that I was, person-
ated Roger; coarse clothes, artificial beard, broad
hat, passed among the unobserving. My accomplice
was —"

" The chest! the chest! — what of it and *its* contents?" groaned the Laird.

"At midnight, we sank it where it stood, and,
always being on the committee of investigation, the
flags remained undisturbed, and the chest undiscovered."

"And that key?"

"It was forgotten at the time; it was subsequently buried in the garden of Hugh Lincoln, by
my order."

· With an effort almost superhuman, the trembling
hand of Lord Glennair noted every particular, and
invited two of the numerous friends who were in
the adjoining apartment, tendering their sympathy
and services to young Robertson, to bear their testimony as witnesses to the signature of the document.
Without glancing at its contents, they signed the
paper, and fearing to disturb the sufferer, silently
withdrew.

There was an unnatural wildness in the eye of
Mr. Robertson, as his head was again laid upon the
pillow, unnoticed by any, until the attention of the
Laird · was · arrested by a low, murmuring sound.
He turned, and saw a frenzied eye gazing upon
him.

" Did you place me in this burning fire, Traquair?
Call Benson. Wretches — miscreants, do you desert
me in this hour of need? You placed the papers —

20
·

you know it. Oh! for some water;—give me
water—I will not betray you. Do not fear—I am
honorable—ha! ha!—the soul of honor—honor—
honor—let the Laird know—your gone, gone,
gone!" With a mighty effort, he sprang from the
bed, and fell heavily upon the floor. The loud call
for assistance alarmed the family. Young Robertson rushed in, followed by the physician and several
friends. He was raised and laid upon the bed, in
a state of entire insensibility.

Lord Glennair, with feigned composure, left the
room, and with hurried step descended the stairway, rushed from the house, and throwing himself
into a seat of the carriage, ordered the man to drive
with all speed to the Court-House. The direction
was obeyed, and with a celerity that startled the
passers-by, they arrived within a few rods of the
building. There their speed was arrested by an
immense concourse of people. The Laird, impatient
at the delay, sprang out, and with difficulty succeeded in reaching the steps; but a further advance
was impossible: a dense mass filled the house, rendering fruitless every effort to obtain an entrance.

"Make way!" he shouted, unconscious of the
impracticability; "make way, my friends; it is necessary—it is of vital importance I should see the
Judge at once."

"Make way for the Laird!" the crowd returned,
endeavoring to force a passage for him; "my Laird
—the Laird Glennair calls for admittance. Wi' ye
nae mak room for the Laird?"

"I *must* obtain an entrance," said the Laird, impatiently; "I have that will prove the innocence of the prisoners."

"Wha'! Of Lincoln and Maister Duncan?" inquired a dozen voices at once.

"The same — the same," he replied, in a voice choked with emotion.

For a moment a buzz only was heard, then a "Lang life tae Maister Lincoln and young Maister Graeme, and tae the Laird wi' the welcome news!" resounded through the building. "Lang life, lang life!" was continued by the multitude without. At the same moment, Lord Glennair was lifted upon the shoulders of those near him, and borne from one to another, until he was placed in safety in the circle of judges and members of the bar, who were endeavoring to learn the meaning of the cheers, and the din of confusion so suddenly bursting upon them.

"My Lord Glennair," exclaimed Judge Scott, as he noticed the unnatural excitement of his manner, "have you tidings for us? What means this wild enthusiasm so impossible to quell? Is there a rescue contemplated? — or is there some further revelation?"

"Lincoln, Neilson, and our boy, are as innocent as ourselves," he replied, in a husky tone, throwing the paper down before him, and rushing into a small room, in which the prisoners were awaiting the dispersal of the crowd. None noticed him; Neilson's eye was riveted upon Mr. Lincoln, with the most intense and absorbing interest, while a tear, stealing silently down his weather-beaten cheek, showed a conflict of emotion. Mr. Lincoln, his eyes cast upon the floor, sat noticing nothing around him. The arm of Duncan rested upon his father's knee, whose face was hidden; but the quiver of the whole frame bore witness to the intensity of his agony. There was a bewildered expression on the ghastly face of the youth, as he looked from the agonized parent to his brother Lochiel, who, in his wild delirium of grief, had thrown himself upon the floor, embracing the feet of his brother, and beseeching him to let him die for him.

"What will life be without my Duncan, my brother?" he moaned, piteously. "I *will* die with you!" he shrieked, starting to his feet. I will—"

The next moment, an arm encircled him, and he was pressed to the bosom of Lord Glennair.

"You will die for none, precious boy," he exclaimed, as the tears streamed down his cheeks; "I have joyful tidings; the powers of darkness have plotted the ruin of the best of men, and this dear youth; but all has been discovered, and the miserable destroyer is now reaping the fruit of his own doing."

The arms of Lochiel were thrown around him with so firm a grasp, it was impossible to free himself.

"An explanation, in mercy, Lord Glennair!" exclaimed Duncan, starting to his feet.

The hold of Lochiel was relinquished, as, with breathless interest, he fastened his gaze upon the Laird.

"Your entire innocence, and that of my dear and

early friend, has been clearly proved," he replied, clasping warmly the hand of Mr. Lincoln. "And Roger, your tried friend and companion through these sore and heavy trials, is proved the same uncompromising, honest man we ever deemed him."

The features of Neilson quivered with convulsive emotion,—a powerful effort was vainly made to reply, but the head bowed, the frame of the strong man was shaken, and a gush of feeling, long pent up, now burst forth unrestrainedly. None interposed to calm the torrent, which continued but a short season, then passed away, and the bright and joyous face of Roger Neilson might be likened to the rays of the glorious sun, as they appear after a storm, scattering the dense masses of clouds that intercepted them from view.

Duncan threw himself upon his knees before his father, saying, "Your blessing, dearest father; a restoration to your confidence is more than life itself: the anguish of the felt separation was worse than the pangs of death." The trembling hand was immediately laid upon his brow.

"My beloved, my stricken one," he murmured, "may the Great Shepherd overshadow thee, and may he shield my child from future injury, and lay up for him a crown imperishable, where no enemy can tarnish his fair fame, where no tear can ever enter, and no rough wind assail his gentle nature."

Tears fell heavily, and arrested the voice of Mr. Graeme; all wept—no dry eye was there, save that of Mr. Lincoln: *his* manner had betrayed no emotion. As Mr. Graeme finished speaking, he arose,

20 *

and in a calm, collected voice, said, "Let us bow the knee and heart to our Great Deliverer."

The warm, fervent petition breathed forth, calmed every Christian spirit, and stilled every conflicting emotion. It told of one purified in the furnace of affliction, sorely tried, yet entirely submissive to the will of his Redeemer.

As they arose, Judge Scott entered. The low, heartfelt, "God be praised," as he clasped the hand of his Pastor, spoke more than many words of gratulation.

"Dear Amy, dear Edith!" exclaimed Lochiel, advancing hastily toward the door, "I must carry the tidings. Such tidings!" he murmured, clasping his hands in ecstasy. "Will I go, father? Will I, Duncan? Am I in a dream?" he said, laying his hand upon the arm of Lord Glennair; "is it a vision from which I shall awake to some dread reality?"

"No, no, my darling boy," he replied, gently; "but no wonder you are in a maze of bewilderment. Await us a few moments, Lochiel, and, in person, the loved ones will proclaim the blessed tidings at the Graeme and Cameron hearthstones."

"The officers have succeeded in dispersing the crowd sufficiently to enable you to leave the place without difficulty," the Judge remarked.

"What meant those groans and hissings, immediately succeeding the loud gratulations?" inquired the Laird.

"Occasioned by my indiscretion. I, of course, read the confession aloud, being anxious at once to place our injured friends in their proper position; but the name of the author of this vile machination so astonished me, that I, with an involuntary exclamation, mentioned it, and produced the manifestation of the revulsion of feeling which met your ears. The carriages are in waiting, gentlemen."

Mr. Lincoln arose; the arm of Judge Scott was immediately extended, to support his feeble steps. Lord Glennair accompanied them. Roger Neilson walked beside his Pastor. The arm of Lochiel was closely linked in that of his brother. Percy Dunbar sprang forward; but a warm pressure of Duncan's hand, as warmly returned, was the only greeting.

A low murmur arose as they appeared, which was as suddenly repressed, and there was perfect silence, as every cap was lifted, in attestation of respect. Many of the members of the bar came forward to greet them; but the bowed head of Mr. Lincoln withheld them. No word passed as they pressed through the crowd to the carriages. The elders of the party, with himself, entered the carriage of Lord Glennair. Percy, with Duncan and Lochiel, followed. A long train of vehicles, filled with friends and strangers, to testify their sympathy, accompanied them to the door of the manse.

The carriage-doors were scarcely closed upon them, ere the multitude burst forth in loud and cheering peals, hundreds of voices simultaneously shouting, "Tae the manse! tae the manse!" There was a general rush in that direction.

"Lang life tae all the house o' Graeme, Lincoln, and Neilson! and mony blessings on the head o' our ain Laird!" was echoed from every quarter.

"To the manse,"—to that hopeless circle mourning despairingly. The few there had clustered in an inner chamber to await the heavy tidings of the doom they dared not hope would be averted. Little Helen was clinging to "dear sister," who had folded her in her arms; Amy, the gentle Amy, was kneeling upon the floor, her head buried in the lap of Mrs. Cameron, whose own grief was too intense to offer one word of consolation. In the heart of Amy was hidden a doubt of their innocence she vainly attempted to resist; the dreadful thought— there it was harbored, and would rise before her in all its blackness. Kathleen and Margaritte were there, with clasped hands and bowed heads, silent in their wretchedness. Dr. McMillan was there; the glance of Amy toward the clock told him the tick was unendurable; he touched the pendulum, and all was still. In quiet expectancy they waited, dreading the sound of the muffled toll of the court-house bell, telling to the distracted survivors that sentence of death had been pronounced. A stifled sob or groan would occasion an anxious look from the Doctor, yet he would but change his position; he could not "minister to the mind diseased." When Amy, completely overwhelmed, with a withering cry of anguish, threw herself upon the floor, he gave way and burst into tears; raising her upon the sofa, he falteringly besought her to be composed.

Clasping her hands wildly together, she exclaimed, "Have you not one word of comfort, James? Oh! no," she murmured, dropping her head again into the lap of Mrs. Cameron; "none, none can save."

"The Lord reigns, Amy, dearest Amy," he ejaculated. "Is it not written, 'the Lord God Omnipotent reigneth'?"

An "amen" groaned from the recesses of the heart of Mrs. Cameron, and all was once again still, and for several hours the stillness was unbroken.

The first peal of the great bell vibrated upon every nerve. In quick succession, stroke after stroke fell upon the ears of the sufferers.

"It is nae the soun' of a boun' clapper, Doctor James," shouted Kathleen, springing to her feet, "and mair than the ane is pealing."

The Doctor heard her not, for he had thrown open the casement, and was breathlessly listening. "Hearken tae the clamor i' the distance," again cried Kathleen, rushing after Margaritte to the front of the house.

Edith stood transfixed, pressing her hands upon her throbbing temples. Amy clung, trembling with hope, to the Doctor's arm. Helen had followed the servants, who were, from the door, endeavoring to look far away into the distance, whence the din proceeded.

"What! oh, what if we are yet disappointed!" murmured Edith, suffering herself to be led to the window.

"The joyous peal of that bell tokens no disappointment, my darling," said her aunt. "Shall we go to the front chamber, Doctor?"

"I would advise not, Mrs. Cameron; the excitement is sufficient here for you, for us all. Amy is trembling as an aspen now, and Edith too; try to be

tranquil. Is not the balmy spring breeze refreshing?"
he said, compassionately.

"The Laird of Glennair's carriage is turning the
Hedge!" Margaritte shouted from the foot of the
stairs, "and Maister Lochiel is waving his kerchief
high in the air." This announcement was scarcely
made, when little Helen burst into the apartment
clapping her hands and exclaiming, "They are
coming! they are coming! I saw Uncle Hugh, I
saw Mr. Duncan, I saw Norval, sister, mother; they
are coming — they are here!"

"Duncan!" gasped Amy, throwing herself into
her brother's arms.

"Father! oh, my father!" Edith murmured.

"My daughter, my treasure," responded Mr. Lincoln, folding her to his heart and kissing her repeatedly.

As Mr. Graeme and Lochiel entered, Dr. McMillan, without being observed, glided out of the room,
saying softly to the latter, "Draw the bolt to prevent intrusion. I will attend to the Laird and the
Neilsons."

Cordial, indeed, was the greeting of the Doctor
and his old friends. "It is sae lang syne I hae slept,
Doctor," said Mr. Neilson, "or I would trow it a'
a dream, the transition was si sudden. It seems
mair like tae a waking nightmare. Some fearfu'
developments hae been made, nae doubt. The Laird
o' Glennair kens the whole matter."

"And would be glad to blot it all from his remembrance, now you are acquitted, Roger," was the
reply. "There have been, verily, fearfully gloomy
developments."

"The name of Robertson I clearly distinguished among the cheers of the throng," rejoined the Doctor. "I suppose he has ferreted out the author of the calumny, and it is a demonstration of their indebtedness to our worthy President."

"Oh! no, no!" Lord Glennair ejaculated. "His name escaped in the court-house inadvertently. Robertson has betrayed the author of all this infamy; has confessed himself the felon, the diabolical perpetrator of the fraud, the false accuser of our much injured friends and relatives. Let wrath, let vengeance be stayed; — Mungo Robertson is a dying man!"

"Was he alone, my Laird, in this dark plot?" asked the Doctor, "or what accomplices did he name in this amazing revelation?"

"Astounding, almost beyond credence, Doctor; from his own lips I have his confession; no names shall pass mine, voluntarily."

Lochiel appeared with a request from his father that the Doctor and his friends would meet them in the sitting-room, whither the family had repaired, leaving Mr. Lincoln, suffering from exhaustion, lying upon the bed in the chamber.

"Dear Edith is nestled beside him," he observed, smiling through his tears, "with an arm closely encircling him, as though she feared another separation."

"Hark!" exclaimed the Laird, "there is evidently a revulsion of feeling among the multitude. Until this moment, the voice of exultation alone filled the air, — now listen!" Lord Glennair turned to the window. "Yes, they have assumed a threatening tone."

A low murmur arose; then, as though one mind swayed the mighty mass, there was a general shout of "Down wi' him!—down, down!" and a general rush in the direction of the dwelling of the President. The officers slowly followed, led by McFin, on whose countenance might be seen a smile very like that of gratification.

"Percy," said the Laird, seizing his hat, "we must be upon the ground at once; our presence may tend to allay the tumult. See, the roads are entirely deserted, and not a sound, save that buzz in the distance, that portends much that is evil."

Percy sprang into the carriage; Lord Glennair followed, giving orders to drive immediately to the house of Mr. Robertson.

There, what a scene awaited them! The mad passions of the populace were roused to frenzy; the glass of every casement in the upper stories was shivered, and the continued cries and execrations were fearful.

"Strenuous measures must be taken to quell these rioters," Lord Glennair remarked to a number of gentlemen who stood calmly looking on, evidently pleased observers of the whole transaction. "The military shall be summoned, rather than permit such shameful violence."

Through the exertions of Lord Glennair and his son, a strong police force was brought upon the field, but it was not until much damage was effected that the assailants were compelled to desist.

A large reward was offered on the following day for the ringleaders of this disgraceful riot, but no informant appeared, where the many would be involved, who doubtless, in their sober moments, sincerely regretted the part they had borne in weakening the laws and casting a stigma upon their much-loved isle. It was a moment of excitement, a moment when the passions are aroused, and, as a writer justly remarks, a moment when a vessel might as well venture upon a tempestuous ocean, as to attempt to guide the helm of reason.

A few days succeeding the riot, great was the amazement of Lord Glennair when the report was brought him that the house of the President was vacated. Whither the occupants had fled, none could ever devise; but the possibility crossed the mind of the Laird that the spirit of the unhappy man had departed, and his friends, dreading a repetition of the tumult, had anticipated the dawn in conveying him to a silent resting-place.

" Miserable being ! " he murmured, as he bent his steps to the house of Mr. Lincoln, where, beside his couch, he now loved to linger, — " he has gone to his own place, mingling with those of kindred spirit. What a deed, blasting the fair fame of such an one as Hugh Lincoln ! A retributive Providence must surely follow, and he is reaping the just reward of his guilt." A hand was laid upon his arm. He turned quickly. A young man, apparently in the humbler walks of life, stood before him ; a mass of sandy hair covered an unusually low forehead, and had been permitted to grow upon the lip and chin until it reached the chest. His countenance expressed the utmost wretchedness. The name of the Laird was pronounced in the lowest tone.

"Have you business with me, my friend?" he inquired.

"Of vital importance," he returned huskily; "I bear a request from the dying."

The voice was perfectly familiar; the truth flashed upon him. Robertson was still alive, and his son addressed him.

"Is not this MacIntosh?" the Laird inquired, kindly.

"Even so," was the reply; "but, oh! delay not, Lord Glennair; my father is in a state bordering on distraction. The daily papers have met the eye of my mother, and a letter has just been received stating that she and sister will return to us without delay. She writes in a state of great excitement, and discredits every evil report, which — alas! — alas! —" The sentence was left unfinished, a deadly paleness overspread the face of the unhappy youth, as he inquired, —

"Shall I conduct you to my father, Laird?"

"It grieves me to add a tittle to your heavy load of sorrow, my dear boy," returned the Laird, "but I cannot accede to this request. I desire to erase his name forever from my remembrance."

"Oh! refuse me not, Laird," exclaimed the agonized youth, "I cannot return alone; further revelation he desires to make that will partially relieve his burdened spirit. Can you not — will you not, for my sake, grant my request?"

"Though my heart bleeds for you, dear MacIntosh, even for your sake, I could not comply; but if there are communications in regard to my dear, injured friends, duty plainly points my course. Lead the way, my son, I will follow."

"The path points to a lowly tenement, Laird, the home of a friend of Katy's. Gratefully we sought its shelter on that eventful night when the excited multitude had retired, and our own friends and domestics had fled, in turn, from our dwelling. Borne by his faithful nurse and myself, he now lies concealed in an upper story there."

He ceased speaking, and the Laird, gently placing his arm within the youth's, silently proceeded with him. No word of consolation was offered — none could be found; but the kind look, the sympathizing manner, struck a chord untouched since his father's downfall. He wept.

"The horrors of that day and night," he said, "beggar description; our house suddenly surrounded, the fiend-like cries of an infuriated mob, the windows crushed to atoms, and missiles hurled even to the very couch of my dying father! With the assistance of Katy, I carried him to the lower story, where the closed windows afforded him temporary protection. There, in that room, from my father's own lips, I first learned the history of — of his — of my — of our family's dishonor; the tidings fell upon my scorched brain with withering power. Despair had set its seal upon me, and my senses would surely have forsaken me had not our extremity forced immediate action. At two in the morning we bore him totally unconscious, to this abode."

They stopped before a cluster of small frame tenements on the borders of the town. "The inmates of the house suppose a female invalid and her son are here," he whispered, as he led the way up a narrow winding staircase. Lord Glennair followed. A door was opened by young Robertson, leading into an apartment of small dimensions, lighted by a single four-paned window. In one corner, on a straw-bed raised upon a cot, lay the wretched sufferer. The flushed cheek and unnatural lustre of the eye, told of burning fever. His nurse, her eyes swollen with weeping, sat beside him.

There was a kind response to her heartfelt "God bless ye," as she arose and retired to a corner of the room. Lord Glennair stood silently awaiting a recognition; no kindly hand was extended, no word of sympathy proffered.

His son leaned over him, and laid his hand upon his burning brow. "Father," he whispered, "Lord Glennair is here; shall Katy and I withdraw?"

"Nae, nae; leave me not again, my son, my injured, my ruined MacIntosh," he replied, with a convulsive grasp of his hand, "until this throbbing pulse ceases to beat, and my spirit has passed into that — that abode of the cursed," he whisperingly added, "of which I am now experiencing so bitter a foretaste."

"Say not so, dearest father," he replied, while his tears bedewed his parent's cheek. "Katy will tell you of a better land — of sins forgiven — of a Saviour's love. Would that I also could point you to a happy home; but alas! alas! I realize it not."

The face of Lord Glennair was averted, and a tear hastily brushed away.

"From my soul I thank you for this visit, Lord Glennair," he said, glancing toward him; but his eye fell as the stern, uncompromising countenance met his view.

"Reserve your thanks for those who merit them," he returned, coldly; "an earnest desire alone to serve my deeply injured friend has brought me here."

A deeper crimson mantled his cheek as he replied, "And ardently do I long to make the utmost restitution in my power, consistently with my duty to those implicated with me."

"In your wanderings, the names of Traquair and Benson were betrayed; but Traquair has fled, and escaped the arm of justice, which he was aware would fall heavily upon him. Information respecting him can no longer affect his safety. Who placed the papers in the dwelling of Hugh Lincoln?"

"Benson, who could feign any hand, lured by the love of gold, forged them; hatred to the house of Lincoln burned in the heart of Traquair. He aspired to the hand of Edith, and was disdainfully rejected. From that hour he breathed revenge. I therefore found in him a fitting tool for my nefarious purposes. In regard to Duncan, I am innocent. On the night of my return, when I bitterly upbraided Traquair for this wicked and useless step, he confessed that rather than see Duncan the preferred suitor of the daughter of Hugh Lincoln, he would bring him to the gallows. His heart was perfectly

21 *

callous to any impression. With a demoniac smile, he left me, saying, 'I am only an apt scholar, trained in the school of Mungo Robertson.'"

"Miserable villain," murmured the Laird; "apt pupil, indeed, for such vile purposes."

"Robert, I deserve it all. I richly merit your heaviest anathemas; but," he added, extending his burning hand, "can you not view me as on the verge of a dread eternity? Can you not bestow one drop of water to cool this parched tongue? I sue for your forgiveness; say, at least, you pity my condition — take but this hand kindly, as of old. I could then more calmly face death, with all its terrors."

The hand of Lord Glennair still rested upon his knee. Without the slightest relaxation of that stern expression, he returned slowly, in an almost whisper, "Had the demon's voice been permitted to speak but once within you, there might have been some palliation; but a succession of acts, cold, deliberate, each transcending the former in its iniquitous conception —may God forgive —*I* cannot."

The face of Mr. Robertson was in a moment concealed from view; his son walked to the window. Lord Glennair arose, and beckoning Katy, placed in her hand a purse of gold, containing a sum far more than equivalent to their present exigencies; and hastily descending the stairway, immediately returned to his own library, where a careful note was made of the information given, and he then retraced his way to the sick-bed of Mr. Lincoln.

CHAPTER XI.

"From jeopardy redeemed,
As from the lion's mouth,
Mercy and truth uphold our life,
And safety guards our path."

IT was the Sabbath; all nature was clothed in
gladness, and the grateful hearts of the inmates
of the Manse and Thistle Hedge beat responsive to
nature's call. Passing strange had been the events
of the preceding week, ushered in by throes of the
most poignant anguish, of intensity of agony, followed by dread suspense, that stilled the life-blood
in its course, and, as though all nature were arrested, heard naught, saw naught, until the truth,
the certainty of what they dared not hope, burst
upon them, robing life in its loveliest hues, and producing unmingled happiness in the bosoms of those
so lately bowed with sorrow. For miles around,
friends and strangers, by words and letters of sympathy, testified their regard, and, by every demonstration of respect, endeavored to atone for their
late distrust — (so unmerited) — of those on whom
it fell so heavily. But the day of rest had arrived,
and not a sound was to be distinguished, save the
footfall of those who were hastening to the house
of God. The excitement being not yet allayed in
the bosom of the multitude, Mr. Graeme declined
filling his pulpit until the following Sabbath. At

the request of Mr. Lincoln, who was still languid,
and unable to leave his couch, the two families were
assembled in the drawing-room at Thistle Hedge.
Lord Glennair and Dr. McMillan were there; Roger,
Norval, and Allan were present also.

"We will set apart this day to praise and thanksgiving," said Mr. Lincoln. "Lochiel, does not your
heart beat in unison with this proposal?"

"Truly," he replied, as his dark eyes beamed with
gladness, "I would praise Him on the harp, I would
praise Him on the psaltery, I would praise Him forever for all his goodness."

"But the Lord will have mercy as well as sacrifice," interposed his father; "can you not say, 'Father, forgive *him* who has so sorely bruised us'?"

The brow of the youth clouded. "That is too
much to demand of me, father," he returned. "Nay,
could that rock before us be loosened from its foundation, fain would I see him crushed beneath its ruin."

"Only as we forgive our debtors, have we the
promise of the great I AM, that our sins shall be
remembered no more against *us*," said Mr. Graeme,
sadly, "and if we regard iniquity in our hearts,
the Lord will not listen to our supplications, my son."

Lochiel was silent.

"Your test is beyond human nature," Lord Glennair remarked to Mr. Graeme. "Lochiel's feeling,
in my view, is both natural and commendable. It
manifests his strong sympathy with those who have
been so unjustly treated, and a proper appreciation
of its author."

"Natural, truly, Laird; but grace will prevail

against nature. Did not our great Exemplar plead forgiveness for those who nailed him to the accursed tree ? "

" Vengeance is mine, saith the Lord," rejoined Mr. Lincoln, " and He has shown himself the avenger here. In viewing the past, present, or future, is there an outlet of hope in the bosom of the unhappy man ? Let us first ask for forgiving spirits, and offer a prayer for Mungo Robertson, ere we render praise and thanksgiving for our many and wonderful mercies. Roger, will you follow Mr. Graeme in prayer ? "

There was a hesitation on the part of Neilson. "I fear I hae nae quite forgiven, Maister Lincoln. For mysel', I hae nae an ill thought toward him, but for ye and Maister Duncan I canna trust my ain heart. The Lord forgive me; I will pray him tae gie me a better mind."

The petitions offered were heartfelt and touching; those of Neilson clothed with humility, mourning his unforgiving, sinful spirit, and pleading that all present might be endued with power to forgive as they hoped to be forgiven. Songs of praise, and the thank-offerings of the heart that followed, showed there was intercession made in Heaven, and unforgiving spirits were cleansed by the blood of atonement, and their sins forgiven even as they heartily forgave.

" I have learned a lesson this day," Lord Glennair remarked, as he warmly shook the hand of Mr. Graeme at parting. " Although baptized in infancy, and partaking, for many years, of the emblems of the Saviour's love, I, this morning, for the first time, was awakened to a sense of the vitality of religion. I am resolved to seek the truth. Pray that I may find it, Mr. Graeme."

"The Lord make you a burning and shining light," ejaculated his Pastor.

Taking his hat, Mr. Graeme rejoined him, as he pursued his way toward the castle. "Are you pledged, Laird," he inquired, "to withhold from all, the place of Mungo Robertson's retreat?"

"Not pledged — but, under his present circumstances, I would not willingly expose him to the rigor of the law; he will shortly appear before another than a human tribunal."

"*I* desire to point him to mercy's path, that he may fling back the sword of justice, and take shelter under the mercy-seat."

"No! not you! so injured — so aggrieved. Would you indeed, in person, offer consolation to one who has so recklessly — so — "

"Stay, my Laird; recount not his misdeeds. In the stillness of the night, my wakeful hours have been passed in the mighty struggle to overcome my natural feeling, to forgive, pity, and even sorrow, over the miserable condition of one on the borders of an eternity of wretchedness. Should I not stretch forth a hand to save? Should not a word of counsel be offered, or a warning given, ere the doom of that spirit is sealed forever?"

"Your high resolve is godlike, Mr. Graeme," returned Lord Glennair, solemnly, "and whatever be the success of your mission, a blessing will redound upon your own head. I will conduct you to his abode."

In silence they proceeded for some time, when the Laird, beckoning Mr. Graeme to follow, ascended the narrow stairway, and, pointing to the door, whispered, "May God speed you," and immediately disappeared.

Mr. Graeme's gentle tap was unanswered; slowly and quietly opening the door, he entered. Young Robertson was sitting beside his father, his head bent upon his hand, apparently in deep thought. Mr. Robertson was sleeping, but the countenance manifested no repose, and his sunken eye and ghastly appearance told of a depth of sorrow.

At a sudden exclamation from the old nurse, the youth started, and casting a look of the utmost anguish upon Mr. Graeme, threw himself at his feet, exclaiming, "Spare, oh spare, my poor, my unhappy father. Let not justice overtake him. Let not—"

"Let me assure you, my child," Mr. Graeme returned, soothingly, "I would not add one drop to *your* cup of affliction, already overflowing."

"Yes, yes," he replied mournfully, "this is to me a world of bitter sorrow."

"Let me point you to a home where sorrow can never enter, and where all tears are wiped away."

The sound of voices breaking in upon the stillness of the apartment, aroused the invalid. Looking fearfully around, he murmured the name of MacIntosh. In a moment, he was leaning over his father.

"Is all over, my son?" he inquired, in a low, tremulous tone. Mr. Graeme advanced to the bedside.

"Alas! alas!" he moaned, "I have forfeited all claim to pity; must I, oh! must I be held up to the gaze of an incensed multitude?"

"No, no, dear father!" exclaimed his son, throwing himself in agony upon him; "they must, they will regard your condition. If not — if they are callous to your sufferings, I will die with you: they cannot separate us."

"I have sought no commission from a human tribunal," interposed Mr. Graeme. "I have come as an ambassador from the great I AM, to offer full and free salvation. Believe on the Lord Jesus Christ, and thou shalt be saved."

Young Robertson threw himself upon his knees, and buried his face in his father's pillow.

There was a look of speechless gratitude as the unhappy man laid his trembling hand upon that of the minister. Mr. Graeme's was not withdrawn as he continued:

"I would not be misunderstood, Mungo Robertson. I came not to palliate crime — crimes of the deepest dye; but I bring an offer of peace and pardon, even for sin, of which the penalty of our law is death. But Jesus is ready to forgive; he is waiting; he is saying, 'Come unto me, all ye that labor and are heavy-laden, and I will give you rest. Knock, and it shall be opened; seek, and ye shall find.'"

"Words of peace from *your* lips," replied Mr. Robertson, as the big tears rolled down his face, "speak only torture to my burdened spirit. Upbraiding I could endure. Can you, indeed, permit my hand to rest within your own, and say that you forgive?"

"Fully and freely," was the reply; "and let us plead forgiveness at the bar of Him with whom the fervent, effectual prayer availeth much."

"Effectual," he murmured; "effectual — no, no, there is nothing will avail; within my bosom there is a fearful looking-for of judgment and fiery indignation. The heavens are as brass over me. I have sinned away my day of grace forever, forever. I will in vain call upon the rocks to cover me from the wrath of my offended Saviour and my God."

"Our Lord God, merciful and gracious," returned Mr. Graeme, "is slow to anger, and plenteous in mercy. Jesus is the mediator, the daysman, that lays his hand upon both; by his stripes all, even the most atrocious sinner, may be healed; those who nailed him to the cross might have had even that crowning guilt washed from their consciences, and their robes made white in the blood of the Lamb."

"*They* sinned in ignorance; *I*, in the face of the highest privileges. My now sainted mother's prayers and counsel were set at nought by my mad ambition and thirst for gold. There is a sin unto death — death eternal. Pray not for me, Mr. Graeme, my destiny is fixed — sealed by my own dark deeds." His chest heaved convulsively.

There was deep sympathy upon the countenance of Mr. Graeme, but he replied not.

Mr. Robertson continued: "Let me tender to you my warmest, heartfelt gratitude for your sympathy, so unprecedented, so like your Master whom you serve so faithfully."

"And can you believe that I more freely pardon than my Master?"

"The Judge of all the earth pierces to the innermost recesses of my heart; He has implanted there remorse — remorse that will scorch and wither in this bosom until — Would that the future could be computed."

"Father, father," whispered young Robertson, "would you madden your only son — your MacIntosh?"

"My ruined, my unfortunate boy —"

Suddenly a murmuring sound was heard beneath the window, and the name of Mungo Robertson pronounced, mingled with threats."

"The infuriated rabble are again upon us," exclaimed young Robertson, springing toward the window.

Mr. Graeme, forcibly drawing him back, threw it open, and inquired the occasion of this unwarrantable violation of the quiet of the Sabbath.

A number of young men from the best families of the place had assembled, and were narrowly surveying the premises. They started with surprise at seeing the well-known face of their minister. One, apparently the leader, came forward, and respectfully raising his cap, expressed his regret that they should so unwittingly have interrupted him while engaged in his parochial duties, and assured him they would at once retire.

"We were searching for the worst, and found

the very best man in Scotland," one of the party remarked pleasantly to his friend as they slowly retreated.

"Shame, shame, young gentlemen," called Mr. Graeme; "shall our law be infringed by those who ought to be its firm supporters?"

"We only wish to aid in enforcing them," the first speaker replied. "We intended bearing Robertson, unharmed, to where he would obtain ample justice of the very nature we desire for him."

There was a general laugh at this sally, and the whole party, raising their hats in token of their respect for Mr. Graeme, quietly dispersed.

The casement was again closed, and Mr. Graeme returned to the bedside. The face of Mr. Robertson was blanched with terror. There was determination written upon the lip of the young man, but the despairing eye that met that of Mr. Graeme was an instant call upon the sympathy of the kind-hearted minister.

"Suspicion is lulled," he remarked kindly to him; "you are for the present perfectly secure in this retreat."

"There will be a struggle — to the death," he returned, almost fiercely, "ere they accomplish their object."

"They purposed no physical injury, my son."

"The countenance of Mungo MacAlpin should scarcely be given to such a mission," he replied, bitterly; "he who was named for my father, and my dearest friend. He should at least remember, if he has forgotten all things else, that I have a nature equally sensitive with his own."

"The powerful excitement of the present moment casts a dark shadow over the past, MacIntosh," returned the Pastor.

"But yesterday he was my warmest friend; the same hour gave us birth, and, ten days since, we celebrated its seventeenth return, at his father's dwelling. Now, how changed — a deadly foe — the leader of a gang to accelerate our ruin. It is base," he continued, striking his clenched hand heavily upon his knee — "heartless, cruel — yea, fiendish. Would that I could have been saved a knowledge of his perfidy!"

Although spoken in the lowest tone, the last word reached the ear of his father.

"Perfidy," he repeated sadly; "yes, perfidy of the deepest dye."

In a moment the cheek of the son was closely laid beside his father's. "Did I disturb you, dear father?" he inquired.

"Those who guide the helm will soon steer her into port," he remarked wildly, without noticing the question. "Make arrangements for their reception, my son — carefully, carefully."

"They shall be made, dear father; give yourself no uneasiness."

"There!" he continued, raising himself as though in the attitude of listening, "their step is upon the stairway. Has the chamber been aired properly for Agnes? Let Katy see to it. The rooms are dark, dreary. Open wide the casements — breath — breath. Agnes is dying — struggling for breath. Quick! quick! give her air."

"These paroxysms are of frequent recurrence, but pass after a brief interval," his son remarked. " I will ask you to retire, Mr. Graeme; I observe his eye intently fixed upon you, and I fear it revives recollections prejudicial to his recovery."

Mr. Graeme quietly arose, and taking the hand of the young man, whispered: "To a throne of grace I will bear all your sorrows. I will plead with Jesus that he may give you the oil of joy for mourning, and the garments of praise for the spirit of heaviness."

The youth, raising the hand to his lips, kissed it passionately.

" Early in the morning I will again see you," said Mr. Graeme, clasping his hand warmly, "and may the peace of God abide with you forever, dear Mac-Intosh."

They separated, and, with a sad heart, Mr. Graeme retraced his steps to the Manse.

A bright and happy group had gathered around a cheerful fire in the study.

"You have overstayed your dinner-hour considerably, dear father," Amy remarked playfully, as she drew his chair closely into the circle and imprinted a warm kiss upon his cheek.

" I have been able to make no computation of time to-day, daughter," he returned; "but why did you permit any detention of dinner? Kathleen and Margaritte will be disappointed in the afternoon service."

"That will scarcely cast a cloud over their joyous

hearts, father," she returned, her eyes filling with tears. "They have had a feast this day in Kirk that has filled their warm hearts with gratitude and love."

"The prayers and thank-offerings that were poured forth," said Kathleen, "nat forgetting our ain Maister Lochiel, were tae much for human nature, Miss Amy; at least," she added, as the apron was put in requisition to arrest the falling tear, "it was tae much for the heart o' Kathleen."

"But I didna like," interposed Margaritte, "the prayin' and a' the guid wishes for that vilest o' sinners, Maister Robertson. *I* dinna want tae see any place that haulds him, here or hereafter."

"When the Spirit has touched your heart, Margie," replied Kathleen, "ye'll gie him a few words yersel'."

Margie shook her head incredulously, and went on to descant on the power that was thought of Mr. Lochiel — just what she had always kenned his wild ways would end in. "And really, father," added Miss Graeme, "they have arrested our attention so pleasantly that two hours have glided imperceptibly."

"Those domestics," remarked Dr. McMillan, "are a treasure in any household."

Kathleen announcing dinner, the conversation was interrupted.

The afternoon was spent by Mr. Graeme in the sacred retirement of his own chamber. What communion he held with his Maker, was never whispered into mortal ear; but when, in the evening,

the two families again assembled in the chamber of
Mr. Lincoln, all noticed the pathos and the depth of
feeling with which he supplicated for him who was
placing an invincible barrier between himself and
his only refuge. There was a plaintive pleading
with his Saviour, as man to man; and when he
sought a blessing, a rich blessing upon the head of
that dear, devoted youth, and prayed, that, if needful, *he* might be made the stay, the protector of one
so stricken in the flower of his days, and bowed
with grief, experiencing no chord of sympathy vi-
brating with his own seared heart, — all were then
fully aware that the occasion of the detention was
a mission of holy love to the unhappy, — a mission
so like him who went about shedding rays of light
on every path.

No inquiry was made and no information proffered, but the Laird remarked to Duncan, that he
always had known his father was the best of men,
but he now doubted there was any human nature
left within him.

At an early hour on the following morning, ere
(with the exception of Mr. Graeme) the family had
arisen, a low knock was heard at the door of the
Manse.

" And wha' may be the ca' at this airly hour ? "
inquired Margaritte, from an upper window.

" I would nae disturb the Maister if he has nae
risen," replied a gentle voice ; " can ye tell me when
I can see him ? "

" As sure as ye are Kathleen," exclaimed Margie,
" Katy McShee is below."

Hastily descending the stairway, the door was immediately opened, and a kind welcome extended to her old friend.

"It's a cauld and dreary house for ye, Katy," she remarked, kindly; "but a blazin' hearth 'ill soon greet you i' the kitchen." So saying, she led the way through the hall, and, throwing open the door, what was her surprise when a bright, crackling fire met her view, imparting its warmth to every corner of the room, while the hissing kettle impatiently awaited its owner's bidding. The smiling face of Allan told a tale that required no unravelling.

"Well, ye're a gude lad, nae doubt o' ye," said the gratified Margie, placing a chair in the warmest corner for her friend, and assisting in the removal of her cloak and bonnet; "but wha' put ye up to a' this, Allan?"

"Norval, and he's done the same for Nanny. He'll ne'er forget the oven, nor the kindness shown him in his time of need. We were up with the Lark, and the wood chopped, he says, it 'll last till the next we split, which will be when that's a lowering. While we're here, Margie, ye need nae blaw yer fingers wi' the cauld, for all the rooms ye'll find as warm as ye do this mornin'."

"Why, are they all warmed, Allan? The study, dining-room — all?"

There was a laugh, and a pleasant nod, as Allan obeyed the summons of Mr. Lincoln.

"A pleasant lad that, Margie," remarked Katy. "Is Norval a brother tae him?"

"Nae, nae; Norval's ane o' them that Maister
Robertson would hae strung upon a gibbet, had n't
the Lord told him anither story. Ye're an angel
frae a den o' wolves, Katy. Could he look ye in
the face after sic a deed?"

"Ah! had ye seen the anguish o' his heart, Margie, ye would hae ministered tae his wants yersel'."

"I!—I have ministered tae his wants? I'd hae
throttled him afore the weight o' this finger had
been lifted in his sairvice. Nae, nae. Was the
dove in my ain cote tae be sacrificed? The lamb in
my ain fold? And could the wail o' my ain nestling, that came frae the depths o' his heart for the
loss o' his brother, sound in my ears, and I minister
tae the want of his murderer?"

"Could ye hae heard the kind words o' the minister, it would hae melted yer heart, Margie."

"The minister!" she exclaimed, removing her
hands from the dough she was lustily kneading,
and coming forward; "ye dinna tell me Maister
Graeme forgive and forget wi' sic a man as that."

"Ah! he would hae led him right awa' tae the
refuge for a' sinners, Margie, and spake of his
death and mighty love in sic a strain, that the
heart of Maister MacIntosh melted wi'in him; but
it fell heavy upon the despairing soul of my puir
maister."

"And did he have the assurance to reject what
the minister carried him sae kindly?"

"Ah! Margie, he could nae receive the promises;
but he looked tae his ain heart, and could nae look
awa' tae Jesus, the sinner's friend."

"And right glad am I he had n't the presumption, for if *he* pushed himsel' in, wha would hae a better right than Lucifer, not half sae bad as sic a demon spirit as Maister Robertson."

"Margie, Margie," said her old friend, solemnly, "ye dinna ken the height or the breadth of the love o' Jesus; he died for the chief of sinners in our ain airth, and he saves us according tae our trust in Him, and not according tae the littleness or greatness of our sins. But there was nae offer of redemption for the hosts of rebels wha went tae their ain place lang syne. But hae ye nae heart tae weep, at least for the bairn sae stricken, Margie?"

"He is but a wee one to bear sic a burden," she replied, in a softened tone; "but a high head *he* always carried, Katy. Ye canna tell anither story than that, can ye?"

"It was his mither's bluid that ran in his veins," her friend returned; "there was nane of it natur; as sweet a lad as ever hanged on the neck of an auld nurse, was Maister MacIntosh, until —"

"Till he was of a size tae ken his rank. Tell me, Katy McShee, did he e'er speak a word of friendship or kindness tae his auld nurse after that?"

With downcast look, Katy remained silent.

Margaritte continued: "I would nae speak the evil word of him in the time of his trouble, Katy; but he brought the fire tae the eye of Kathleen, not many months since, by his high words about our ain household."

"Was it about the wildness of Maister Lochiel?" inquired Katy.

"Nae, nae sae bad as that; nane would hae stood a word upon our ain bairn; but he could not bide for worship, for he could not brook the servants takin' sittins in the same room, and haulding their heads like lairds and ladies. Ah! it would hae gladdened yer heart tae see the scorn o' Maister Lochiel. 'Our domestics, Maister MacIntosh,' he answered, 'I'd have ye tae ken, are our friends, and are lairds and ladies in their position, and if ye dinna like our worship, why ye ken absent yersel' frae it.'

"The color was pretty high, and the rebuke was felt, but he left the hall with a toss of the head, meant for contempt; but our ain bairn stood his ground, and read him a wholesome lecture on his sinful pride, so unbecoming a gentleman of his good standing."

The tinkle of a small bell in a corner of the kitchen checked the volubility of the old woman. Turning quickly, she said, "Ye are frae now tae see the minister, Katy; a touch of his bell lets us ken he is ready to receive any message, or call, if need be."

With a kind, benignant smile, the hand of Mr. Graeme was extended to the timid woman as she entered his study.

"Your visit portends no evil, I trust, Mrs. McShee?" he inquired, kindly, as he drew a chair for her beside the fire. "Have the people again threatened the cottage?"

"Maister Graeme," she returned, her voice trembling with agitation, "they are all gane — Maister

Robertson, Maister MacIntosh, Mistress, and Miss Agnes."

"Your Mistress and Miss Agnes were not, surely, here?"

"Maister MacIntosh did not tell the likes of me about all their doins; but in the dead hour of the night he was awa', and when he returned, his face was swelled with weeping, and in a low and hurried tone he bid me assist, with noiseless tread, fearin' tae disturb the sleepers, in bearin' my puir sufferin' Maister down the stairway and along the path some distance. There a horse and wagon, wi' a small bed, was awaitin' him, and wi'out speakin', we laid him on it, and beconin' me tae follow, he seated himsel' beside him, supportin' his puir head upon his bosom. The man drove slow and carefu', but his groans sank tae the heart of the bairn, and his sobs just mingled wi' the ither troubles. I could nat scan the distance, but in nae wee time we stopped wi' our burden. It was a dark and cheerless night, the wind whistled past us, and I kenned neither man nor beast in the darkness. My heart quaked for fear, and my feet a'most sunk under me."

"'Tak' a firm and gentle hold, Katy,' whispered the young Maister, 'bear him a short distance and we'll soon be out of the way of all danger.'

"The sound of water made me ken we neared the sea, and, followin' his lead, a bright light pointed the way tae the cabin of a large vessel. There was a mournfu' cry as we entered, and the fairst thing that met my eye was Miss Agnes. The pale cheek and sunken eye were sad tae look upon, and her

piercin' cries and sobs, as she hanged over her puir
father, made us all tremble for grief. But all her
trouble and pleadin' wi' him did not bring life tae
Maister Robertson, neither a word to his lips. There
was nae word of comfort gien tae her, for her mither
and brother both needed consolation, and had nane
to offer.

" ' Will ye nae speak tae yer ain bairn, dear father?'
she sobbed, piteously; ' will ye nae gie a word of
blessing tae Agnes?'

" The mither's face was hid in the lap of Maister
MacIntosh; nae word escaped her lips, but the heavin'
of her bosom spake her bitter sorrow. I made frae
tae whisper softly in the ear of the sweet young
leddy a few words of truth frae the lips of Jesus,—
' Come unto me, all ye that labor and are heavy-
laden, and I will gie ye rest.'

" Then she raised her head frae the cheek of her
father, where it was resting, and her sweet blue eye
turned right upon me.

" ' Did ye speak of a rest, Katy,' she inquired
gently; ' a rest frae all sorrow?'

" Then the Lord put into my heart many words
of his own framin', and her eye fell softly, and the
tears that wet her cheek were not as the former—
wild and bitter.

" ' Mansions of rest,' she murmured, ' for all who
love him. May I enter into that rest, Katy?'

" My tears fell sae thick I could not answer the
dear young leddy, but her mother raised her head
and said sternly,—

" ' Ye will hae a rest wi'out the seekin,' Agnes;

23

dinna listen tae the tales of any, as though ye were a sinner.'

"'Dinna stay the words of Katy, mither,' she said, wi' a pleadin' look; 'she tells me of a rest for a weary spirit in a better land. I would seek it, mither, and Katy can point the way.'

"'Ye will find it, darling, in yer father's mansion, when he's well and righted.'

"'Katy's words are the words of Holy Writ, mither,' said Maister MacIntosh, 'and the same words of our ain minister tae our dear father, on yestermorn.'

"'They are good words, my son,' she retairned, 'and well fitting Katy; but our bairn has nae need, for she has ne'er sinned, and canna need a Saviour.'

"'I have long since wanted the thing Katy has brought me, mither; I want tae be a lamb of Christ's fold.'

"The tears came, and her coughin' wi' it, and a deep groan frae the bosom of Maister Robertson startled us. Maister MacIntosh arose quickly, and beckonin' me tae the stairway of the cabin, whispered, 'The boy and the wagon are baith in waitin' for ye, Katy.'

"Walkin' back a wee space, I slipped into the hand of the young lady my ain little Scripture promises, gien to me by yersel'; and only sayin', 'Pray tae Jesus, and he'll be yer friend in sorrow and in joy,' I followed Maister MacIntosh tae the wagon, tae which he led me in the darkness; and, takin' my hand kindly, he whispered, 'May God bless yer kindness tae us, and reward ye for it. Ask the gude minister to pray for us.'"

" Let *your* prayers arise, without ceasing, for them," said Mr. Graeme. " Miss Agnes is perhaps fitting for a blessed home, and I trust Mr. MacIntosh is not far from the kingdom of Heaven. But what arrangement have you made for your own comfort here, Katy ?"

" If the gude quality ladies could gie us needle-work, my friend and I could manage finely ; the cot is my Laird's, and we' hae no landlord to pinch us."

Miss Amy and Miss Edith will see to that matter, Mrs. McShee. In the meantime, bide with Kathleen and Margaritte a few days ; the change will benefit you."

With a grateful smile and a low curtsy, Katy left the apartment and hastily proceeded to the kitchen, to impart to her friends the kind invitation and promises of her good minister, adding, " A wee time in this pleasant and comfortable house will build me up, and mak' me feel strong and well again, and fit me for all the work the ladies will hae the kindness to gie us. The Lord bless them for all their goodness."

CHAPTER XII

"Something mournful and profound,
Saddens all her beauty now;
Weds her dark eye to the ground,
Flings a shadow o'er her brow."

IT cannot be possible you so soon leave us, Percy,'
Miss Graeme remarked, as she entered the parlor,
and her friend, with extended hand, arose to meet
her, — "Duncan's announcement of your intention
was the first intimation of it to us."

"It requires some effort to leave all we hold dear,"
he returned, with a sad smile, "and the thought of
my father's lonely hours in my absence presses
heavily upon me; but it is in accordance with his
earnest wish that I sail in the steamer *Mungo*, at
eight in the morning."

"Will not the Lady Gertrude shortly return to
cheer the hearthstone at the castle?" Miss Graeme
inquired, as the color mounted, and a slight tremor
was visible upon her lip.

"The day after my departure. I would gladly have
awaited her return, but pleasant friends as fellow-
passengers held out a strong inducement. But a
few added thorns in life's pathway seem not to me
very material," he added sadly.

"I imagined only flowers strewing your path,
Percy. But should clouds gather around you, the
Sun of Righteousness will soon dissipate them. Your

268

faith has always been simple and abiding. I should
grieve to know that Percy Dunbar was unhappy."

" And far be it from Percy Dunbar to cast a shade
upon the cloudless brow of Amy Graeme. That
title you will scarcely bear on my return," he observed, with forced gayety ; " as it will have been
exchanged for one of more matronly dignity. Will
it not be so, my friend ? "

The crimson mantled her cheek, as she replied
laughingly, " Amy Graeme has vowed eternal fidel-
ity to her father."

" Well, well ; then as a friendly seer, I warn you.
Beware of the fascinations and importunities of one
James McMillan."

" If it depend upon *that* tie," she replied, coldly,
" Amy Graeme will bear the same title on your return."

A footstep was heard by Amy in the upper part
of the hall, as they left the parlor, and Dr. McMillan passed into the study.

Percy, without observing him, continued, — " I
must tear myself away, Amy ; time is waning, and
numberless cares devolve upon me ere I leave these
shores ; but may I be permitted to inform Amy
Graeme of my welfare and whereabouts, from time
to time ? "

" Intercourse with an early friend is always pleasant, Percy ; I shall esteem it highly."

" And will a line sometimes be penned by the hand
of my old friend, to cheer my wanderings ? "

" Of course your epistles shall not remain unanswered."

23 *

" Thank you, thank you. And will you promise
sometimes to breathe a prayer for the absent one ? "

The head of Amy bowed. Raising her hand to his
lips, he whispered, " Say farewell to Edith," and hastily left the hall. Miss Graeme returned to the parlor.

The voice of Dr. McMillan was distinctly heard
in conversation with her father. She lingered, she
scarcely knew why. She felt depressed, sad, unhappy. Was it that the friend of her early childhood was about leaving them ? No; for him she
had every kindly feeling, but upon him she was not
dependent for happiness.

But his communication, — " Lady Gertrude was
about returning." Of what moment was this to
her ? Was not Dr. McMillan free to act as he deemed
fitting ? But *was* it fitting that his attention should
be proffered to another ? Was not his attention
marked ? his leisure hours always spent in her society ? Did he attempt to conceal his interest in
everything relating to her ? When she was called
to agony of spirit, who manifested deeper sympathy ? and, when the cup of rejoicing was filled to
overflowing, whose heart beat more in unison with
her own ? " It cannot, cannot be," she murmured ;
her head was bowed upon her hand. She was
aroused by a voice addressing her.

Starting from her reverie, she perceived Dr. Mc-
Millan standing before her.

" Edith requested me to see you, Amy," he observed, with an evidently restrained manner, " and
say to you that, for the first time, her father would
walk in the garden this morning, and she desired
you would join them there." -

"I will be with them in a few moments," she returned, hastily dashing a not unobserved tear aside, and throwing a shawl carelessly over her shoulders.

"Shall I accompany you?" the Doctor inquired hesitatingly. "Helen is upon my list of patients; I must see her this morning."

"I trust she is not seriously sick, as Mr. Lincoln dines with us to-morrow. It would much mar our pleasure should Mrs. Cameron be detained at home."

"Not at all — a slight cold merely. I regret I shall not be able to accept your father's kind invitation; some transactions with Lord Glennair will prevent my doing so."

Only the compressed lip of Miss Graeme told any impression had been made. The garden-gate was reached, and, in silence, they entered Thistle Hedge together.

Mr. Lincoln was already walking over the grounds supported by the strong arm of Duncan Graeme, while Edith, with glad countenance and joyous step, watched every movement of her beloved father. A warm and kindly greeting was given and returned.

"How pleasant," said Mr. Lincoln, "to enjoy once more the breath of heaven. When restored to my former vigor, Doctor, I shall need your counsel in the arrangement of my garden-plot, and these little girls shall adorn it with the choicest plants their taste can select, or the green-house furnish. Allan shall be our executive, as I intend retaining him as gardener."

"A more willing heart could scarcely be obtained,"

returned the Doctor, "though others may be found better skilled in horticulture."

"But here comes our friend, Lord Glennair," Miss Lincoln remarked, springing forward to meet him as he came through the garden-gate, and placing her arm playfully within his. "An early convention, Laird, to consult on the contemplated improvements of the grounds of Thistle Hedge. Shall your opinion be withheld on such a grave question?"

"By no means," he returned pleasantly, imprinting a kiss upon her cheek, "only postponed until a more pressing matter is settled. My honor is now pledged, and my reward is given in advance of my services. But my business matter this morning is, to offer, in the name of the Directors of the Bank, the Presidency of that Institution to Mr. Hugh Lincoln, and to say to Master Duncan here, that the office of Cashier is open to his acceptance."

"My Laird!" exclaimed the youth, flushed with surprise and pleasure, "by whose instrumentality was such a nomination obtained? I am overwhelmed with gratitude, and will labor to prove myself worthy of such confidence."

"The acknowledged worth of Duncan Graeme bears its own testimony. Will Mr. Hugh Lincoln consent to preside over us?"

"You will present to the Board my warmest acknowledgments, Laird; but a few books, a few friends, and the cultivation of this little spot, will bound my future course. I shall not again take any part in public life."

"Recall that present resolve, Hugh Lincoln;

there is not a heart in that Bank but beats in unison with your own, and you have no right to confine your talents within so narrow limits. When health is restored fully, your energy will return with it, and you may regret so hasty a determination. Does not James McMillan agree with me in opinion?"

"When health is restored, my mission is at an end," the Doctor replied. "I would not presume to prescribe further; but I must see Helen for a moment, and, as I have some urgent cases, I must say good morning. At eight o'clock I will be with you, Laird." Without another glance at Amy, he left the garden.

"Has Roger yet returned from his visit to his people?" the Laird inquired.

"Last evening, and is now in the house with Norval."

"Will he accede to my proposition?"

"He is filled with gratitude. Gardening has always been his favorite calling;—failing to obtain such a situation induced him to enter the Bank as porter."

"Then shall I see, and make some arrangements with him? As Percy and I both leave here to-morrow, the hours to-day will be fully occupied."

"_You_, Laird," inquired Duncan; "you surely do not leave us?"

"The Doctor and I propose being escort to my runaway Gertrude. It is time she was turning her face homeward."

There was evident surprise and chagrin upon the

s

face of Duncan. "Does Dr. McMillan accompany you?" he inquired.

"He does. We shall put the carriage in requisition, and will not return until the following day."

"I believe it is twenty miles distant. Is it not, Laird?" inquired Edith.

"Just twenty; but through a pleasant country there is little fatigue. Shall we see Roger?"

Duncan, with Mr. Lincoln, led the way. Edith and Amy retired to Helen's chamber.

The summons of Lord Glennair was answered with alacrity by Roger and Norval.

"I am happy to hear, Roger," the Laird observed, "that my offer meets with a hearty response from you and Norval."

"We could nae hae thought o' sic a hame," replied Neilson, a bright smile illuminating his naturally grave face. "Tae be the gardener i' the manor of my Laird, and the bairn wi' me, is past my ken. We thank ye frae our hearts, Laird; but I would mak' frae tae speak, would not there be feelin' o' the part o' Robin, or could not we smooth his auld age as he gangs toward the better land?"

"Robin's faithful services will not go unrequited," returned the Laird; "but if a housekeeper could be obtained," he observed, looking archly toward Norval, "perhaps a corner of his old cottage might yet be spared him. Have you no word to offer, my lad?"

The eyes of Norval sought the floor, but making a great effort to overcome his natural timidity, he replied, "Lang afore our sair trouble, Laird, Jennie gie me a promise, and a tried friend she stood when my weary spirit was well-nigh crushed; and," he continued, lowering his voice, " as our hearts are ane, could not she be the housekeeper o' my father's hame, and make the latter days o' Robin quite content ? "

"A bright vision, that of yours, Norval," returned the Laird, taking his hand kindly. "Roger, do you approve this step ? "

"I have lang felt for Jennie as her ain father, and if it meet your approval, I am but tae well content."

"Then we must await the return of Miss Gertrude, for her consent to the loss of her favorite housemaid; and as soon as may be, the knot must be tied. And when the day is settled, you may promise your faithful clan a hearty greeting and good cheer in the Hall of Glennair Manor, and the bans shall be published with the good will of all parties."

There was an effort to reply on the part of Norval, but the Laird, observing his embarrassment, merely said, kindly, laying his hand upon his arm, "A son such as Norval Neilson is worthy of our faithful Jennie. May you be long spared one to the other."

The hand of the Laird was seized by Norval. "Thank ye, thank ye," he murmured; "but I hae nae words tae thank ye as I would."

"I know it, I know it, my lad, and will receive it as though expressed. You will take this note to Miss Ellen, Norval; your father will accompany you. Await my return at the manor."

With a heartfelt acknowledgment, Roger Neilson followed his son, and Lord Glennair took his leave also.

Mr. Lincoln and Duncan were left alone. The door opened, and Edith entered.

"Where is Amy?" her brother inquired.

"Entertaining her little favorite, who pronounces 'Cousin Amy's' stories 'the sweetest in the world.' I left her inviting her to 'come and live all the time' with her."

"Our friend James, I fear, would put a veto upon that proposition," Mr. Lincoln remarked, laughing; "has he not yet declared himself, Duncan?"

"Perhaps so," returned the youth; "to Miss Gertrude Dunbar."

"What!" exclaimed Mr. Lincoln, starting with amazement; "your words are a profound enigma to me. The heart of James McMillan belongs to none other than Amy Graeme."

"Then rank and fortune, I imagine, have induced a proffer of his hand where the heart is lacking."

"Never. The Doctor has a high-souled sense of honor, and, at any rate, would not so miserably wreck his own happiness."

"Of late his attentions have been too glaring to be mistaken, Mr. Lincoln; twice a week, during the last month, he has ridden with Lord Glennair to visit her, and to-morrow accompanies her father to return with her to the manor."

"I have observed an almost melancholy look on his countenance of late, and have also noticed an abstracted air when Amy is in the circle. But for the last two years he has scarcely breathed out of her presence."

"His feelings must have marvellously changed.

In my daily ride with Amy, in which Percy Dunbar usually accompanies us, if he happen to cross our path, a cold bow to Amy is the only recognition, and he always turns from his course, rather than join our party. His own conveyance has, to be sure, been several times offered to her, but, of course, declined."

"Time will reveal — it is impossible. There is an end of all perfection, truly, if James has swerved from the path of honor. I will ask him —"

"Nay, Mr. Lincoln; give me your word you will not so compromise the dignity of Amy."

"Well, I will watch every word and look; — I will know the truth. My almost daughter and beloved friend shall not be the victim of a fatal error."

"I am confident I need warn you no further, Mr. Lincoln; the refinement of your own nature would prompt you aright. I will now urge a plea in my own behalf. Mr. Lincoln, must your promise much longer remain unfulfilled? Edith is perfectly callous to my entreaties, only remarking, 'My first duty is to my invalid father.' My salary will now enable me to rent the house upon the hillside, which you know Mr. Davidson vacates in two weeks. It has been my beau ideal of all that is pleasant and comfortable; but I was aware it was beyond my grasp. Does it accord with your views also, Edith?"

"The arrangements of the house and grounds manifest decided taste, Duncan, and the site is unsurpassed."

24

"As the field joins Thistle Hedge, it can be common property, under the supervision of Mr. Lincoln. Shall it be so, Edith?"

"Let us defer the subject, Duncan, until the former vigor of father is restored."

"I should be truly selfish and unjust to Duncan, my darling," returned Mr. Lincoln, drawing her tenderly toward him, "did I detain you longer; and the tie that binds you to one I so much love and honor, will not sever mine. Take her, Duncan," he continued, with a slight quiver of the lip, as he placed her hand within that of the youth, "love her, cherish her, guard the precious boon as the apple of your eye; and may you both walk in wisdom's path, and may the lives of my two children be living epistles, known and read of all men."

The arm of Edith rested upon the neck of her father; her hand was closely clasped by Duncan.

"Guard her," he repeated warmly. "Would that I could be to her a covert from every storm, a shield from every sorrow. But my heart, my life, shall be devoted to *my* Edith; mine by her own solemn pledge, and mine, bestowed by a father's hand." Bending over her, he kissed her brow.

"The Laird requires your presence at the Bank, Duncan," Mr. Lincoln remarked; "he desired you would meet the Board in one hour."

"Expulsive power is irresistible," Duncan returned, as he gayly took his hat and hurried to join the directors, fifteen minutes after the time appointed.

The evening had almost closed, when Dr. McMillan, worn with the fatigue of the day, entered the manse. Mr. Graeme was occupying his large arm-chair, while Amy sat beside him with her knitting. Lochiel was reading aloud.

"Why, Doctor," observed the youth, "I left you so comfortably ensconced in cushions at the manor, I scarcely thought we should have had the pleasure of a visit this evening. I mistook your footstep for that of Percy, in the passage."

"I fear *my* footfall may have occasioned some disappointment," the Doctor observed, slightly glancing toward Amy.

"None could ever find a truer welcome than James McMillan, in the house of his Pastor," Mr. Graeme returned kindly, "but the heart of Lochiel is so absorbed in the departure of his friend, he has scarcely leisure to lend his father a moment. Is it not so, my son?"

"Not at all, father; but Percy told me he should see sister before our hour for retiring, and I naturally supposed it was he."

They were interrupted by the entrance of Kathleen. "Mr. Dunbar bid me ask ye, Miss Amy, if he could see you in the study for a wee time. He seems hurried, and wi' not e'en be seated."

Miss Graeme, laying aside her knitting, with a slight "Excuse me for a few moments," left the room.

"Mrs. Percy Dunbar will be a well-sounding title," said Lochiel, looking archly toward the door. "Do you not think so, father?"

"Your remark only proves the truth of my assertion, Lochiel. Certainly, in your esteem, it is the only name upon the Island."

Dr. McMillan immediately arose. "It is approaching ten," he remarked, with some excitement that he endeavored vainly to conceal, "I will not await the return of Amy. You will say good evening for me."

Shaking hands with Mr. Graeme, he immediately left the room.

Animated voices were distinctly heard in the study, which were hushed as the door opened, and a low, gentle "Farewell, dear Amy," was heard, and the youth joined the Doctor in the hall.

"I scarcely hoped to find you here, Doctor," he remarked; "but my father desired me to see you at your lodgings, and say that he had, to-day, received a letter from Gertrude, in which she entreats you will not accompany him in the morning, if interfering with your numerous engagements."

"She has a prior claim, Percy; and my visit to her is certainly at no self-sacrifice. Moreover, a few days' absence will involve no neglect of duty."

"Thank you, my dear Doctor,—and the peculiar situation in which you stand in regard to her," he added, in the lowest tone, "renders you doubly dear to us all. We never hoped to find a friend on whom we could so fully rely, and in whose bosom our sad secret would be entirely sacred."

The few last sentences did not reach the ear of Amy, as the door closed upon them while they were yet speaking.

The package left by Percy almost fell from her trembling hand. A small silver desk, of exquisite workmanship, supplied with golden implements for writing, had been placed in her charge for Edith's acceptance when the union should be formed with Duncan; and, before parting, a word was whispered pleasantly in her ear, that its counterpart was awaiting "Amy McMillan."

"What motive can actuate Percy in practising such duplicity?" she murmured. "His sister is evidently the betrothed of James McMillan. His conduct is unworthy himself, and to me far more than offensive."

With difficulty reaching her chamber, and laying aside her burden, she threw herself upon the bed, and gave way to a torrent of grief. All suspense was at an end. The almost avowed attachment for *her* had been transferred to another, and he whose character she had so revered now stood in the light of a deceiver.

In vain, pride sought to assert its place. Had she not been cast aside as a thing of naught? Would she desire to assume a position not offered her? But the warm, the ardent, the loving James McMillan of former times stood vividly before her, and his tender sympathy in time of overwhelming sorrow. And was it only sympathy, commiseration for suffering, that induced the fatal error?

Then starting from the bed, she exclaimed, "Ungrateful being! Is my brother yet alive — free — honored — and I mourning my unhappy fate?"

Falling upon her knees, she implored forgiveness,

24 *

and recollecting the family would be awaiting her for worship, with a great effort she assumed her usual calmness, and descended to the study.

Early on the following morning a messenger entered the dining-room, saying that Dr. McMillan desired to speak with Miss Graeme in the study.

"Say to him that I am particularly engaged," she returned, while a deadly paleness overspread her cheek; but none were present to witness her emotion. The servant withdrew — the hall-door closed immediately. Hearing Lochiel in the passage, fearing he would perceive her agitation, she retreated to the study.

The first thing that met her eye was a miniature of Percy Dunbar, beautifully set with pearls, appended to a finely wrought golden chain. It was intended as a surprise present for his sister on her return, and had been brought to Amy to obtain her opinion of the correctness of the likeness. It had been unintentionally left when he, in haste, joined the Doctor in the hall.

Enclosing it carefully in a small envelope, she directed Lochiel, without delay, to place it in the hands of Percy.

"Your order shall be obeyed to the letter, sister," he returned. "Thank you for the mission. I much desired an excuse to offer for an early visit at the manor, but feared intruding. I promised, after the departure of the family, to break the loneliness of Ellen by a pleasant book. Amy," he added, in a low tone, stepping back as he was about leaving the room, "there are mysterious doings at the Castle, and if report has any foundation, or actions any meaning, bridal attire will soon be needed there."

"And is Lochiel to be the favored one?" she inquired, with a forced smile.

"Only in a bright future. There is a responsive chord in the bosom of Ellen, and the Laird gives it his countenance. But, sister, I supposed formerly that *you* smiled upon our Doctor."

"And to what ancient time may your 'formerly' allude?" Miss Graeme inquired, pleasantly, though the color forsook her cheek, and her voice trembled as she spoke.

"Previous to his entire devotion to the inmates of the manor,— before time, thought,— yea, his very life was laid at the feet of Miss Gertrude. He has accompanied the Laird in every visit to his daughter, and when with Percy, supposing himself not noticed, his whole theme is 'Miss Gertrude.' Yesterday I heard him remark, 'On her return, Percy, I trust you will exert your influence with the Laird to permit me to bring Mr. Graeme to the manor. My anxiety increases daily. He remains deaf to every entreaty of mine.'

" 'There is an undefined feeling in the bosom of my father,' was the return, 'that such a step will more speedily deprive him of his treasure.'

" 'That can scarcely be, Percy; her mind is settled upon the subject; but she desires herself to have the union sealed. I was not aware, until a few days since, that Gertrude had never professed religion.' "

"They then turned to spiritual matters, incomprehensible to me, and I lost my interest in the conversation. But I trust my dear sister will not break the heart of Percy Dunbar," he added, archly, as he left the apartment, "by declining the future title of Lady Glennair."

The last remark passed unnoticed. Lochiel, unaware of the anguish he had caused, closed the door, leaving Amy to her own reflections. Until this moment there had been a lingering hope within her bosom; now that had fled; a heart-sickening realizing of the truth came over her — the bitter thought that her heart's idol must be renounced forever. Her physician — her support and comforter in every trial. Could she endure to see herself forsaken? Could she survive his union with another? The bare idea was madness. Clasping her hands upon her throbbing temples, she was conscious of nothing further until she felt the arm of her brother supporting her.

"Where am I?" she inquired, as her eye rested upon that of Duncan. "Have I been sick — ill? My mind is a perfect chaos."

"Not ill, I trust, my darling sister; but I found you here much enfeebled, and feared alarming father — therefore called none to our aid."

"Thank you, thank you, dear Duncan," she murmured, rising, as the bell rang for breakfast; and supported by her brother's arm, with trembling step reached the room. "I shall soon, very soon be better."

"The bloom must be restored to that pallid cheek,

Amy. The events of this winter have been too much for your sensitive frame. Change of scene is imperative. Does not a visit of a few weeks to Uncle Rushbrook's commend itself to your judgment?"

"I could scarcely be wanted at Thistle Hedge, Duncan. Your demands upon Edith are so urgent," she added, with a faint smile, "that her efforts to meet them single-handed would hardly be successful."

"But your health, Amy?"

"But your wishes, Duncan?"

"— Shall always succumb to the comfort of my only, my precious sister."

"Then permit me to remain quietly at my own home for the present. In six weeks I shall be called to part with you, Duncan. I must remain this short season with you."

"Part?— never! Though the same roof may not shelter us, whilst this pulse beats, Amy will not be second, even to Edith Lincoln. Nor would *she* desire it. No, no, Amy. You gain a loving, affectionate sister by our union, and the heart of Duncan Graeme will always beat in entire unison with that of his beloved sister."

"I know it, Duncan, and only rejoice in the happiness of Edith and yourself."

"Then speak not of parting, Amy; it wounds me to suppose there can any different feeling exist between my sister and myself. Mr. Davidson laughingly remarked, when in treaty with me for the house, 'I scarcely supposed the heart of Duncan

Graeme could be attuned to other than his sister
Amy. The fascinations of Miss Edith must have
exercised a magic power.'

"As you desire to remain at home, I shall have
sufficient apology to offer Laird Glennair."

"In what way am I implicated with the Laird?"
she inquired, as the color suffused her face.

"In none whatever; but he left an urgent request
last night, that, on the return of Miss Gertrude, you
and Edith would pass a few days with her."

"That was somewhat gratuitous," she replied
coldly, "as our calls have neither been received nor
reciprocated, for a length of time, by Miss Dunbar."

"Yes," returned her brother, "her habits were
quite changed for some time previous to her departure; her long walks were discontinued, and an
early ride was her principal exercise."

"Riding? With whom, Duncan?"

Her brother hesitated, — at length replied, "I was
not a little surprised myself when I saw with whom,
Amy."

"Was it with James?" she inquired, faintly.

"It was. His conduct is inexplicable. As he
was circumstanced, mere words were of little moment; but if there be not some wide misunderstanding, he is unworthy the hand of my Amy.
One who could be guilty of so dishonorable an act
must have a low standard of morality, indeed."

"There is no mistake, Duncan; and I desire that
his name should cease to be mentioned in the presence of your sister."

"Are my suspicions, then, confirmed, Amy?"

"It is possible, yea, probable, the union will take place on the return of Miss Gertrude," she replied, with a face of ashen hue.

"By whom was so passing strange information conveyed to you, Amy?"

"From Lochiel — who received the communication from his own lips."

"No! He surely did not dare speak so plainly to our brother?"

"No, — he says the matter has been quietly progressing; it was only from conversations he could not avoid overhearing, that he came to a knowledge of the state of affairs at the manor. But Duncan, the subject which I considered nearest his heart was never broached to me. May we not ascribe his attentions to other motives?"

Duncan shook his head. "His very silence in regard to Miss Dunbar is sufficient to condemn him. No, Amy, — frame no excuses; he is a dishonorable trifler with the affections of another, and has been lured by the glare of birth and fortune. Such a deed will never render him a happy man. As you propose, with us let his name be forgotten. I will never again intrude the painful subject upon you. No marvel his face is blanched, and his countenance sad and gloomy."

"Yet, Duncan, is it not a cause for thanksgiving that such a support was given us in the time of our grievous sorrow; when his kind, heartfelt sympathy smoothed our thorny road, and, it may be, prevented us sinking altogether?"

"True, Amy. When incarcerated in that gloomy

prison, from what a mountain of responsibility was
I relieved when I realized the strong earthly arm to
which I could consign my sister so confidingly.
But," he added, "the Lord has restored this arm
that can support her at all times; and this heart,
that can rejoice with her in every joy, and sympathize in every sorrow. And at the cross we can
both ask guidance, and lay all our wants."

A tear stole down her cheek, but there was no
reply, and they joined their father at the table.

CHAPTER XIII

" My heart is weary, and my spirit pants
Beneath the heat and burden of the day."

WELL," remarked Lochiel, as, toward the close of the day, he entered the study of his father, — " of all changes in this eventful world, the changes at the manor are the most wonderful. Change of purpose, change of place, change of time. The earth would surely never roll steadily did the Laird direct its course."

" And what wonders have transpired to-day, to produce such intense excitement?" inquired his brother.

" In the first place, Percy has relinquished all idea of a sea-voyage for the present, and has accompanied his father and the Doctor in their visit to the lady-love of the latter."

There was a flash in the eye of Duncan as he glanced toward his sister. Neither spoke.

Lochiel continued, — " Then their return is postponed for a week, and Ellen whispered in my ear that the Doctor proposes a trip to the Continent, in which he will be very happy to join them."

" And leave Ellen to her loneliness?" inquired Duncan.

" Not at all. She is, of course, to make one of their party. • Would that I were wealthy, Duncan.

What advantage I should derive from visiting foreign climes in such society."

" A far broader foundation than that upon which you are resting may be laid in your native soil, my son," Mr. Graeme observed.

" Why, father, do not the reports of Monsieur Alençon show some proficiency in my Greek, Latin, and French studies? Neither is my time, as you feared, frittered at the manor. Ellen and I have taken up Charles XII., in the original. Of course, the guests who will remain with her until the Laird's return will oblige us to defer it."

" And what profit may have been derived to-day from your lengthy visit?"

" Won a game of chess from Miss MacAlpin, the most notable player in Scotland, and left her not yet recovered from her chagrin at her defeat."

" Then," returned Duncan, " the most glorious deed you can recall on this eventful day, is producing a cloud upon the brow of a beautiful damsel."

" A result I did not foresee, Duncan," he returned, good-humoredly. " By the voice of the whole party it was won honorably and fairly. Six times I have seen James McMillan make the same effort with the same opponent, and fail. Sister," he inquired, turning suddenly toward her, " did n't Percy advise you of his change of purpose?"

" I received a business note this morning, in which he named it," she replied.

There was an arch smile, as he said, " He will probably have much business of the same nature to transact during his absence."

"Lochiel,— my son," said Mr. Graeme, very gravely.

The youth turned instantly.

"Progress in your studies may and will fit you for society, for visiting foreign climes, and will enable you to enjoy what otherwise would be a blank to you. But that alone will not suffice. Steadiness of purpose, and obedience to a parent's will, will render you a far happier man. You are but a youth, Lochiel; I should be very reprehensible did I permit you to guide the helm of your own destiny. Henceforth, your seat at your father's table must not be vacant without a reason previously assigned."

A dark cloud gathered upon the brow of Lochiel, foreboding a storm, unnoticed by his father, who had taken up the paper, when Duncan whispered gently,—

"Your mother's wishes, Lochiel."

A softened expression succeeded. Only murmuring, "I supposed when in such society as James McMillan, who dines there almost daily, father would be content,"— he slowly left the apartment.

Anxiously the eye of Duncan turned upon Amy; the compressed, quivering lip told the impression the last few words had made.

Days passed on; great and many were the preparations for the anticipated removal to Pleasant Slope. None studied with more interest to gratify the taste and please the fancy of Edith, than Amy; and the pleasant smile of the unselfish girl beguiled all, excepting Duncan, into the belief that her heart was light and buoyant. Anxiously he watched that cheek, daily becoming more pallid, and when secluded, as she supposed, from human view, the bitter tear told of a grief upon which no stranger might intrude.

At the solicitation of her brother, her daily ride with him was continued, but the bloom produced by the fresh mountain air faded ere they reached their home.

The week had passed, and the return of the inmates of the manor was hourly expected.

"More than ordinary preparations are being made at the castle," Lochiel remarked. "*I* presume the grand denouement will not take place until it is divulged by father's call. With due deference to the Laird's judgment and Dr. McMillan's sense of propriety, this profound mystery seems to me passing strange. *I* would hail the peal of every bell in Scotland, to celebrate my nuptials."

" 'T is time Margie had ceased talking o' the sweet bairn i' the cradle," Duncan returned pleasantly, "when he is making such strides toward manhood. Wedding-bells for our Lochiel! To use your own words, sound so 'passing strange' to our ears that we could scarcely do honor to our bridegroom."

"Well, well, Duncan, though you may be somewhat in advance of the 'sweet bairn,' yet in a few brief years your remark will not apply to the present company; neither will Miss Gertrude so facetiously inquire whether Lochiel had not better tarry at the manse, until, as a bearded youth, he could pay his respects at the manor. She has certainly, herself, not erred in that respect; the Doctor is full five years her senior. Was it his advanced age that induced your rejection, sister?"

"As my decision was never required, I, of course, never gave a verdict," she replied, plying her needle closely.

"Then you accepted Percy merely from fancy, without allusion to age?"

"On that question, either, I have not been invited to decide."

"You amaze me, sister. I was so certain of the result in that case, that I told the Doctor, when he made inquiry upon the subject, that, although you had never favored me with your confidence, I was sure Percy's attentions were not hidden under a bushel, and would at some future day be proclaimed upon the housetop."

"When you are again invited to solve the grave question, Lochiel," his sister observed, excitedly, "say that Percy never was, neither is, nor will be any other than a common friend to your sister."

"Well, well, sister," replied Lochiel, springing up and tossing his hat into the air, then catching it and placing it upon his head to leave the room, "I will never be guilty of offending father by disseminating false doctrines; opportunity and importunity may have a magical effect, even upon the stony heart of Amy Graeme."

With a "Good night, Duncan; good night, sister," he closed the door, and Amy and Duncan were left alone.

"Shall we rise with the lark, and view the sun-

25 *

rise, Amy?" he inquired, willing to divert the current of her thoughts; "we will, from the hillside, once more enjoy the prospect together. We will test the mettle, also, of Mr. Lincoln's gift, and see what comparison he bears to my Raven."

There was a careless assent, as though the thoughts were far away, and they separated for the night.

The heavy mist upon the mountain on the following morning gave no promise of a glorious view; but Duncan, hoping at least to beguile the depression of his sister, knocked at her door, to say that Raven and her pony were impatiently awaiting them. But the listless eye and fevered cheek alarmed him.

"Are you unwell, Amy?" he inquired.

"No, Duncan, not at all," she returned, pleasantly; "not sleeping particularly well last night, I feel languid, and require just what you have prescribed for me. How does my milk-white contrast with Raven?".

"Beautifully. They remind me of tiny Fawn tripping in the garden beside her uncle. Raven bends his neck and waves his tail, as though he felt she really needed his protection."

Amy, with gentle care, was placed upon little Blanche by Duncan. In a low voice, his sister inquired, "Was there not a note awaiting father this morning?"

"I saw several upon the table," he replied, evasively. "Shall we take the direction toward the cottage of widow Milln, Amy? I have a little package to deliver from Mr. Lincoln. His charities are as extended as ever."

The flush was brighter upon Amy's cheek as she murmured, "Then they have arrived." Her head sank for a moment, but recovering herself, she made a passing remark upon the mistiness of the morning, and slowly followed her brother along the mountain path.

"Miserable poltroon," thought Duncan; "would that I could blot his unworthy name from her remembrance forever."

They had reached the cottage, and, throwing her the reins, saying he would return in a few moments, he disappeared.

In vain was the head of Raven laid upon the shoulder of his young mistress, in the hope of obtaining some notice; her head had fallen upon her hand, and all surrounding objects were for the present excluded.

She was startled by a well-known voice. It was Percy. By a great effort, she succeeded in recovering her composure.

"This is an unexpected gratification, Amy. I did not anticipate meeting you at this early hour."

The hand of Miss Graeme rested but a moment within the one so kindly extended; her rein was immediately resumed as she coldly observed, "Lochiel did not report your return last evening. Was he aware of it?"

"It was past eleven ere we reached our home," he returned, while a deep shadow crossed his brow. "Amy," he continued, "we must soon resign our darling sister. We can no longer withhold the truth. It has been my father's earnest desire that no report should reach the ear of the community, and the domestics were bound, by promise, to reveal nothing. I always felt it was a mistaken step in father; but you know, with us, his wishes have always been respected. The entire devotion of the Doctor has won every heart; and in him we can place, and have placed, entire confidence; but the thought of the desolation of the house, bereft of Gertrude, wrings my father's heart; his grief is wild, unrestrained — yea, I fear rebellious."

"Could not other less painful arrangements be devised, that would not bring a blight upon the inmates of the Manor?" she inquired, very coldly.

The question was unnoticed; the head of Percy was bent low beside her, while his hand entwined itself through the mane of her palfrey.

At this moment a horseman issued from the forest skirting the road. An intent and earnest gaze was fixed upon them for an instant, then crossing the path, he disappeared around the foot of the mountain. Dr. McMillan (for he it was) was on his road to the Castle of Glennair.

The whole movement was silently witnessed by Miss Graeme. Taking a small piece of paper, she wrote upon it: "Allow me to request that the desk, similar to that for Edith, may, at the close of this day, be placed in the hand of Mrs. James McMillan."

With a lofty bearing, foreign to the character of Amy Graeme, she gave it him, saying, "It is my desire this paper may not be read until Miss Gertrude Dunbar no longer bears that title."

There was a surprised and wounded expression upon the countenance of the youth as he hesitatingly received it.

"Your sympathy would have been a cordial to my soul, Amy," he said, mournfully, as he merely touched his hat on leaving her; "for withholding it, you, of course, must have good reasons."

There was no reply, and the youth slowly and silently withdrew.

"What has happened? Who has molested you, Amy?" inquired Duncan, who at that moment joined her. "If anything has occurred to give you uneasiness, I shall ever regret having left you."

"It was nothing, Duncan—nothing new. I have been slightly excited, and felt somewhat uncomfortable. Percy was here—spoke freely, frankly, on the subject still so painful to me."

"Shall we secure our horses, and ascend the mountain, Amy?"

His sister shook her head. "Take me home, Duncan; the keen air does not brace me this morning. I am sick—I fear ill; take me home, brother."

A slight glance at that cheek alarmed Duncan, and, without further remark, he turned with her toward their home. With the assistance of his arm, Amy with difficulty ascended the stairway, and entered her chamber.

"Leave me now, Duncan," she said; "my pillow, I trust, will soothe my aching head, and I shall, in the course of an hour, rejoin you and father in the dining-room. Do not name my indisposition to him."

"Promise me you will attempt no further exertion," he said, as he felt her throbbing pulse.

"But father?"

"Leave that all to me; he shall not be unnecessarily alarmed."

A very short time had elapsed ere Kathleen appeared, bearing a small tray, on which she had nicely arranged a few delicacies, to tempt the palate of her young mistress.

"Maister Graeme will be here presently, Miss Amy," she said; "he is keen for ye seein' the Doctor right awa', and tauld Maister Lochiel tae gang at once and bring him tae ye."

"Is Duncan there, Kathleen?" Miss Graeme inquired, anxiously.

"Here he is tae answer for himsel', Miss Amy," she replied, as Mr. Graeme and Duncan entered.

"I fear Duncan was unwise in exposing you on this chilly, misty morning, daughter," the former remarked, as he bent over her and kissed her forehead. "I am confident James will approve the use of the lancet where the pulse beats so heavily."

"Do not, do not, dear father, permit him to be called," she returned, with an imploring look toward Duncan. "Rest is all that I require;—promise me, dear father."

"Lochiel awaited not a second bidding, daughter; he was out of sight ere your brother could recall him."

The head of Amy was instantly buried in the pillow.

"I have sent a messenger for him," Duncan whispered.

"Will, oh! will he overtake him!"

"Why so unwilling to have medical aid, Amy, daughter?"

Amy made no reply, but the trembling hand showed her anxiety.

The step of Lochiel was heard on the stairway. The next moment the door opened.

"A wild-goose chase, truly," he remarked, as he threw himself beside his sister. "Off to the manor, I suppose before daylight, or at peep of dawn, for which he had doubtless been awaiting anxiously. Bernard had been ordered to drive home, and announce his intention of breakfasting with the Laird; then who should meet me on my return but Allan, with countermanding orders from 'Maister Duncan.'"

"Your voice scarcely accords with your sister's pain, Lochiel," his father observed, while in the corner of the room he prepared a simple remedy for her.

"And I marvel that Lochiel's constant theme does not become wearisome, even to himself," returned Duncan.

"It was consistent with my mission, Duncan," he replied, half rising, and speaking in the lowest tone, "as it is my duty to account for not fulfilling it. I was unable to obtain the Doctor to administer to the physical wants of sister, as I presume the darts of Cupid have driven him to pay homage at the feet of his lady love. Doubtless when she is bone of his bone, and flesh of his flesh, there will be a spare moment for objects of less interest."

The head of Miss Graeme fell wearily upon her pillow, from which she had arisen to receive some refreshment, and the color that overspread her cheek showed some mental as well as feverish excitement.

"Have I wearied you, dear Amy?" inquired Lochiel, laying his cheek closely beside that of his sister. "It was thoughtless—very thoughtless."

"Leave me, Lochiel," she said, faintly; "my head aches intensely; I require not medical aid, but entire repose."

"And may I not remain quietly beside you? Duncan goes to the Bank, and father—let me see—father, at what hour do you go to the manor?"

"Not until eleven; but there is a prayer-meeting at the Kirk before that time."

"Will the carriage of the Laird be sent?"

"Of course, my son. But is this the quietness you yourself proposed, and your sister so much needs?"

Duncan beckoned Lochiel from the room.

"I am not absolutely needed at the Bank this morning, Lochiel. Will you say to Mr. MacAlpin that I am detained at home, unexpectedly? Do not mention sickness; and, if you desire to see Amy better, do not again enter her chamber. Your efforts to refrain your speech will be, as heretofore, unavailing."

Lochiel laughed, and promising future amendment, went to fulfil the request of his brother. Mr. Graeme, whose fears in regard to Amy were set at rest by Duncan, withdrew to his study, and Duncan returned to his sister's apartment.

"Was the purpose for which father's presence was required mentioned in the note?" Amy asked when they were alone.

"No; it merely stated that at ten the carriage would be here to convey him to the manor, if convenient to father. The messenger waited this morning until his signal — the little bell — sounded to obtain an answer."

There was a strong effort to conceal her agitation. Her brother, taking his Bible, sat silently beside her. For hours the stillness remained unbroken, save by the gentle footfall of Mr. Graeme, Kathleen, or Margey.

The hour of ten had arrived. The ponderous wheels of a heavy carriage were heard rolling toward the manse. It stopped; as the step fell noisily, Miss · Graeme tremblingly inquired, "Have you any suspicion that father will request medical advice for me, Duncan? I fear I could scarcely survive an interview. I long for their departure. I shall then not dread collision. I saw him this morning, Duncan."

"When, Amy? — where? — under what circumstances?"

"It was but for a moment, when Percy was with me. His face was pale, ashy-pale, and, strange to say, his countenance bore rather an air of upbraiding than any compunction. He is an enigma altogether, but his whole demeanor, as, without any recognition of either, he turned his horse suddenly from us, is impressed so vividly that I cannot obliterate it. That look, that reproachful look. It seemed to say,

26

'Why have you so deeply injured me?' What could it mean, Duncan?"

"He is a riddle I cannot solve, Amy. Would that he had never entered this dwelling. Lochiel is hurt, evidently, that he should be excluded from confidence to-day. He told me that if I had any orders for him, he was at perfect leisure after college hours, as he should not, of course, intrude upon the inmates of the manor whilst their mysterious rites were performing."

"The bells will probably be our first informants, unless father should return immediately. But you must see Edith, Duncan; mention merely a violent headache detaining me from her. I will endeavor to obtain some sleep that I may be fitted to receive her this evening."

"Can you not let your mind rest upon our signal mercies, Amy? We had tidings of the family of the unhappy President last evening. I neglected mentioning it. Percy received a letter from a clergyman, speaking of an interesting event which occurred on board the vessel in which he took passage as a missionary to Australia. Meeting with some accident, they put into a neighboring port to repair, from whence he wrote. He mentioned, with much interest, the devotion of a young man — a fellow-passenger — to his sister, the most beautiful young lady his eyes had ever beheld, though attenuated to a shadow. Daily he carried her on deck to obtain fresh air, supporting her in a large arm-chair. The few words the minister caught, breathed of heaven and heavenly things. He ventured to address her upon the foundation of her hope.

"'In this little book,' she returned, with the sweetest smile, pointing to a small text-book held by her brother, 'I have learned of Jesus, the sinner's friend. Can you tell me more of Him?' she inquired, as her large blue eyes rested earnestly upon him.

"'I spoke gently, and at intervals,' he said, 'as her strength would permit, of the love of Jesus, of His agony in the garden, of His death upon the cross, of His resurrection, of His mediation at the right hand of God, for all who call upon His name.'

"'Upon her brother's bosom she wept.

"'When I ceased speaking, she asked me to intercede for her with that Redeemer.

"'I commended her to His care, and plead with Jesus that she might be a lamb of His fold. Her fervent 'amen,' touched our hearts; her brother was deeply affected.

"'It was our only interview. In a few days I was called to perform the last rites, as we consigned her body to the deep. Her brother, whom I noticed she addressed as MacIntosh, was her only relative present. Her parents remained below, but their piteous moans told the intensity of their grief.

"'The name entered upon the books was Gordon. You may perhaps have a knowledge of them.'

"Will not a comparison lessen the weight of our present burdens, Amy?" inquired Duncan, fondly kissing her cheek.

"I desire to have a grateful spirit for my unnumbered blessings," returned his sister; "the Spirit is willing, but the flesh is weak, Duncan. It shall be my aim, in future, to lighten father's weight of cares, and find happiness in ministering to other's wants."

" *Your* happiness always was reflected, Amy," returned Duncan, affectionately ; " when did you seek your own, rather than another's wealth ? "

The morning passed, the dinner-hour arrived. Duncan and Lochiel, vainly awaiting their father's return, partook of the meal alone. Day closed in ; darkness gathered around them. Duncan had left home on some important business, and Lochiel, feeling somewhat anxious, acceded to the proposal of Edith, who was sitting with her friend, to dispatch Allan to the manor to learn the cause of his detention, and hastened to Thistle Hedge to ask the consent of Mr. Lincoln. Scarcely had he left the house before the ponderous wheels of the carriage were heard approaching. Edith sprang to the window ; Mr. Graeme alighted.

" Dr. McMillan is with him," she observed, " but he has driven on to Thistle Hedge. Helen is quite unwell, and father desired Mr. Graeme to mention, that if he could not conveniently see her, he would ask Dr. Gordon to prescribe."

Amy was silent ; there was a quickly drawn breath. It was unobserved by her friends. The next moment Mr. Graeme stood beside them.

" What has happened, dear father ? " Amy inquired, as she noticed the sadness of his countenance.

" A most unexpected event has transpired this day at the manor, my darling daughter. I have been exceedingly anxious about you, but my detention was unavoidable."

Kathleen opened the door to say that tea was waiting Maister Graeme.

As he arose, a hand was laid upon the head of Edith and Amy. "How rich a treasure I possess in these precious boons. How willingly would Glennair's Laird have parted with his broad lands to retain his child."

"It is of almost universal occurrence in every family," observed Miss Lincoln; "his case is not a peculiar one."

"Certainly not; man is born to trouble as the sparks fly upward; but Lord Glennair is a nervously sensitive, warm, tender-hearted, idolizing father, and has not placed his hopes, his trust, his heart, where alone he will find consolation. Yet he clung to me as a tendril to an oak; besought my sympathy, my prayers, and plead with me to remain and be his solace in his extremity."

"I will return home for a few moments and hear the Doctor's opinion of Helen. Will you not recount to us all the troubles of the manor when I return, Mr. Graeme? There must be something we have not anticipated. Amy, have you not an interest in hearing the detail? The Laird was evidently partial to the Doctor." Mr. Graeme left the room.

"His conduct is incomprehensible. It is unworthy a man of sense such as Lord Glennair," she added, as she threw her shawl around her and left the room.

Dr. McMillan, when she entered, was in earnest conversation with her father. He immediately arose to receive her. Should she offer him her congratulations? No,—she would not—could not; it was impossible.

"How is Helen, Doctor?" she inquired.

"Better, much better. A mother's solicitude," he added, smiling, "renders Mrs. Cameron almost too watchful over her little daughter."

"Perhaps so; and her cousin walks too closely in her mother's footsteps. But you will excuse me, Doctor; I will see little Helen for a moment; I have then promised to return to the manse."

"And Amy?" inquired the Doctor, hesitatingly.

—"Is better,—decidedly better. Her physical strength has been too heavily taxed of late. She requires rest,—absolute rest, rather than medical aid."

"So I should judge," he returned, as a cloud gathered on his brow; "as Mr. Graeme did not invite me to prescribe, delicacy, of course, prevented any proffer of my services."

"We all supposed *you* would leave us immediately, and it required some consideration to consult a comparative stranger."

"I was not aware I had confided to any my intention of settling in the capital; but so unceremonious a leave-taking of my friends at Thistle Hedge, you must have considered rather a curious proceeding. This sickness of Miss Dunbar alone has detained me this long; her death now frees me from every obligation."

"Her death!" exclaimed Mr. and Miss Lincoln at the same moment.

"We supposed for the last six months," observed

the latter, "that the occasion of your devotion at the manor was of a far different nature."

"Of what possible nature?" he remarked, with surprised inquiry.

"Not a doubt ever suggested itself to our minds that Miss Gertrude was the affianced of James Mc-Millan, and that to-day their destinies were to be united."

The eye of Dr. McMillan flashed. "Then why was the hand of friendship still extended me by those of this dwelling?" he inquired. "Was such a craven fitted to be the companion of any actuated only by a sense of honor? True, there had been no promise asked or given, but were not my attentions fully understood and silently encouraged by Miss Graeme? For whom did I inquire in my daily visits, and with whom was almost every leisure moment passed? No, no," he continued, sadly; "until cast aside as a thing of nought, by her who was, and is, my life's —" he paused. "I desire only to bury in oblivion all that she has ever been to me. May she be happy as the chosen one of Percy — the future mistress of Glennair."

There was a tight clasp of the hand by Mr. Lincoln.

"Most thankful am I," he said, "that James Mc-Millan has brought no dishonor upon his fair name. Let me disabuse your mind, also, in regard to Amy. The hand of Percy has never been received, nor proffered! I have it from the lips of Duncan."

"And why was my name almost blasted, Mr. Lincoln? Why was not inquiry made as to my real position?"

"The feminine delicacy of Amy, and the proud spirit of Duncan, forbade it."

"And has she indeed viewed me in the light of a trifler? I have in vain sought an interview with Amy. Her cold denial only confirmed the testimony of Lochiel. But is she indeed free? — and may I hope — "

His voice denied him further utterance. He grasped more closely the hand of Mr. Lincoln.

"You must plead your own cause, my friend," he returned, pleasantly. "In the midst of so strange a succession of events, I scarcely realize my own identity. Do not oblige me, therefore, to answer for another. Why was the sickness of Gertrude shrouded in such mystery?"

"Owing to the Laird's peculiar temperament, and his idolatry, — his perfect idolatry of Gertrude. In the manor, you know, all his domestics are bound by the closest of all ties, — that of affection, — and his slightest wish is to them a law. It was his earnest desire that no report of her illness should go forth. Percy was much opposed to the secrecy; but his objections were overruled by the fallacious arguments of the old gentlemen. Such was his dread of its being even whispered, that it rendered him perfectly miserable. The secret has been kept at an immense amount of self-sacrifice, — conversing pleasantly, — yea, even gayly with his friends, while his heart was bleeding. It was sad, indeed, to see the strong man bowed, when none were with him but Percy and myself. At the manor, I was obliged to remain continually, as the Laird was never satis-

fied unless I were within his call. In regard to my
practice, as soon as I should be freed from my duty
at the Castle, I resolved to place it in the charge of
Dr. Gordon, and leave forever my home, and all my
early associations, and retire to where I might have
no reminder of my loss. "I must see Amy at once.
Edith, I will accompany you."

"But the Laird's carriage is still waiting for you,
James," said Mr. Lincoln.

"We will ride to Mr. Graeme's, and then dismiss
it. I have promised to remain the night with the
Laird, but I will defer my visit until a later hour.
Suspense is intolerable; there must be mutual explanation. I cannot, will not, should not delay it a
moment longer. I must know whether—"

The veins were swollen almost to bursting. His
voice quivered as he spoke.

"James, James," said Mr. Lincoln, "you are in
no frame to visit Amy. Your excitement might
produce evil consequences. The pallor of her cheek
has long told me she is not indifferent to you. Let
Allan dismiss the carriage; do you walk slowly
with Edith to the manse, that the balmy air of this
evening may allay your feverish impatience. Be
guided, young man, by one more versed in life's
sober realities. Make a calm, dispassionate state-
ment to Amy, who at present feels, no doubt, sorely
aggrieved. All will be well, dear youth; and may
God smile upon your future prospects."

There was a heartfelt "Thank you," as Mr. Lincoln shook his hand at parting, and he proceeded
silently with Miss Lincoln to the manse.

"Dr. McMillan sought Mr. Graeme in the dining-room; Edith went to her friend's chamber. Amy had risen, and was reclining in an arm-chair.

"Did Duncan see you from Thistle Hedge, Edith?" she inquired; "I supposed he was engaged for the evening."

"He told me, Amy, he would not return until ten o'clock."

"Then who came in with you? I certainly heard a familiar footstep."

"Dr. McMillan is with Mr. Graeme."

"Not James!" she exclaimed, as her face crimsoned with excitement; "I cannot see him, Edith. Frame what excuse you will, I cannot see him."

"At Thistle Hedge he announced the tidings of the death of Gertrude Dunbar, Amy."

"Death! So immediately after the nuptials? And he with us to-night? How strange,—how passing strange."

"No, Amy, no—" There was a gentle tap at the door. Dr. McMillan entered. Miss Lincoln immediately withdrew.

There was a cold recognition on the part of Miss Graeme, as he seated himself closely beside her, and laid his hand gently upon her own. Her eye was raised for a moment, then sought the floor.

"Why have I been so lightly esteemed, dear Amy?" he inquired, "that a breath, an idle tale, should drive me from you?"

"In none did I place more confidence," she returned, coldly, "until—"

"Until," he interrupted, "I proved myself no

longer worthy of that confidence. Until my base
conduct rendered me unworthy of the friendship of
Amy Graeme. Until this hand, proffered to Miss
Dunbar, rendered me, in your estimation, a paltry,
miserable trifler. Was it not so, Amy?"

"The hand of Dr. McMillan might be proffered
to whom he would, she replied, haughtily, "if he
were bound by no tie to another. *I* am not aware
of any such restriction."

"And if a sense of honor had not restrained me,
why should I have rendered myself the most miserable of men?—why voluntarily have relinquished
what has been the beau ideal of my life? The first,
the last, the only being in existence, who has it in
her power to render my life's pathway bright and
joyous, is yourself. My time, my skill, have been
most willingly spent in endeavoring to rescue that
young, that lovely flower from the grave; but my
heart has been filled with distress, and my days and
nights passed in wretched sorrow, that Amy Graeme
could have permitted me to hope, have smiled upon
my efforts to win her affections, and then cast a
cloud over my path forever, by her acceptance of
the hand of Percy."

"Never!" she exclaimed; "never!" as the tears
fell rapidly down her cheek.

"I know it; I know it all, dear Amy," he returned, gently; "my mind has been fully disabused.
Within this hour, I have obtained permission of
Mr. Graeme to ask a boon, that, if granted, will
dissipate every cloud, and render me the happiest
of men. May I hope to call you mine, Amy?" he
inquired, as he bent anxiously over her.

A faint smile played over her pallid face. Her head slightly bowed.

Her hand was raised, and clasped warmly.

"One hour since," he continued, "I was on the eve of forsaking home, fleeing from self, seeking, — alas! how vainly, — forgetfulness of the past in new scenes, while my heart remained buried with you, my own, my precious Amy. Now, how changed, — my path is indeed cloudless. But your fluttering pulse needs rest, Amy, and I can scarcely be wanted longer at the manor. I will prescribe a trifling opiate, which I will leave with Mr. Graeme in the study. But the physician invariably anticipates a fee," he added, smiling archly; "shall it be withheld in this instance?"

There was a very bright smile as the deep color suffused her face, but whether the fee was obtained, I will leave my readers to determine.

CHAPTER XIV

"So he stood in his integrity,
Just and firm of purpose,
Aiding many, fearing none,
A spectacle to angels and to men."

BRIGHT, indeed, shone the sun on the succeeding morning, as Amy with a light and gladsome spirit, opened wide her casement to invite its beams, and sweet was the carol of the little birds, as from the hand of their young mistress they pecked the crumbs she offered ; and as the rich and melodious notes of Duncan, in the adjoining chamber, singing a favorite air, fell upon her ear, she raised a tearful eye and grateful heart to the Author of every good and perfect gift.

Seating herself with her Bible in her hand, she was interrupted by a gentle tap, and a pleasant inquiry from Duncan whether he might come in.

"I could scarcely await the morning, dear Amy, to meet you," he said, clasping her warmly to his bosom. "Mr. Lincoln told me all ; and father sympathized deeply with the happiness of James, when, on leaving you last evening, he joined him in the study. He said that he sealed with his full consent his fondest wishes."

The face of Amy was hidden ; the tears upon her

27   313

cheek told not of sorrow, but a heart overflowing
with happy feeling.

" The transition is so sudden," she at length remarked, " that the revulsion is almost painful. Such
a tide of unexpected happiness unnerves me."

" The reality," returned her brother, " is more
wonderful than the vagaries of a disordered imagination. Through the past year, our fortunes have
been indeed varied. All is now sunshine, Amy; I
trust no cloud will intervene to mar our prospect.
The Lord reigns; He will always bring good out of
evil. If misfortune had not beset our path, we
should not have nestled so closely to the cross."

" Are not afflictions always sanctified to the believing heart, Duncan? I trust we have that evidence of being the children of the covenant."

" Doubt it not, Amy; though sinning daily,
hourly, yea, at every moment ready to mourn some
sad defection, yet I know that my Redeemer liveth,
and that in my flesh I shall see God."

" *My* assurance has been clouded of late, Duncan.
I feared my good estate was not firmly founded."

" Distrust not your Redeemer's word, dear Amy.
' He that cometh to me I will in no wise cast out.'
Go to Him; cling to His cross; look away from self;
rely upon His precious promises, and trust Him for
time and eternity. *Your* home is prepared in that
abode which He died to secure you. Wound Him not
by doubting for a moment your safety. But there
is the bell. Father is no doubt awaiting us impatiently in the breakfast-room."

A very bright smile was returned for the warm

kiss of Amy, as she bade her father "good morning."

"And did the anodyne have the desired effect? or had other causes a magic charm to produce so bright a glow this morning?" he inquired.

"The anodyne stilled my nerves, father," she replied, as the color deepened, "and I slept very calmly."

"And may life's pathway be calm and peaceful, daughter," he returned, as he laid his hand affectionately upon her head, "and may you be gently led on the heavenward road, where all is perfect peace, and may your mind ever be stayed on the Almighty arm. None can better point the way than he whom Providence has allotted as your protector. James is all I could desire, in every point of view; and it is in my Amy's power still to be the life, the stay of her father's home. James has promised never to separate her from those dependent upon her for many comforts."

"And on no other terms would I ever consent to his wishes, dear father," she returned; "and nothing but death will ever separate Amy Graeme from her dear, her only parent."

And I trust, daughter, I will always keep in view the hand which has bestowed so inestimable a gift, and be resigned to His holy will, should He see fit to remove my treasure. But," he added, "while we are living under a cloudless heaven, let us not overlook the command to 'mourn with those who mourn.' The poor Laird now demands our sympathy, our kindest attention. Mr. Lincoln, at early dawn, ordered his carriage made ready, and, with

Lochiel, has gone to offer his sympathy to his friend."

"And Lochiel came to my door, father," interrupted Duncan, "to say that the Laird required his services when freed from college duties; he would therefore remain for a few days at the Manor."

"And I have promised again to see him after attending to some parochial duties this morning. I long to impart consolation to his crushed spirit. He is stricken to the earth, realizing not the hand that has so sorely bruised him. With one having so high a moral sense as Lord Glennair, (like him who touched the heart of the Redeemer, yet left him sorrowing, unwilling to fulfil His one command,) it is difficult to minister comfort; but I trust he will be led to see mercy even in this severe dispensation,— which may be instrumental in his own sanctification."

The heart of Amy bounded, as a familiar footfall met her ear. Dr. McMillan entered. The chastened expression of his countenance showed the impression left by the sad scenes in which he had, of late, been so prominent an actor; but his face lighted with pleasure as his eye met that of Amy—which told only of sympathy for the sorrows of others; and his heart was now gladdened by her welcome, the benignant smile of Mr. Graeme, and the cordial greeting of Duncan.

"Do you feel equal to a short drive, Amy?" he inquired, "my carriage is in waiting, and I have an hour at your service. Mr. MacAlpin has purchased a house among the mountains, five miles from this. We will take a survey, and, if satisfactory, I will convey your opinion to sister on our return."

A ready assent was given, and Amy, when equipped, was placed with care in the wagon, by the Doctor, who dismissed Bernard to Thistle Hedge, to render any assistance in his power until his return.

"What magic charm has not that little assent of last evening wrought, Amy," he whispered, as he seated himself beside her; "could you have imagined my days and nights of anguish while sitting beside the couch of the dear sufferer at the Manor, you would then realize the happiness, the—truly, my lot is cast in pleasant places. Must I await the rising and setting of many suns, Amy, ere I may call you mine?"

"In six weeks, Duncan removes to Pleasant Slope," she replied.

"Then permit Duncan to be my first groomsman previously," he interrupted, with an arch smile.

The eye of Amy fell as she falteringly replied, "It cannot be, James; it is impossible."

"And why impossible?" he inquired, playfully taking her hand. "Mr. Graeme has promised me shelter;—will you be less hospitable? Would that I could see that pallid cheek always so deeply tinted as now. Well, we will for the present (but remember, only for the present) dismiss the subject, and pass an opinion on the rural cottage before us."

The beautiful mansion was duly examined and admired.

"I have promised sister a month of our society each summer, Amy. It is due. A sister, in every sense, she has been, and is to me. Impatient to have her sympathy, I saw her ere she arose this

27 *

morning. She now rejoices with me, even as she has, in some bitterness of spirit, I fear, mourned with me. She reflected upon you sorely, Amy."

"I observed her changed manner, and could not divine the cause."

The conversation was interrupted as they arrived at the door of the manse, and Mr. Graeme appeared, to assist Amy in alighting. There was a silent thanksgiving offered as he noticed the bright and happy face of his daughter, and a silent prayer for him to whom he had resigned his treasure.

After many precautions given Amy, the Doctor set forth to pursue a round of duties, rather distasteful at the present moment; and toward evening, after dining with the afflicted inmates of the Manor, returned to his desired haven, to enjoy with Amy the few hours he could call his own.

"There has been some misunderstanding on the part of Percy, Amy," the Doctor remarked, as they sat together in the study; "he evidently is sorely grieved at receiving coldness, rather than sympathy, from you. I much fear," he added, sadly, "his heart is centred in Amy Graeme."

"The charms of Amy Graeme," she returned, pleasantly, "if they have forced others to bow to their supremacy, have certainly had no effect upon the heart of Percy; but I fully comprehend his meaning: there was mutual misunderstanding, and I will at once, by a kind note, disabuse his mind of the idea that sincere sympathy is lacking on my part."

The note was written, and the Doctor deputed to

be the bearer, with any further explanation he
deemed advisable.

Some days had passed, and the hour, that dreaded
hour, had arrived, in which the first-born of the
Laird was to be conveyed to the silent tomb. Many
sad hearts were there, to pay respect to the memory
of the departed. Many social ties were broken, and
many mourned the loss of a kind benefactress; but
by this afflictive dispensation the heart of the Laird
was led to higher aspirations, and bowing submis-
sively to the chastening rod, he was enabled to say,
"Though He slay me, yet will I trust in Him."

On the day succeeding the burial, Lochiel left the
Manor, and on the following morning, at the door
of the manse, met his sister returning from her ride,
accompanied by her brother and Doctor McMillan.
After assisting Amy to dismount, he followed Duncan, who was leading Raven to the stable. So soon
as they were alone, he drew his brother's attention
by suddenly dropping the rein of Blanche, exclaiming, " Do, in pity, Duncan, explain to me the new
witchcraft that has taken possession of sister and
Doctor McMillan!"

"Any maze regarding either can readily be cleared
away, my dear brother," replied Duncan, calmly.
"What is the trouble?"

"Why, Duncan, when the Doctor left us last
evening, he kissed sister as if he had our birthright."

Duncan laughed outright; Lochiel colored indig-
nantly, and resumed: "Surely, Duncan, you, with
all of us, are fully aware of the claim of Percy Dunbar; you certainly believe Amy is affianced to him?"

"I *know*, certainly, to the contrary, Lochiel. I know Amy never accepted addresses that were never proffered, nor even thought of."

"You amaze me, Duncan: then why was sister, and sister only, inquired for so constantly by Percy?"

"That may have reasonably occurred, as Amy was *confidante* in some affair of his,—neither of her own or of Cupid's. It is my brother's habit to rush at a conclusion: a single query would have satisfactorily solved the seeming mystery."

"Admitting this a possibility, Duncan," resumed the lad, in a hushed voice, and hesitatingly, "Gertrude Dunbar is scarcely consigned to the tomb, and you will not tell me there was no betrothal there?"

"With the same confidence, my mistaken brother. The almost exclusive attentions, and constant visits of our Doctor, were earnestly entreated by the Laird; his abhorrence to the publicity of his daughter's failing strength induced this requirement, and also his secrecy: from the implicit adherence of the Doctor to all these injunctions, originated the report which others than yourself credited. James has explained all so satisfactorily, that father has consented cordially to receive him as a third son at as early a period as Amy Graeme chooses to name."

Lochiel silently led Blanche into the stable, smoothed her down, and joined his brother again.

"Any objection, Lochiel, to the increase of the brotherhood?" Duncan asked pleasantly, as they were nearing the house.

"There could be none to James McMillan, in any situation, Duncan; but to fling away all my speculations, and overthrow all my expectations, will require time and reflection."

"The Doctor is coming,—be careful how you express yourself to *him;* go forward and offer your hand and congratulations, Lochiel."

"From the sudden cessation of conversation," the Doctor remarked, taking the extended hand of the younger Graeme, "I conclude I have been the subject. Surprise still is uppermost in the mind of Lochiel. I trust the happiest man in Glennair has created no contrary feeling,—no disappointment?" He regarded Lochiel earnestly.

"Oh! no, no!" exclaimed the warm-hearted youth, "it is just as I could have wished it; but 'Who is it?' has been so often the question in our Parish, I am perfectly bewildered." Grasping the hand of the Doctor, and throwing his sister's riding-whip to his brother, he rushed into the house.

"Such excitability will destroy that frail form;—what could have induced it in this instance?" inquired the Doctor.

"He was among the misled by your constant visits at the Manor; and your position in our family could not remain undiscovered, after the manner of your parting with our sister last evening: that led to his inquiries, and the dénouement. He is still suffering from the bewilderment caused by learning that Percy and Amy had not formed a contract for life, which he implicitly believed. To reason with Lochiel will be unavailing; he will become calm in a little while, if left to himself."

"Lochiel, with a noble intellect, and a warm,

affectionate heart," returned the Doctor, " has always been the slave of an unfettered will of late, influenced, in a measure, by his devotion to a wayward girl. I feared the helm would scarcely guide to a propitious haven; but since this sore trial has mellowed Ellen's temper, and brought her, with a meek and chastened spirit, to the foot of the cross, I doubt not it will tell upon the character of Lochiel for time, and when time shall be no longer."

" I have always marvelled, Doctor, that a fetter could be drawn so firmly by one so inferior to our boy."

The Doctor smiled. " It is a chain whose links often bind closely ere reason is consulted," he replied; " but the appreciation of Lord Glennair is much increased in consequence of the excellent taste he has shown in his selection; and the sincere sympathy of Lochiel, in this trying season, has so won the heart of the Laird, that he is resolved, if he obtain the consent of Mr. Graeme, that he shall share with Percy and Ellen the advantages of visiting foreign parts. He intends broaching the subject to-day when Mr. Graeme pays his customary visit."

"And the Laird has fully determined to accompany Percy ? "

" He is not willing to retain Percy at home, and cannot endure the thought of separation."

For a moment there was a troubled expression upon the brow of young Graeme, then, as though a sudden thought had arrested him, his countenance brightened. " I will see the Laird with father," he remarked. " Under such auspices the advantages would be incalculable. Lochiel must avail himself of them."

There was an arch, meaning expression upon the face of the Doctor as he called, on mounting his horse, "The Graeme spirit, Duncan." There was no reply; and waving his hand pleasantly, he rode away.

On the same evening, young Graeme accompanied his father to the Manor.

"Your daily kindness is a balm to my wounded spirit, my dear Pastor," the Laird remarked, as he warmly pressed his hand; "and my poor son cannot too highly commend the attentions of his most beloved friend, Duncan Graeme; but I have yet another favor to ask at your hands. Lochiel, of late, has been to me as one of my own family, and I desire that he, as my guest, may accompany us to the Continent. Mr. Turnbull, as private tutor, will be with us, and no loss in regard to his regular routine of education shall accrue."

"Your kind wish was mentioned to Duncan, Laird; his object in accompanying me this morning was to have some conversation with you upon the subject."

"Pardon this seeming intrusion, Laird," said Duncan, "when my father alone was addressed;—but if such advantageous arrangements can be made for Lochiel, the responsibility and trouble he will cost you will be more than he can ever possibly repay: will you not, therefore, permit me to defray all personal expenses?"

"So spoke the grandson of Campbell Dunwiddie!"

he exclaimed — " that maternal grandsire, loved by all, respected by all, and whose only failing was an intense desire to bestow, rather than to receive. But, Duncan Graeme, as I am already under the deepest obligation to your house for your unwearied attentions, I must be gratified in this instance. Lochiel goes as my guest."

"We duly appreciate your kindness, Laird," returned Mr. Graeme, " and do most sincerely thank you; but the expenses of Duncan have been light for some previous years, and he has reserved from his salary a sum sufficient for this purpose. Will you not allow him the gratification? His heart is set upon it."

Lord Glennair hesitated. "I am fully aware, my boy," he remarked, laying his hand kindly on his arm, " that an urged favor is no favor; therefore, let the matter rest as you would have it; it is of trivial importance, and scarcely worthy a contest; but to my dear Pastor," he added, turning to him, " *my* obligation will never cease. No, when time shall be no longer with me; when this heart and voice shall join in rapturous strain to praise redeeming love, I will still bless the hand that, in my sore bereavement, pointed to a Friend that sticketh closer than a brother; to a Physician able to bind up the broken in spirit; to a Redeemer able to save to the uttermost; and led me to the foot of the cross, from which nothing can ever separate me. Yes, I bless affliction, that it has led me to know myself,—to know my God, — my —" Overcome by his emotion, he wept.

With instinctive delicacy, Duncan silently withdrew from the apartment.

The eye of Lochiel beamed with pleasure and gratitude as Duncan opened up to him the proposal of the Laird, and the terms on which *he* had acceded to it.

"It is noble, Duncan," he returned, resting his hand affectionately on his shoulder; "just like you, and the deeds of your whole life. You were born for the happiness of others, and have faithfully fulfilled your mission. It is not given from your abundance, Duncan, and shall not be lightly esteemed. It will incite me to more industry, more perseverance, and," he added, striking his hand heavily upon the table, "as sure as Lochiel Graeme is Lochiel Graeme, it shall be returned to its present owner. The first,—yea, second, third, and fourth fees of Dr. Lochiel Graeme shall be held sacred for this purpose. None shall say that the scapegrace, Lochiel, has appropriated the hard earnings of the best of brothers, to his own selfish purposes."

"Well, well, Lochiel, all I desire in return is to see you a Christian gentleman, striving to benefit others; and, like your Master, going about doing good."

"The atmosphere I breathe ought to render me all you wish, and, if affliction sanctifies, surely I have born the yoke in my youth."

A smile played upon the face of Duncan as he replied, "That passage, as I apprehend it, alludes not to trial, Lochiel, but to the yoke of the Saviour."

"A yoke that I am resolved to bear," he returned,

28

seriously. "But I must at once see Ellen; she has sorely mourned with me the prospect of a separation. Her mind must be relieved without delay."

"Dinner is waiting us; you will remember father's injunction, Lochiel."

"Explain to him the urgency of my engagement, Duncan."

"The urgency, in your esteem," his brother replied, pleasantly.

"And, Duncan," he added, returning as he was about leaving the room, "ask sister to break it gently to Margey. I cannot be the first bearer of the intelligence; her grief would entirely unman me. Or will you do me this favor, if sister is unwilling?"

"The information had better be conveyed gradually."

"No, Duncan, no; she will be hurt—deeply hurt, unless apprised of it immediately. On second thought, I will be my own messenger."

"Your thoughts and intentions are so swift-winged, Lochiel, that we can hardly distinguish them by number."

Lochiel, only replying by a laugh, crossed the hall hastily, and disappeared in the kitchen.

"You are going to lose me, Margey,—a certain case," he said,—"all settled between father and the Laird. It can't be helped, Margey, and we must all submit to whatever may befall us."

"Lose ye, Master Lochiel?" exclaimed the old woman, letting fall the spoon within her fingers; "lose ye! Heaven bless ye, what mean ye by sic a thing?"

"Why I mean, Margey, that I am going to England, and many other places, with the Laird, and —"

"And wha wi' hae the care o' ye should ye be ill?" she inquired, laying her trembling hand upon his arm; "and wha wi' care for a' your wee comforts, my bonnie bairn?"

"Well, we must trust, Margey, and I have no doubt the Laird will have an eye to all these matters."

The old woman shook her head sadly, while tears coursed down her cheeks. "And hae ye nae thought," she inquired, reproachfully, "for the mony lonely hours of puir auld Margey? And hae ye nae care for a' the sad forebodings that hae come to me o' late? It's a' out; ye may gang, Maister Lochiel: but your return wi' nae be sae blythe and happy; the sod will be lang o'er the grave o' auld Margey; how wi' she live wi' the thought of Maister Lochiel's illness, or may be death, in the land o' strangers?" Covering her face with her apron, she sobbed aloud.

"But, Margie," he returned, placing his arm kindly around her, "it is so usual to travel, and persons constantly return safely."

"But it's nae the kind thing o' ye, Maister Lochiel. Wha stood up for ye when ye've been called names that's made me hate 'em, and watched o'er ye night and day when ye've been sorely ailin'? 'T is nae the kind thing o' ye. And ye cannot find a blyther spot than our ain isle. What will ye gain by a' your trampin's?"

"You will think better of it, I know you will," he replied, as the tear started to his own eye; "and the first letter written shall be to my own Margey, and the first purchase in foreign parts shall be for you. You cannot long think hard of your own Lochiel; and when I come back, safe and sound, think of the stories I shall have to tell you."

"And wi' ye tarry lang?" she inquired, somewhat soothed; "or wi' it be weeks and months afore your sweet face blesses me wi' its sight?"

"There is no certainty; and I could not be rude enough to worry the Laird with many questions. You have taught me differently from that, Margey."

"Nae, I'd gie any the lie that said nae tae that, Maister Lochiel; and ye'll bear yoursel' the gentleman in the face of Laird or sairvants. Never fear ye. But in a strange land, where they dinna ken ye, ye'll hae tae be a wee mair like Maister Duncan, and nae the less like yoursel', either; but you're a gentleman, and nane 'ill e'er dispute it in this, or any land ye'll travel, till ye arrive at the gate o' the Celestial City."

"And the way to that gate I am now seeking, Margey," he returned, gravely.

"And I'll seek it with ye," she replied, warmly. "I'll ne'er see ye enter, and be left out mysel'."

"God grant we may both seek aright," he returned, shaking her hand affectionately; "but father will be the better teacher."

"And ye'll hae a cauld dinner, Maister Lochiel," interrupted Kathleen, who came in at that moment, "if ye dinna hasten tae it. Maister Duncan said ye were gane tae the Manor."

"And I have a pressing engagement that forbids

my remaining longer," he said, hurrying toward the front door.

As far as sight had the faculty of discerning, the eye of the old nurse followed him as he bent his steps toward the manor; then, slowly returning, as she closed the door, she murmured, "May the Lord keep him frae harm i' the midst o' strangers; but we'll hae a lane time, even wi' Maister McMillan and Bernard."

. The evening brought Lochiel home, enthusiastic in the praises of the Laird and the Directors of the Bank, placing, at the same time, a package in the hand of Duncan. What was his brother's astonishment on opening it, to find enclosed a deed conveying Pleasant Slope to Duncan Graeme, and a kind note from the Directors, asking his acceptance of it as a token of their sincere regard and high appreciation. Mr. Graeme was not at home to sympathize with the feelings of the gratified youth, and, accompanied by Lochiel and his sister, he proceeded immediately to Thistle Hedge.

" It is just the purchase I wished to make," said Mr. Lincoln, " but could not see my way clear in doing so at present; but the Lord will always provide for his own people. We seem to be peculiarly his care, Duncan; and how his judgments have followed in every step of the path of our miserably unhappy persecutor! Percy placed this letter in my hand this morning, desiring me to send it to the manor for perusal. It is from the same correspondent who described, so feelingly, the last hours of the young and beautiful daughter of Mungo Robertson. He says, —

28 *

" ' Several months elapsed, after arriving in Australia, before I had any tidings of the surviving members of the family of the interesting young lady I mentioned in my last; and the sad event had almost passed from my mind, when a stranger came to my house with a request that I would at once see a man in the last agonies of death. "He has mentioned you by name," he said, " and desires you would come to him."

" ' Without a moment's delay, I followed him to a small cabin. There, what a scene presented itself! Stretched upon the ground floor, lay a miserably haggard being, the wildness of whose eye startled me. I seated myself upon a low stool beside him, and laying my hand upon his forehead, clammy in death, I said, " Though we pass through the valley of the shadow of death, the Lord has promised to be with all who love Him, and put their trust in Him."

" ' The lip quivered, and the eye closed, as he murmured, "The eternal horrors of a second death; a dread abyss; dark, deep, eternal!"

" ' I replied not, but kneeling beside him, was about offering a supplication in his behalf, when, with unnatural strength, he seized my hand.

" ' " You will call in vain," he said, bitterly. "Vain, vain, is the help of man. But I have a request, a message —" His voice sunk, and I supposed him dying; but rallying, he continued, — "Do you remember consigning one to the deep on board the *Congo?*" he inquired.

" ' " Perfectly. Where is her brother?"

" ' " Gone to an early grave ; a victim to the ambition of a cruel parent."

" ' " And are his parents still living ? " I inquired.

" ' " Her mother, with a crushed spirit, followed her idolized son and daughter." "And her father?" "Would you know his fate ? Tell *him* — tell Percy — tell him," he whispered in a voice almost spent, "to intercede for me ; I know you are his friend ; I therefore sent for you to ask, to plead, at the hand of Robert Dunbar, forgiveness for the perjured, miserable, unhappy, and justly execrated Mungo Robertson."

" ' I started from my seat with amazement. "Not," I exclaimed, "Not — " Large drops now stood upon his forehead. I again sank upon my knees. I pleaded as a man pleadeth with his brother, for the dying man. I felt that an immortal spirit was about entering the eternal world, without resting upon that arm extended to receive the chief of sinners. "Lord, thine arm is not shortened," I said.

" ' The hand of the stranger was gently laid upon my arm ; his finger pointed to the lifeless tenement. So quietly had the spirit passed, I was not conscious of the change. May I never again be called to witness such a scene.' "

" Truly," said Mr. Lincoln, "the hand of the avenger of blood will not be stayed without the walls of the city of refuge."

" And truly," exclaimed Lochiel, as the big tears rolled down his face, "any resentment I may have harbored, is at an end. I feel only the greatest commiseration, and Lord Glennair will weep over so terrible a retribution."

For some days there was a sad impression; a feeling of compassion — but it passed away; and with hearts overflowing with thankfulness, they blessed the hand that was now strewing only flowers in their path.

With redoubled zest, as the possessors of Pleasant Slope, Duncan and Edith suggested improvements in the house and grounds; and the changed appearance of the manse also told that something more than usual was about transpiring there. An addition of a large wing appeared, which was certainly not needed by the Pastor, and might possibly be for the accommodation of one of another profession.

"Wonderful, indeed, have been the checkered events of the last few years of our lives," Lochiel remarked to Mr. Lincoln, as they stood viewing the enchanting prospect from the window of Pleasant Slope; " and through what a different medium do I now see the power that rules the universe and guides the destinies of men. Since the still, small voice has spoken, peace has reigned over the troubled waters, and my soul is stayed on Christ my God. I leave these shores with new aspirations, new hopes, a new and happy future opening up before me."

"Here, viewing such a scene," returned Mr. Lincoln, solemnly, " our heart may be stirred to its inmost depths, revering the hand that formed it; but on Calvary alone will we be melted with the consciousness of our own sinfulness, and cling as humble suppliants to that cross, finding a balm for every sorrow, and the bright prospect of a crown beyond the skies."

www.ingramcontent.com/pod-product-compliance
Lightning Source LLC
Chambersburg PA
CBHW020949030726
47496CB00005B/1432